FILMMAKERS SERIES

edited by
ANTHONY SLIDE

In Preparation

MARTIN SCORSESE
and
MICHAEL CIMINO

Filmmakers, No. 8

by

MICHAEL BLISS

The Scarecrow Press, Inc.

Metuchen, N.J., & London 1985

Library of Congress Cataloging in Publication Data

Bliss, Michael, 1947–
    Martin Scorsese and Michael Cimino.

    (Filmmakers ; no. 8)
    Bibliography: p.
    Filmography: p.
    Includes index.
    1. Scorsese, Martin. 2. Cimino, Michael. I. Title.
II. Series: Filmmakers (Scarecrow Press) ; no. 8.
PN1998.A3S3483 1985   791.43'0233'0922   85-2276
ISBN 0-8108-1783-7

99310

DEDICATION

This book is dedicated to Nathan and Sophia Bliss,
and to Ruth, Charles, and Ethel Sheirr.

CONTENTS

v

ACKNOWLEDGMENTS

My thanks to Morison Buell for a special favor, and for publicity material on Who's That Knocking At My Door?; Stephen Mann of Midwest Entertainment and David Sikech of Orion Pictures for access to a print of Boxcar Bertha; Bingham Ray of New Yorker Films for that elusive photo from Heaven's Gate; Richard Peterson of the Walker Art Center for background information on Michael Cimino; Alicia Rothman for photos and extraordinary exertion; Peter Bateman for repeated searches for illustrations; Scott Levine of 20th Century-Fox for publicity material on The King of Comedy; Audree Malkin of UCLA's Theatre Arts Library.

Thanks also to Christina Banks for going out of her way for me; and to Tim Grady, Mark Bishop, Eddie Brandt, and New York's Movie Still Archives.

Michael Bliss

EDITOR'S FOREWORD

At the 1979 New York Film Festival a film on Martin Scorsese as seen by his friends was screened. Its title was Movies Are My Life, which describes both Scorsese and Michael Cimino very well. Both spent their formative years learning about film, and both became major figures in the new Hollywood. Martin Scorsese's list of credits is much longer than Michael Cimino's, yet both have experienced their share of success--Scorsese particularly with Taxi Driver and Raging Bull, Cimino with The Deer Hunter --and both have known failure: Cimino, of course, with Heaven's Gate and Scorsese with the quickly forgotten The King of Comedy.

Martin Scorsese and Michael Cimino have brought much to the art and craft of filmmaking. They have also, unconsciously, borrowed from the past, particularly in their manipulation of performers and their use of the same actors (notably Robert De Niro), a format adopted years before by the likes of John Ford and Frank Capra (whose styles are, of course, diametrically opposed to those of Scorsese and Cimino).

Michael Bliss analyzes the work of both directors in depth, devoting chapters to each of their feature films, noting opposites in their styles and finding a number of similarities in their work. Additionally, he devotes a chapter to the scandalous handling of Heaven's Gate by United Artists, and offers biographical notes and detailed filmographies for each director. Here is a major study of two leading figures in contemporary American cinema, written by a teacher of English and film, based in Minneapolis, who has written an earlier volume in this series, on Brian De Palma.

Anthony Slide

INTRODUCTION

Scorsese and Cimino--Why This Pairing?

At first glance, Martin Scorsese and Michael Cimino may seem a rather odd couple to consider together in a critical study, since their cinematic styles appear to be widely divergent. Scorsese may at present justifiably be referred to as the contemporary master of American idiosyncratic filmmaking. His works usually deal with the psychology of unusual individuals in unusual circumstances, the specifics of whose personalities become the focal point and motivating principle behind the action of each of his films. As a consequence of their concern with inner states, Scorsese's films are by definition small, by which I mean that they focus on limited time spans; the films' events generally take place within precisely (one might almost say tragically) limited locales over a usually circumscribed period of time. [1]

Alternatively, Cimino has already evidenced in his three films a desire to concentrate on more grandiose structures. His films are concerned with many individuals rather than few. These individuals' activities are portrayed against epically large canvases of events (the Vietnam War in The Deer Hunter, the Johnson County Wars in Heaven's Gate). Even in his first film, Thunderbolt and Lightfoot, with its comparatively limited budget and cast, one can see Cimino attempting to stretch the boundaries of the film's structure and plot. Instead of concentrating predominantly on one person (e. g. , J. R. , Alice, Jake La Motta, Rupert Pupkin) or a pair of characters (most notably, the alienated--and therefore basically lonely--couples, such as Jimmy and Francine, Rupert and Masha) as Scorsese might, Cimino comple-

---

Opposite: Above, Michael Cimino with Robert De Niro during production of The Deer Hunter. Below, Martin Scorsese with De Niro on the set of Taxi Driver.

ments Thunderbolt and Lightfoot's two central characters
with an additional pair of individuals, has their activities
take place against the screen of a grandiose cross-country
trip along the nation's highways, and climaxes the film with
a theft whose very daring and scope introduce elements of
expansive ambition into what might otherwise have been a
modest drama. [2]

While both Scorsese and Cimino are interested in
events as they affect individuals in the United States, their
realization of this concern differs strikingly. A brief discussion of the characters portrayed for Scorsese and Cimino
by Robert De Niro will illustrate this distinction.

De Niro's ineffable mixture of grim humor and usually contained hostility is certainly a characteristic upon
which both directors draw. However, in The Deer Hunter
Cimino was able to elicit an additional quality from De Niro
that the actor had never previously shown. By simultaneously placing De Niro's Michael Vronsky in direct and close
affiliation with a number of male friends, and then setting
Michael against the alienating backdrop of an international
event--the Vietnam war--Cimino, working along with De
Niro and encouraging him to assume semi-mythic postures,
extended the quintessential De Niro character's inherent
loneliness and simultaneous desire for companionship to embody a statement, not about the American psyche (as Scorsese would have done, e. g. , Taxi Driver's Travis Bickle as
the hostile soul of the United States; Raging Bull's Jake La
Motta as the archetypical American, literally and figuratively fighting his way to the top and then characteristically losing everything before redemption occurs) but about the United
States as a nationalistic (as opposed to, as it would be in
Scorsese, a psychological) whole. Thus where, as in Taxi
Driver, Scorsese with his microcosmic focus tells us (by
extension) much about Americans, Cimino, with his macro-
cosmic bias, will produce a film like The Deer Hunter,
which is more concerned with telling us about America.

As we might expect, this contrast of thematic concerns is mirrored in Scorsese and Cimino's cinematography. True, both men demonstrate a fair amount of boldness
when using color. One immediately thinks of the intentionally exaggerated tones of the opening of Alice Doesn't Live
Here Anymore, the sickening greenish tinge to many of Taxi
Driver's images, and the garish tones employed in The King
of Comedy. In Cimino, there are the beautiful colors of The

Deer Hunter and Heaven's Gate. Moreover, even in the absence or suppression of color the directors are similar;
compare, for example, the stunning black and white cinematography of Who's That Knocking At My Door? and Raging
Bull (the latter usage evokes a newsreel-like atmosphere)
with the intentional muting of color--achieved by shooting
through dust and haze--to suggest both reminiscence and
historicity in Heaven's Gate.

However, Scorsese and Cimino differ significantly
with respect to the frames within which their films' action
takes place. Scorsese's frame is intentionally limited. He
shoots his films either flat (in the standard 1.37:1 Academy
aspect ratio) or in Panavision's 1.85:1 format, the latter a
compromise widescreen aspect ratio that hardly introduces
any real expansiveness into the film's frame of action. As
with the conceptual scope of his films' plots, this self-imposed limitation is in keeping with Scorsese's intense focus
on the psychological nuances of individual characters.

Given Cimino's bias in favor of events writ large,
one should not be surprised by his favoring Panavision's
2.35:1 anamorphic format for his films. The interesting
consideration here is that, like Scorsese, Cimino never
draws overt attention to the shape of the frame he employs.
Quite often, Cimino uses static camera set-ups and lets his
set-pieces speak for themselves, an approach that may be
seen as a correlative of Scorsese's extremely restrained
use of the moving camera throughout his films (only Raging
Bull is notoriously stylized in this respect). Although there
are certain notable camera movements in Scorsese's work
(e.g., the dramatic slow motion drawback shot towards the
end of Taxi Driver and the use of the hand-held camera to
accentuate either chaos or drunkenness in Mean Streets),
for the most part Scorsese, like Cimino, is quite conservative with his camera work.

Despite the apparent differences in Scorsese and
Cimino's cinematic styles, their films can nevertheless be
seen as strikingly complementary. Both Scorsese and Cimino are concerned with dislocation, either psychological or
geographical, or in some cases both. Generally, the protagonists in Scorsese and Cimino's films are tragically, one
might say almost marvelously, alienated from their surroundings, their society, their fellow human beings, and
themselves. All of the central characters in these films
are, to appropriate Travis Bickle's description of himself,

"God's lonely m[e]n" (or, in the cases of Boxcar Bertha
Thompson, Alice Hyatt, Francine Evans, The Deer Hunter's
Linda, and Heaven's Gate's Ella, all of whom are displaced
from relationships with men, God's lonely women). This
three-word assessment of these characters' situations is significant for each of its component parts: religion, isolation,
and homophilia.

Religion. It's important to note that the universe in
which the actions of these films take place is not devoid of
a deity. There is a God that watches over Scorsese's and
Cimino's characters, although he may be represented either
in traditional forms (the church and priest references in Who's
That Knocking At My Door?, Mean Streets, Raging Bull,
Thunderbolt and Lightfoot, The Deer Hunter, and Heaven's
Gate) or in the form of virtually religious obsessions (e. g. ,
the private and often destructively devotional practices of
characters like Taxi Driver's Travis Bickle, who refers to
God either explicitly or implicitly through his longing for some
sort of deliverance and scourge, as in the city washed clean
of its sins through violence; and the constructive/destructive
religio-mythic pursuits engaged in by The Deer Hunter's Michael).

The essential point to keep in mind is that for both
directors, traditional religion's promise of deliverance from
or transcendence of earthly anxieties is shown to be simply
impossible. In essence, the church can offer only empty
solace, not salvation, a realization that the characters in
these films come to in unusually painful ways. These characters are alone in a universe from which God's grace has
been withdrawn (assuming, of course, that such grace was
ever in force to begin with). As a result, in a religious
sense these characters are alone. In a physical sense, they
are alone as well. There are two ways of reading the last
two words in Travis' equation, either with the emphasis on
"lonely" or the accent on "man." Both readings aptly describe the majority of Scorsese's and Cimino's characters and
both ways are equally tragic.

Isolation. Certainly, the striking personality aberra-
tions evidenced by most of Scorsese's characters threaten to
consign them to a lifetime of loneliness, even if we only read
loneliness as an enduring awareness of one's difference from
the "normal," well-integrated, and thereby supposedly happy
members of society. Yet this loneliness goes further than
an alienation from one's contemporaries, because almost uni-

formly (with the exceptions of <u>Boxcar Bertha</u> and <u>Alica Doesn't</u> <u>Live Here Anymore</u>, whose peculiarities will later be discussed), Scorsese's lonely people are lonely men, men alienated from the company of women. In Cimino's films it is also men (with the exception of the minor female characters in <u>The Deer Hunter</u> and <u>Heaven's Gate</u>) who are, as a result of their obsessive quests, lonely as well.

<u>Homophilia</u>. Men's preference for the company of other men, as opposed to associating with women, is a thematic concern of American literature that has been noted by numerous commentators, notably by Leslie Fiedler in his <u>Love and Death in the American Novel</u>.[3] The homophilic relationship, a rather blatant emblematization of the fear of procreation (childbirth opens the gateway to death; participation in the reproductive cycle affirms one's transient nature, attitudes coupled with the Old Testament view of women's disobedience bringing, as John Milton put it in <u>Paradise Lost</u>: "death into the world and all our woe"--Line 3), is seen by Fiedler as a desire for an escape into a deathless, and thereby changeless, world, a move achieved through a homophilic relationship which, because it excludes procreation, is (mis)-conceived as perfect. However, the irony of homophilic relationships is that the precise qualities that attract men to them--their lack of productivity and consummation--signify death. It is notable that none of Scorsese's or Cimino's homophilic couples manage to escape death or near-death. Indeed, all of these characters seem able to bring their relationships to fruition only through some form of death. The ultimately loveless pairings in Scorsese of J.R. and Joey (<u>Who's That Knocking At My Door?</u>), Charlie and Johnny Boy (<u>Mean Streets</u>), Jake and his brother (<u>Raging Bull</u>) and, in Cimino, of Thunderbolt and Lightfoot (in the film of the same name), Michael and Nicky (<u>The Deer Hunter</u>), and Jim (with both Billy and, potentially, Nate in <u>Heaven's Gate</u>) attest to homophilia's deadly orientation.

Even representations of traditional sexuality in Scorsese's and Cimino's films suggest a linkage between sex and death that cannot be ignored. In <u>Who's That Knocking At My Door?</u> we have the morbidly tinged "fantasy" scene between <u>J.R.</u> and the whores; in <u>Boxcar Bertha</u> we witness the growth of passion between Bertha and Bill occurring simultaneously with the gang's move towards destruction. <u>Mean Streets</u> gives us a femininely-coiffed assassin who turns murder into a sexual encounter; Charlie's death dream, which associates sex and death; the sexual gestures invoked by Giovanni when discussing morbid topics; and a mock death threat (against Michael) from Johnny Boy that involves sexual movements. Alice Doesn't Live Here Anymore contains a memorable scene between Alice and her deadly lover, Ben. In Taxi Driver, Travis Bickle's homicidal obsession is seen to derive in part from his misdirected sexual energy. A grim antithesis between heterosexual romantic satisfaction and artistic expression seems to exist in New York, New York. The Last Waltz finds a rock star telling an unintentionally grim "joke" about the cheapness of human sexual interaction. Raging Bull implies that an opposition exists between culminated sexual relations and athletic potency; while The King of Comedy shows sexual (on Masha's part) and near-sexual (on Rupert's part) adulation mutating into a grim charade.

In Cimino's films a similar relationship between sex and death is exemplified through the unfulfilling, dead-end heterosexual relationships experienced by Thunderbolt and Lightfoot; the awkward, morbidly-associated couplings in which Michael, Nicky, Steven, Angela, and Linda are involved (The Deer Hunter); and the unproductive relationships experienced by Jim, Ella, and Nate in Heaven's Gate.

Nevertheless, it is homophilia--its significance and consequences--that emerges as the most strikingly similar element among the films of Scorsese and Cimino, one that brands them as companion filmmakers, different in style and technique but alike in theme. There are no women in Scorsese's or Cimino's films who act as integral parts of the action. With the notable exceptions of Boxcar Bertha (an atypical political film) and Alice Doesn't Live Here Anymore (a woman's film that nevertheless leaves us with a flawed view of female emotions and sexuality), no Scorsese or Cimino film gives us a female character who is essential either to a film's plot or thematic focus (although New York, New York's Francine Evans shares equal screen time with Jimmy Doyle, the film's bias towards innovative music and in favor of Jimmy's point of view emphasizes the primacy of the male character's wishes and desires). Instead, these films concentrate mainly on either solitary men or men and their relationships with other men. In fact, the women in these men's films are depicted as detrimental to the male characters' desires for what they view as constructive relationships (in Jimmy's case this involves his relationship with his music and the men who play it). Certainly, the women in Who's That Knocking At My Door?, Mean Streets, Raging Bull, The King of Comedy, and all three of Cimino's films are not only tangentially related to these films' central relationships (those among their men) but are portrayed as virtually identity-free abstractions.

Additionally, the women in many of these films (with whom the male characters cannot for various reasons establish and maintain relationships) are often viewed by these characters as wanton or, in some traditional sense, debased. Thus, Knocking's J. R. reverts to calling his girlfriend a "whore" when he is confronted with his inability to relate empathetically to her; Mean Streets' Charlie tells Teresa he doesn't love her because she's "a cunt"; Taxi Driver's Travis Bickle damns Betsy to Hell when their relationship fails, while Iris is initially seen as living in the midst of corruption; Robbie Robertson in The Last Waltz seems to find amusing the fact that musicians get, as a fellow musician puts it, plenty of "pussy"; Raging Bull's Jake La Motta continually accuses his wife (who in his eyes is a virgin-turned-whore) of infidelities; while King of Comedy's Masha is seen reverting to cheap theatrics during her striptease in front of Jerry Langford.

In Cimino, we are given Thunderbolt and Lightfoot's briefly glimpsed Melody and Gloria, the latter protesting her integrity when Lightfoot says "she has a great ass," to which she replies, "I didn't get out of one bed to crawl back into another one," although this is precisely what she is seen doing in the very next shot; Linda's possibly questionable transferring of affection from Nicky to Michael in The Deer Hunter; and the only important female character in Heaven's Gate, Ella, who winds up making a living as a madam.[4] All of these women attest to the similarity of Cimino's and Scorsese's female characters. Alone among all of these women in her emotional integrity and ability effectively to establish and maintain a positive, supportive sexual relationship is Boxcar Bertha's Bertha Thompson. One can only assume that Bertha's healthy adjustment in this respect is a function of her allegiance to a cause greater than herself--in this case, the rights of the disadvantaged. Bertha's commitment to something meaningful outside of herself apparently frees her from what we must view as the essentially self-centered concerns that contribute to these other characters' apparently unresolved dilemmas.

The conceptual transition of woman from virgin to whore is a further important similarity among Scorsese's and Cimino's films. Indeed, with the understandable exception of Boxcar Bertha, all of their work exhibits this quality.

"The girl" in Knocking is first seen as a virginal symbol of
innocence, then as a whore-like font of corruption. For
Mean Streets' Charlie, Teresa represents both purity (he
dreams of her on white sheets) and corruption through morbidity ("I came blood"). The main character of Alice Doesn't
Live Here Anymore passes from a flawed but nonetheless socially sanctioned marriage (in which she strives for the "ideal"
union) and through various corrupting trials (sordid nightclubs;
a physically violent sexual relationship), only to emerge fortunately into what superficially appears to be an extremely
promising relationship with the supposedly new kind of man
that Kris Kristofferson's David ostensibly represents. Taxi
Driver's Betsy initially appears virginal (Travis notes how
she is dressed all in white); later, Travis consigns her to
a whore's Hell (in complementary fashion, Iris is in Travis's
eyes first a whore and then, ostensibly through his efforts--
which ironically result in her restoration to her family--a
virgin once more). The promised innocence of the relationship between Francine and Jimmy in New York, New York
soon degenerates into Jimmy's viewing Francine's pregnancy
not only as an annoyance but as some sort of betrayal of
their marriage's sanctity. In his remark about "pussy," Robbie Robertson in The Last Waltz reminds us of the at-first-
innocent state within which the groupies to which he alludes
must at one time have existed. Raging Bull's Jake La Motta
jettisons his first argument-corrupted marriage in favor of
a union with the virginal Vickie, whom Jake later suspects
of whore-like liaisons with his friends and brother. Before
her transformation to pseudo-siren, The King of Comedy's
Masha is seen dressed in what appears to be innocent pre-
paratory school garb; while in the same film, the supposedly
wizened Rita traces a mirror-image movement from experience (her role as a skeptical bartender) to innocence (evident
in her light and airy attire for the supposed weekend jaunt at
Langford's).

    In Cimino, we have Gloria's (in Thunderbolt and Light-
foot) already-noted initial protestations of innocence, which
are followed by her sexual dalliance with Thunderbolt. The
Deer Hunter's Angela has her innocence (suggested not only
by her name but specifically noted in Steven's remark that
the couple have not had sexual relations before their marriage) destroyed, not only through her white bridal gown's
receiving the red wine stain, which signifies both deflowering
and the corruption of death, but also by the depressing personal effect on her of the Vietnam war. The same film gives
us Linda's suspicious movement from a relationship with Nicky

to one with his friend, Michael.   Finally, Heaven's Gate bears
witness to Jim Averill's passage from a relationship with the
innocent coed with whom he dances on graduation day to his
involvement with Ella,[5] the town whore, a move that signals
the eventual loss of Jim's already shaky ideals.   In all of
these instances we can see the filmmakers' work not only as
appropriations of an important symbolic dichotomy but also
as examples of attempts to come to grips with the notion of
redemption, with attendant inquiries into questions concerning
good and evil, the possibility of maintaining ideals in the face
of a debased universe, and (depending, of course, on the degree of pessimism of the film involved) the inevitability of
corruption.   These themes will be dealt with in the individual
chapters on the films.

    These views of women not only involve a cooptation of
traditional attitudes concerning women's threat to male camaraderie but additionally suggest that for deep-rooted cultural
and psychological reasons American men are incapable of successfully relating emotionally to their traditional sexual counterparts.   In keeping with both mythic and literary tradition,
Scorsese and Cimino depict women as not only antipathetic to
camaraderie, but also (again with the notable exceptions of
Boxcar Bertha and to a degree, Alice) as harbingers, not of
continuity and reconciliation but of displacement and death.
From the morbid associations involved with "the girl" in
Knocking through Mean Streets' death dream about Teresa,
the essentially destructive impulses catalyzed by Betsy and
Iris in Taxi Driver, the intrusive child in New York, New
York, to the supposed threat to Jake La Motta's potency in
the form of the desire for his wife in Raging Bull, Scorsese
has shown himself to be allied with the view of women as
symbolic of death and destruction.   The fact that King of
Comedy's Masha aids Rupert in his morbid plot, while Cimino's
female characters are all somehow associated with unproductive, often deadly relationships (the dead-end liaisons in Thunderbolt and Lightfoot; the juxtaposition of grief and tenderness
in Linda and Michael's affair in The Deer Hunter; Nick's love
for Ella, which involves him in Heaven's Gate's land war in
a way that leads to his death), only further establishes this
characteristic's significance.

    Women in Cimino's films are either tangential to the
thrust of human relationships (as in Thunderbolt and Lightfoot)
or uninvolved with what is represented as the only significant
kind of human affection (as in The Deer Hunter, with its notably ambiguous sexual relationship between Michael and Linda,

a relationship that pales beside those among the male characters; and Heaven's Gate, whose only important female character, Ella, not only acts as an obstacle to male friendship--
in this case, between Jim and Nate--but is additionally portrayed as a fallen woman, a prostitute).

It is essential to note when discussing Scorsese's and
Cimino's films the techniques for closure that each director
employs. In some cases, Scorsese ends his films in rather
conventional ways. The shots at the end of Knocking and
New York, New York not only mirror the films' respective
openings, but also (with their depiction of people walking out
of the scene of action) reaffirm the essentially lonely and
alienated nature of the films' protagonists. Additionally interesting are the relatively traditional closings of Mean Streets
and Alice Doesn't Live Here Anymore. Both films end with
the main character (Charlie in the former case, Alice in the
latter) walking away from the camera. And though Charlie,
a directionless figure throughout the film, staggers away,
while Alice Hyatt, apparently moving towards the sign trumpeting Monterey (her supposed destination throughout the film),
walks with determination, given their films' events, both
characters can be seen as making at best halting progress
towards their vaguely defined goals. Like Knocking's J.R.
and New York, New York's Jimmy Doyle, each character is
destined to remain essentially alone and unfulfilled.

Most notable in Scorsese's work is the ironic closing
device, which first surfaces in Taxi Driver and subsequently
has been in evidence at the ends of The Last Waltz, Raging
Bull, and The King of Comedy. In Taxi Driver, Travis Bickle
inadvertently becomes a media hero instead of being revealed
as the desperately maladjusted individual that he is; the same
fate is visited on King of Comedy's Rupert Pupkin. The Last
Waltz leaves us with an ambiguous vision of The Band gracefully playing a waltz in a carefully controlled environment that
seems to pale beside the adventurous surroundings within
which they played their farewell concert; the ending seems
melancholy, enervated, depressing.

Raging Bull's case is more problematic since, perhaps
unintentionally, it is unclear in what fashion Jake La Motta's
final manifestation--as cabaret performer reading from literary works that supposedly reflect on his own life--is meant
to be taken. Has Jake, after all, attained self-consciousness,
or is his act merely another grandstand role in his continuing
bid for the affections of the crowd? (The chapter on Raging

Bull will investigate this question in detail).   In any case,
we are left with a picture of the resurrected Jake as a "star"
that invites comparison with the kind of status that Travis
and Rupert achieve.

The net effect of these ironic endings is two-fold.
On the one hand, they call into question the type of morality
that we bring to bear on these characters.   Not satisfied in
these films with the kind of pat endings present in his other
works, Scorsese here compels the viewer to question which
judgments on the characters are apt--our own or those of
the celebrants who applaud these strikingly disturbed individuals' activities.

These ironic endings also bring into question the rather
pat conclusions of the Scorsese films with which they implicitly contrast.   These closures almost compel us to ask:
which are the more real resolutions, and which the over-
romanticized dramatizations that, while pleasant during the
viewing, fail to endure on closer examination?   With two
such widely divergent aesthetics operating in his films (all
of which fall into one or the other category), can such comparisons, and the questions they raise, be avoided?   Through
these endings Scorsese provides us with two divergent views
of the universe--one integrated and well-adjusted, in which
the thematic thrust of the film supports traditional values
(Alice, The Last Waltz, New York, New York) and one in
which aberration seems to be the dominant ethic (Knocking,
Mean Streets, Taxi Driver, Raging Bull, and King of Comedy).

Since music functions as an essential part of each of
the "integrative" films, one might hypothesize that there is
in these works a figurative harmony being played out, and
that when discords in these films occur, they do so as a
result of the characters' moving away from and forgetting the
type of harmonious attitudes and activities that would result
in a more balanced and traditionally well-adjusted existence.

In this sense, each of Scorsese's characters can be
viewed as yearning for what New York, New York's Jimmy
Doyle refers to as "a major chord"; when this major chord
is forgotten or overlooked, serious problems result.   Characters who appear in films in which the music complements
their actions (Bertha, Alice, Travis, Jimmy Doyle, The Band,
Jack La Motta, and Rupert) are seen to prosper (this in spite
of the fact that their ends may be viewed by Scorsese as
ironic).   However, characters appearing in films in which

the music acts as a counterpoint to their activities (J. R.,
Charlie) suffer at the end of their respective films, almost
as though by being out of step with the music they are, in
some sense, out of step with themselves as well.

Music in Cimino's films also serves two divergent
functions: acting in concert with closure devices, it reflects
tendencies towards either integration (harmony) or dispersal
(discord). The difference from Scorsese is that in Cimino,
both tendencies are contained within the same films.

The music toward the beginning of Thunderbolt and
Lightfoot (the first music we hear in the film is the congregational singing, which Cimino blends in after about a minute
of screen time--punctuated by natural sounds--has elapsed);
the touching "Sarabande" (heard during the opening credits),
"Can't Take My Eyes Off Of You" barroom sing-along, wedding reception music, piano solo interlude, and "God Bless
America" sing of The Deer Hunter; the marching band tune,
waltz music, and peasant band melodies of Heaven's Gate,
are all examples of strongly integrative music that connotes
beauty, tenderness and unity. These associations are complemented throughout the films by the depiction of communal
events (e. g., the united flock at Thunderbolt and Lightfoot's
beginning; the wedding and reception in The Deer Hunter; the
commencement hall and Heaven's Gate meeting hall gatherings
in Heaven's Gate).

However, by the ends of Cimino's films, with all possibility of total reconciliation and integration destroyed, music
returns with a different effect. Paul Williams' "Where Do I
Go From Here," which ends Thunderbolt and Lightfoot, reflects the ultimate pointlessness of Thunderbolt's existence.
Stanley Myers' "Sarabande" returns at The Deer Hunter's
conclusion; "Ella's Waltz" (a slow version of the "Mamou
Two-Step," to which the peasants joyfully roller skate) is reprised for Heaven's Gate's finale. Each film's melancholy
close is heightened by the music that accompanies it; and in
the latter two films, music heard earlier achieves a new,
bittersweet resonance when experienced in tandem with the
films' conclusions.

Unlike Scorsese, Cimino employs the same structure
in each of his films, one that can be viewed as a dramatization of a natural process: birth, development, death, and
decay. The relationships among the principals in each of
Cimino's films follow this pattern, with emotions of anticipation, joy, and comedy followed by tragedy and regret. As

one might expect, the films' music complements these emotions.

Another characteristic quality of Cimino's films is his protagonists' reluctance to become directly involved in relationships, a trait manifested through a recurrent paradigm of behavior. Like Shoot The Piano Player's Charlie, all of Cimino's central characters--Thunderbolt and Lightfoot's Thunderbolt, The Deer Hunter's Michael, and Heaven's Gate's Jim Averill--move from non-involvement in emotional events (Thunderbolt is hiding out in the guise of a preacher; Michael is only seen enjoying the benefits, and not performing the duties, of friendship; Jim is delightfully carefree at the film's beginning) to participation (Thunderbolt's accepted responsibility toward Lightfoot; Michael's acting on his promise to bring Nicky home from Vietnam; Jim's decision to help the peasants by directly opposing the stockgrowers) and then, after the death of a "lover" (Lightfoot, Nicky, Ella, Nate, J.R., and Billy) back to non-involvement.

The lesson Cimino seems to be communicating through this dialectic structure is clear: none of us can really help anyone else. Indeed, our well-intentioned (although probably hubristically motivated) actions only result in tragedy for others (Thunderbolt is responsible for Lightfoot's participation in the robbery, which leads to the youth's death; Michael "causes" Nicky's death, as the chapter on The Deer Hunter will demonstrate; Jim exacerbates the peasants/stockgrowers conflict, thereby indirectly hastening the deaths of Ella, Billy, J.R., and Nate). The withdrawn individual may be pitiful in his loneliness, but his withdrawal is (apparently) the only sensible mode of behavior. As a result, Cimino's already melancholic films, with their accent on past events and fated action, take on a note of tragedy that appreciably adds to their dramatic stature.

Indeed, each of Cimino's films ends with a bittersweet resolution, one so strongly tinged with regret (and, usually, despair) that Cimino must be judged a maker of decidedly tragic films. We find here no ironic celebration such as those that occur at the end of many of Scorsese's works but an overwhelming sense of loss and sorrow (even the supposedly celebratory "God Bless America" at The Deer Hunter's end evokes its share of pity). As one of the epigrams for the promotion of Heaven's Gate, Cimino coined the slogan, "what one loves about life are the things that fade," an assertion that brands Cimino as a man overtly concerned with both ro-

mance (evidenced through myth) and melancholy, qualities we
will discuss in greater detail in the chapters on his films.

Judging by the resolutions of their films' plots, Scorsese and Cimino are interested in charting the course of emotion's death. The protagonists in all of the films discussed
in this book (again with the curious exceptions of Boxcar Bertha and Alice, whose peculiarities will be noted in their respective chapters) are not only alone at the end, but disappointed in love as well. Ultimately, the protagonists'
loved ones are either dead or beyond their reach; as a consequence, these physically isolated men (even The Deer Hunter's Michael, although among his friends, seems alone without Nicky beside him) appear to be fated to dwell apart.

While fate in Cimino continually manifests itself as
an expected presence (man seems doomed to live alone; the
things that one loves seem destined to erode), it works on
Scorsese's characters solely through chance. The cruel twist
endings in Scorsese's films are the gods' black jokes on the
wanton humans who, if not killed for their sport, are rele-
gated to a useless (because essentially lonely) notoriety. 6
In fact, the greater the success that Scorsese's male characters manage to achieve, the wider the anxious gap between
what the characters desire and what they actually receive.
Despite appearances, neither Travis, nor Jake, nor Rupert
is any happier at the end than throughout their respective
films. Travis's notoriety, Jake's suspiciously arrived at self-
awareness, and Rupert's attainment of his long-sought-after
fame do nothing to rectify the essential personality maladjust-
ments that will always consign these men to a state of unfulfilled yearning.

For all of the similarities, there are nevertheless
important differences between Scorsese's and Cimino's work.
With the exception of Boxcar Bertha (his only proletarian film
and a striking thematic departure, since it is the sole Scorsese film with a pronounced political stance), all of Scorsese's
films are situated in big-city environments. Truly, Scorsese
may be considered the poet of urban anxiety. It would be
difficult to conceive of characters like J. R. , Johnny Boy,
Charlie, Alice, Travis, Jimmy Doyle, Jake, or Rupert exist-
ing outside of cities (although there are doubtless unfortunate
women like Alice in many sectors).

Without exception, Cimino's films take place in small
towns:7 the Montana communities in Thunderbolt and Light-

foot; the small-town steel-producing region of Clairton, Penn-
sylvania in The Deer Hunter; the essentially still-small Johnson County of Heaven's Gate. Where Scorsese's films feed
off of the urban milieu, exploiting the city's confined spaces
and hectic pace (correlative reflections of the characters'
entrapped behavior and manic obsessiveness), Cimino opts
for the more expansive vistas and leisurely style of the country. Even a film like Thunderbolt and Lightfoot, which is
charged with the high-powered energy of Thunderbolt's ambition and Lightfoot's yearning, is slowed down not only by the
film's casual pacing (up until the de rigeur fast cutting rhythms
of its robbery sequence) but by the casting of Clint Eastwood
in the lead. Eastwood's unhurried verbal delivery and off-
the-beat reactions lend an appreciable degree of casualness
to the film's anxious emotions.

It is here that the importance of the aspect ratios
employed by Scorsese and Cimino surfaces once again. As
I have noted, Scorsese invariably limits the frame's potential
for expansiveness; he has never shot a film in an anamorphic
format, whereas all three Cimino films were shot in 'scope,
within which spacious frame Cimino situates his characters
against the great natural set pieces he prefers. The choice
of frame sizes here is not arbitrary; though both directors'
films are usually about limitations, Scorsese concentrates on
protagonists whose very surroundings limit their possibilities,
and seem to loom ominously over them at every turn. Even
Alice Hyatt, in the West's open spaces, is straining against
the limitations of the life she leads; while Bertha Thompson,
in predominantly rural settings, only moves beyond the bounds
of her outlaw life style at her film's end, when she significantly passes out of the frame's field of view. In contrast,
Cimino's protagonists, although they are essentially doomed
to failure in their quests, struggle in the midst of large,
cataclysmic events: daring robberies (Thunderbolt and Lightfoot), wars (The Deer Hunter), land feuds (Heaven's Gate).
Cimino's characters' frustrations and desires may be just as
personal as those of Scorsese's characters, but given the
greater room that they have to develop, such yearnings tend
to take on comprehensive--as opposed to merely personal--
overtones. As a result, the failure of love in Thunderbolt
and Lightfoot is the failure of all homophilic love; the tragedy
in The Deer Hunter is America's sorrow; the corruption and
inherent injustice in Heaven's Gate is the country's disgrace.

It is an individual characteristic of Cimino's films that
he employs within them a perpetual paradigm: that of the

ritualistic event, occurring towards each film's beginning
(and echoed in later occurrences), which is used by the characters to create a semblance of normalcy in an attempt to
establish social and cultural cohesion for both the individual
and the group. The congregational gathering at Thunderbolt
and Lightfoot's beginning, the wedding ceremony and reception/
going away party early in The Deer Hunter, the graduation
exercise and dance in Heaven's Gate and the peasants' meetings in the Heaven's Gate meeting hall (where the gates that
are opened for the peasants are those of military confronta-
tional hell, not peaceable heaven) are all mythical ceremonies
that work towards establishing a sense of community.

     Yet it is precisely these acts that strongly presage
the undoing of cohesion by the end of these films. Thunderbolt, rapidly abandoning his congregation, picks up a disciple
(Lightfoot) on the road, and even doubles the number of his
itinerant congregation when two former accomplice/disciples-
turned-enemies (Red and Goody) are brought back into the
fold for the second armored car company heist. Yet by the
film's end, the ejection from the place of worship and the
loss of the flock are repeated in the three disciples' deaths,
which once again leave the morose preacher/leader alone.

     The Deer Hunter's wedding reception/party presages
the un-wedding of the band of male friends, three of whom
are exposed to the cruelties of the Vietnam War. The coffin-
like pews in the church, the appearance at the reception/party
of the taciturn Green Beret, and the symbolic spilling of the
blood-like wine seem to seal the fate of the departing warrior/
heroes.

     In Heaven's Gate, the commencement ceremony in the
chapel anticipates the gatherings in the Heaven's Gate meeting
hall, where the peasants graduate from passive suffering at
the stockgrowers' hands to a mature (albeit deadly) conflict.
Similarly, the peasants' middle-class counterparts, the Harvard students, shockingly prefigure the ends of their two representatives, Jim Averill and Billy Irvine, in the patterns
they describe in both their waltz and their fight (the circling
dancers and circling defending students become the circles
of the attacking peasants and defending cavalry during the
film's massacre sequence). Jim's student date's literal distance from the students' rituals prefigures Ella's unsuccessful attempt to figuratively distance herself from the peasants/
stockgrowers dispute, while the shot of this young coed leaning out of a candle-fringed window presages the assault against
her counterpart's (Ella's) lover, Nate, in a burning house.

In another sense, this paradigm assumes the form of a dialectic: order followed by disorder followed by a reestablishment of order. Thus in Thunderbolt and Lightfoot, Thunderbolt is first placidly alone, then embroiled with male friends in a cataclysmic robbery, then (at the film's end) alone once again. The male friends in The Deer Hunter are first amicably together, then separated by the Vietnam War, then re-united. Heaven's Gate first finds Jim Averill alone (running down the street to join the graduation parade), then in the company of friends (first with his fellow students and Billy, then among the peasants and Ella), and finally, at the film's conclusion, alone again. Given the ultimately solitary status of these films' male protagonists (even at The Deer Hunter's end, Michael still seems the most individual and distant member of the group) and the fact that all of these men are left alone as a result of the deaths of friends and lovers, we must conclude that Cimino views the isolation which often results from a loved one's death as the foregone conclusion of every human relationship.

The deaths of loved ones in Cimino's films seem to act as some sort of appeasing sacrifices, something we might expect in the films of a man concerned with ritualistic behavior. However, although the sacrifices occur, they produce no appreciable results. All of Cimino's protagonists end as they began--essentially alone, either as a man forever separated from his flock (Thunderbolt and Lightfoot), a man toiling in the hell-fires of steeltown (The Deer Hunter) or a man solitarily pacing the deck of his yacht (Heaven's Gate). Cimino apparently believes in ritual but despairs of its positive consequences. The result is that he produces films filled with their settings' grandeur but tinged with melancholy and regret--emotions so fully realized that they demand our attention to the films that evoke them so well.

NOTES

1. Both New York, New York and Raging Bull span a number of years, but the manner in which each film's scenes have their action compressed destroys any sensation of chronologic expansiveness that might otherwise have been created.

2. As he continued working, though, Cimino began to further emphasize his films' backdrops, and thereby implicitly diminish the stature of his characters. The Deer Hunter has only two central presences (Michael and Nicky), while Heaven's Gate has just one (Jim Averill). Interestingly, this shift in

characterization emphasis produces a concurrent change in
contextual emphasis, since the settings in which Cimino's
films take place become physically larger (Thunderbolt and
Lightfoot's small Montana town yields to The Deer Hunter's
somewhat more extended Clairton, which is itself dwarfed
by the broad vistas of Heaven's Gate's locales) as the number of each film's prominent characters shrinks. This progression is in keeping with Cimino's development as a mythic
filmmaker, an aspect of the director's that is investigated
further in the chapter introducing Part Two of this book.

3.   Leslie Fiedler, Love and Death in the American Novel
(New York: Dell Publishing, 1969).   One should also note
the stress that Fiedler places on the theme of the doppelganger
or double as an important element in American literature.
The notion of doubles is not only inherently related to the
homophilic pairings in our literature but also links up with
the doubles that we see constantly reappearing in the films
of Scorsese and Cimino.   Thus, we have the two J.R.s and
the two "girls," each pair containing one "pure" and one
"corrupt" member) in Knocking; Charlie's pure and corrupt
selves and the Charlie/Johnny Boy pairing in Mean Streets;
the two Travises (pure/corrupt as well as the public and
the private selves) in Taxi Driver; the Francine/Jimmy pairing in New York, New York; Raging Bull's two Jakes (before
and after the championship), along with Jake's two wives;
and King of Comedy's Rupert/Masha, Rupert/Rita relationships.   In Cimino, we see the doubles theme emerging in
the persons of Thunderbolt and Lightfoot; The Deer Hunter's
Michael and Nicky; and Heaven's Gate's various personal com-
binations (Jim and Billy, Jim and Nate, Jim and Ella, Ella
and Nate).   The significance of these pairings is explored in
the individual chapters on the films.

4.   The fact that Ella is the heir to the role of Jim Averill's
female love interest--a role initially played by an innocent-
looking coed--suggests that in Cimino's view, woman's transition from innocence to corruption is virtually inevitable.

5.   Nate's offer of marriage to Ella can be profitably viewed
as an attempt symbolically to redeem her from the corruption
of prostitution (through a legitimate coupling: marriage) back
to innocence, in essence, as the expression of a desire to
turn the whore back into a virgin.   In a comparable (but vin-
dictive) way, Knocking's J.R. offers to legitimize "the girl,"
whom he now recognizes as having lost her virginity, by offering to marry her.

Of course, the virgin/whore conceptualization is a basic aspect of much world literature, especially American; the notion roughly parallels American literature's city/forest dichotomy (Hawthorne's "Young Goodman Brown" is without doubt the most successful and effective representation of this theme).   Additionally, one can see the theme's repeated appearance in the scripts of Taxi Driver's author: Paul Schrader.

6.   "As flies to wanton boys, are we to th' gods, They kill us for their sport." King Lear, Act IV, Scene I, 36-7.

7.   Heaven's Gate's Harvard University and men's club sequences function only as relatively brief contrasts to the film's predominant concern with rural activities, although implicit in Heaven's Gate is the threat of urbanization (represented by Canton, Billy Irvine and, to a significant extent, Jim Averill as well) and the move towards big-city centralization and development, which is seen as a symbol of moral paralysis.

PART ONE

MARTIN SCORSESE

INTRODUCTION

In a 1982 interview, Brian De Palma delivered what is probably an accurate assessment of Martin Scorsese's work when he said that "Marty's work will always be interesting because he has such a bizarre sensibility." Naturally, the terms that define this sensibility need to be adequately explored. Nevertheless, at the outset it may be instructive to gauge and evaluate what the general reactions to Scorsese's work are.

Most filmgoers are probably familiar with Scorsese through seeing either Mean Streets, Taxi Driver, or Raging Bull. It is easy from these productions to assume that Scorsese is a filmmaker overtly concerned with violence, yet such a conclusion overlooks the unusual tonal range of his films, from the urban tensions of Who's That Knocking At My Door?, Mean Streets, Taxi Driver, and The King of Comedy; to the rebellious proletarian mood of Boxcar Bertha and the essentially humanistic themes explored in Alice Doesn't Live Here Anymore; to the contemplative atmosphere of The Last Waltz and the melancholy feelings engendered by New York, New York.

Actually, most of Scorsese's work does not depict explicit violence at all. The Last Waltz and New York, New York contain no violent confrontations (although admittedly, some of Jimmy and Francine's fights seem a bit excessive). Knocking contains only the non-contact gang fight and the fragmented rape scene memory sequence; while the violence in Mean Streets, Alice, Taxi Driver, and King of Comedy is carefully counterbalanced by scenes of comedy and camaraderie. Only Raging Bull, unique among Scorsese's films, places physical confrontation at the film's thematic center. Yet even here, the emphasis on brutality is ostensibly the result of the anti-violence didactic intention that the director seems to have in mind.

What seems most disturbing about the violence in Scorsese's films is not only its immediacy but the implied forms that it takes, usually in the persons of characters who, while not acting violently, nevertheless seem to embody extremely aggressive tendencies. Much of Scorsese's cinematic violence results from the almost impossible demands that a society which views itself as orderly and organized imposes on individuals who, through socialization, are expected to suppress hostile tendencies in favor of correct and polite responses.

For many of Scorsese's protagonists, though, successful socialization has simply not taken place. As a consequence, social aberrants like Johnny Boy, Travis Bickle, and Jake La Motta make a living by harnessing their hostile or aggressive tendencies. Johnny Boy exists by dangerously juggling the demands of the various people to whom he owes money. Travis recklessly confronts his hatred of blacks and minorities by using his cab to pick up anyone, anywhere. Jake, more animal than man (although Raging Bull's end attempts to contradict this view), seems suited for little other than fighting. Like Johnny Boy, Travis, and King of Comedy's Rupert Pupkin (who only achieves fame through excessive means), La Motta is an outcast and a loner; and since these characters' interactions with other people are limited, they are free to pursue their unusual, untested ideas.

The result of these characters' socially disfunctional status is violence--a violence, however, that presages readjustment. Charlie's and Johnny Boy's shooting at Mean Streets' end teaches them a cruel lesson; the same may be said of Alice Hyatt (who learns a great deal about trust at the hands of Harvey Keitel's Ben), and of Jake (at least, we are expected to feel that Jake's incarceration initiates his moral recovery). What can we conclude, then, but that violence is meant to act as a redemptive force in these films, both alleviating socially induced tensions (this effect is especially present in Rupert's case) as well as acting as a cohesive agent that re-integrates the aberrant individual?

In Scorsese's canon, only Who's That Knocking at My Door? shows us a character for whom self-recognition is not offered as a necessary corollary to violence (in this case, J.R.'s hostility towards "the girl"). Knocking's J.R. is still a lonely man at the film's end; unable to resolve his problems with "the girl," he is left isolated and miserable. With the exception of this film (and, as I argue in a later chapter, Raging Bull as well), this pattern of violence followed by en-

lightenment continually reasserts itself, a horrifying situation
since it makes violence a necessary prerequisite to self-
awareness. Moreover, given the depicted regenerative capabilities of violence, we may infer that it is thereby not only
an essential part of existence but a part that affirms, through
its curative powers, society's basic healthiness--that it is,
in effect, a sane response to conditions that are quite often
offensive or intolerable.

As a consequence, the violent individual, unfettered
by restrictions on his behavior, becomes a lone avenger for
justice, a cowboy affirming his right to bear arms.   It must
be noted that in many of these films (Knocking, Boxcar, Mean
Streets), weapons are readily available despite the legal restrictions placed on their possession. To take the prime
example: not only does Taxi Driver's Travis Bickle find it
quite easy to purchase any weapon (or drug for that matter)
that he cares to, but he is seen practicing his marksmanship
skills in a shooting gallery that uses the kinds of targets employed on police academy firing ranges. The suggestion here
is shocking: by virtue of his actions, Travis invites comparison with another armed segment of society--the police--
who, like him, see their mission as one of patrolling and
cleaning up the crime-infested city. The manner in which
the film thus suggests by implication that the police are as
aberrant as Travis (and vice-versa) thereby produces a ter-
rifying view of society completely out of control and headed,
if we are to judge by the film's indecisive cataclysm, towards
some vague, apocalyptic end.

While only separable from social-disfunctional violence
in a conceptual way, the erotic violence in Scorsese's films
is nevertheless such a characteristic and powerful force that
it deserves individual attention. Erotic violence in these
films is that violence, either actual or implied, that arises
out of sexual relationships. In its most restrained form it
consists of jousts for control within heterosexual relationships. Erotic violence is present in J. R.'s refusal of the
girl's tendered affection (an act that thereby establishes him
as the relationship's dominant partner); in Alice's husband's
insistent demands at the dinner table and his initial refusal
to make love to her; in the power plays (most notably the
argument about who "counts down the band") between Jimmy
and Francine (power plays that re-surface in the love/hate
relationship between King of Comedy's Rupert and Masha);
in the constant bickering between Jake and each of his two
wives.

The most notable exception to the prevalence of this
characteristic is in Boxcar Bertha.   The relationship between
Bertha and Bill is strikingly balanced.   It is only when Bertha
is involved with other men that jockeying for dominance (always practiced by the men, not Bertha) asserts itself.   The
conclusion here is obvious: it is traditional, male-oriented
capitalist politics that creates and sustains antagonisms among
people; aggression between sexual partners is a microcosmic
repetition of hostilities between entrepreneurs and workers.
Boxcar Bertha's gang, though, is notably egalitarian; it contains a woman, a black, and a Jew as equal partners, and
thereby gives us a view of a non-oppressive (and non-capitalistic,
at least in structure) society that would be possible if robber
barons like Sartoris, who exploit the poor and powerless, were
ejected from the country.

We are thus led to conclude that sexual inequality,
and thereby inequality with respect to position or power, is
a necessary outgrowth of the country's political inequality.
As a consequence, the erotic violence in Scorsese's films--
the rape scenes (Knocking), the scenes of assault against
women (Boxcar Bertha, Alice, Raging Bull, King of Comedy),
the scenes depicting oppression of females (Iris in Taxi
Driver)--can be viewed as integral reflections of American
society.

The anger and violence directed against women in
these films is as an extension of the anger and violence that
the films' male protagonists feel against the society as a
whole, a society whose oppression is so anonymous that it is
virtually impossible to rebel against it.   As a result, these
men take out their frustrations against the most accessible
and available target, the enemy whose obvious sexual difference brands them as a force that both attracts and repels:
women.

Nor does it matter whether these women are viewed
as either virgins ("the girl" at Knocking's beginning; Betsy
when we first see her in Taxi Driver; Masha early in The
King of Comedy) or whores ("the girl" at Knocking's end;
Betsy after her break-up with Travis; Masha during her se-
duction of Jerry).   Taxi Driver even gives us a character
who occupies both worlds: Iris, while clearly a whore, exhibits in Travis' eyes such a potential for redemption that
he works to restore her to her original state of essential
virginity.   It is but the cruel black joke irony of Taxi Driver's
end that this recovery is allowed actually to take place, as

though only through Travis' murderous activities could Iris
have been pried loose from Sport's clutches (when in fact,
Iris previously indicated a willingness to leave the city and
live on a commune, that is if Travis would accompany her).

These polarized views of women are, naturally, those
of Scorsese's characters, whose sensibilities color most of
what these films show us. In the typical Scorsese protagonist's view, everything is exaggerated: people are either
friends or enemies; politics is either good or bad; total success is either completely unattainable (e. g. , Jake La Motta's
lament that he'll never be able to fight Joe Louis, "the best
there is") or just barely out of reach. The characteristic
forms that these Manichean conceptions take are examined
in the chapters on the individual films.

The meanings of Scorsese's films do not reside predominantly in the director's use of overt cinematic technique.
One would be hard pressed to find in Scorsese's work many
examples of symbolic framing or allusive camera movement.
Instead, Scorsese's most striking films (Knocking, Mean
Streets, Taxi Driver) leave the viewer with the sensation of
having been exposed to a milieu of evil that serves as the
overall communicator of the films' meanings.

We thus return to De Palma's observation about Scorsese's cinematic sensibility. Although Scorsese's work is
extraordinarily rich in symbol and structure, we are initially
impressed in a Scorsese film by two things: the acting and
the script. The two actors who figure most prominently in
Scorsese films are Harvey Keitel (Knocking; Mean Streets;
Alice; Taxi Driver) and Robert De Niro (Mean Streets; Taxi
Driver; New York, New York; Raging Bull; and The King of
Comedy). Both actors might on first glance seem to be exhibiting characterizations dictated by the scripts and suggested
by the director. Yet a glance at the important work of Keitel
and De Niro for other directors (Keitel in James Toback's
Fingers, Ridley Scott's The Duellists, and Nicolas Roeg's
Bad Timing; De Niro in De Palma's Greetings and Hi, Mom,
Coppola's The Godfather Part II, Kazan's The Last Tycoon,
and Grosbard's True Confessions)[1] should indicate that both
actors' mannerisms appear so consistent and firmly fixed that
we must assume that Scorsese merely drew upon Keitel's and
De Niro's ability to project menace and elicit sympathy at the
same time.

Much has been made of Scorsese's association with
scriptwriter Paul Schrader, who wrote Taxi Driver and helped
in rewriting Mardik Martin's script for Raging Bull; for the
most part, though, only Taxi Driver represents a fully realized Scorsese/Schrader production. Yet viewed alongside
such other typical Schrader scripts as Blue Collar, Hard-
core, and American Gigolo, Taxi Driver seems curiously
different. There is a subtle but significant distinction
between Schrader's view of violence as a necessary part
of some great schema and Scorsese's view that violence
is an integrated form of behavior which seems to be a part
of regular existence. In essence, Schrader makes of violence
a religious artefact, part of a ceremony whose expected outcome is redemption. For Scorsese, violence--although it
may lead to some change in a character--is not a tool to be
exploited, but merely a normal part of existence.

Moreover, in Schrader's universe there is virtually
no room for humor, even of the dark variety. Only Taxi
Driver exhibits a dark humor, a characteristic very possibly
introduced into the film by the director since Schrader's own
films do not contain humor, only small bits of comic relief
as though it were an expected device tossed in solely for its
entertainment value.

In Scorsese's work, though, violence and comedy are
linked in frightening juxtapositions. The bad joke gun-taunting
in Knocking, the robbery hijinks in Boxcar Bertha, the pool
room fight and Charlie's pretend shooting of Teresa in Mean
Streets, Ben's emotional explosion in Alice, Travis's ridiculing of the Secret Service agent in Taxi Driver (which reveals
his potential for controlled violence), Jimmy and Francine's
tumultuous disagreements in New York, New York, the abduction of Jerry Langford in The King of Comedy--all of these
events, excessive though they may be, have their impact per-
ceptibly altered by the humor that characterizes them. In
essence, by juxtaposing violence (either real or implied) and
comedy, Scorsese implicitly ridicules exaggerated actions,
although he notably complicates this schema by continuing to
depict violence as a prelude to the attainment of the qualities--
(a modicum of) peace (Taxi Driver), self-consciousness (Mean
Streets, Raging Bull), or fame (King of Comedy)--that his
characters desire.

I like to refer to Scorsese as the poet of violence because of the way that he stylizes exaggerated behavior in his
films. It should be understood here that I am not talking about

the kind of representation of homicide exemplified in the work
of Sam Peckinpah. Peckinpah's use of slow motion romanticizes violence in an attempt to reveal what the director sees
as the balletic grace inherent in it. In contrast, even when
he employs slow motion, Scorsese sees nothing romantic about
violence at all. Thus, when Gaga is threatened with a gun
during one of Knocking's party sequences, the scene's slow
motion only compounds the terror. The slow motion backward track away from Taxi Driver's final blow-out increases
the horror by allowing time for a more extended audience reaction; while in The King of Comedy, Rupert's time-expanded
move through the crowd towards Jerry Langford produces an
appreciable uneasiness resulting, in part, from the sequence's
protraction.

The poetry of Scorsese's filmic violence is a function
of the manner in which violence is so well integrated into the
films that it becomes appreciated as a part of life's continuum. Characters in Scorsese films often seem to derive
their most attractive qualities from a font of near-violent,
aggressive behavior that is represented as an integral part
of their personalities; thus, the volatile temper of men like
J. R. , Charlie, Johnny Boy, Travis, Jimmy, Jake, and Rupert both motivates them in playful moments and fuels their
violent outbursts.

In all, Scorsese warrants our attention for his dedication to his craft, for the perceptive messages about human
relations and their curious mixture of tenderness and aggression, and for his admirable penchant for experimenting with
different genres (drama, musical comedy, documentary). If
only for the reason that he has yet to receive the kind of detailed treatment that his work deserves, a book such as this
one would be warranted. The fact that he is considered one
of our most important living filmmakers makes such a study
virtually imperative.

One final note: it is not the purpose of this book to
detail exhaustively the similarities between Scorsese's and
Cimino's work; my overriding intent is to systematically and
individually investigate their films. That there are striking
similarities between their films appears to be true. However, Cimino is not afforded a place in the book solely for
that reason, but also for two other considerations: first because, despite having only produced three films to date, he
is--as numerous critics and reviewers have noted--a major
talent who is therefore deserving of study. Also, in a prac-

tical sense, given the absolutely shameful and unwarranted
reception that Heaven's Gate received, there is obviously a
need for a less narrow, more comprehensive view of this
director's work. To the extent that it is possible within a
critical study to redress such glaring injustices, I have attempted to do so (see, especially, Chapter 12). Both Scorsese
and Cimino, though, are neglected masters deserving of greater
study, a shortcoming this book attempts to rectify.

On the following pages all of the feature films directed
by Martin Scorsese and Michael Cimino are discussed in chronological order. I stress once again, as I did implicitly in
Brian De Palma,[2] that a single-featured study of films yields
an appreciation of a work's organizational and symbolic complexity that simply cannot be gained by any other comparable
method. I generally proceed from the assumption that a film
is a unified text, one that should be read comprehensively in
order that from its structure, symbology, and rhetoric (dialogue, editing, camerawork, lighting) may be derived the
work's essential themes and meanings. I trust that the insights produced by the application of my method more than
justify its use, and that when viewed in tandem with other
approaches to a filmic work, such a method may broaden our
comprehensive understanding of just how rich and complex
the work of important directors like Martin Scorsese and
Michael Cimino really is, yielding through an appreciation
of networks of symbol and suggestivity a range of meanings
that are far too often overlooked in reviewers' hasty judgments.

NOTES

1.   The reader is referred back to page 2 for observations
on the differences between De Niro's work for Scorsese and
his work for Cimino. An interesting study could also be made
of the distinctions between the uses to which each director put
actor Kris Kristofferson. Characteristically, Scorsese (in
Alice Doesn't Live Here Anymore) uses Kristofferson for his
individualistic earthiness, a typical microcosmic quality. In
contrast Cimino, in Heaven's Gate, turns Kristofferson into
a representation of the macrocosm, in this case the emerging
American industrial nation.

2.   Michael Bliss, Brian De Palma (Metuchen, N. J. : Scarecrow Press, 1983).

Chapter One

LET ME IN; LET ME OUT

As a debut feature film, Who's That Knocking At My Door? is a remarkable achievement. Shot in black-and-white on a low budget, the film emerges as not only an important work that comments on male bonding and the influences of religion on Italian-Americans, but also as a striking precursor of most of Scorsese's future work. Knocking contains virtually all of the major themes that are prevalent in Scorsese's later films: the insular integrity of the Italian-American community; the difficulty of establishing an extended relationship with a member of the opposite sex; the anxieties of urban life; and the yearning for union with kindred spirits (always male) as opposed to the desires of the flesh for sexual satisfaction. The latter tendency subjects Knocking's (and, later, Mean Streets') characters to the stresses to which Italian-American Catholics are exposed as a result of an upbringing that condemns their physical desires without making available to them anything other than the most enervated alternative to these problems: the supposed solace of the church, which Scorsese shows is unequal to the task of providing spiritual or physical comfort to the afflicted in this life.

Knocking's action begins in a shabby tenement apartment, where a grandmotherly woman[1] is preparing a breadlike pastry. While the soundtrack incessantly hammers out a series of noises that sound like some grinding, insistent machinery at work, the woman prepares, kneads, and shapes the dough, and then bakes it. Then, after a short dissolve, she distributes the cake to four young children.

Throughout the scene we are given indications of just how pervasive the religious influence is going to be in this film. We pass from a close-up shot of a votive candle in

31

the apartment to shots of a statue of the Virgin Mary. These latter shots then dissolve into a view of the elderly woman, suggesting a relationship between the two figures, the one Jesus' mother, the second the maternal moving force behind what we must, given the scene's ecclesiastical trappings, view as a religiously tinged breaking and distributing of the loaves among the faithful. Indeed, throughout the eating scene Scorsese places the camera in a position from which the Virgin's statue is either glimpsed in the background or situated in the foreground; in the latter case, the Virgin appears to be looking down on, and perhaps approving of, the communion-like sharing of food that is going on here.

The implications of this short scene are striking: the old woman assumes the role of the elder, the progenitor of the tribe, supposedly imbued with wisdom and grace; the young children who eat the bread are the congregation or disciples. The bread-breaking, then, symbolizes the passing on of religion and knowledge to the next generation.

What this religion and knowledge yield, and what the next generation is up to, are made clear in Knocking's next shot as we see two of the film's principals, Joey (Lennard Kuras) and J. R. (Harvey Keitel), preparing for a street fight with a Puerto Rican opponent who kisses his cross before beginning the altercation. Thus far, then, the results of religion are violence, not peace.

Scorsese then cuts from the street fight (glimpsed only briefly) to a shot of a butcher chopping meat. The butcher's dividing of the meat into sections with his cleaver invites comparison between his activities and those of the old woman, who cuts the bread with a knife. The fact that the grandmother and butcher sequences bracket the street fight further suggests that the street scene's symbolic action is somehow "enclosed" by these two figuratively rich activities.

Both the old woman and butcher sequences involve food and the dividing of edibles for ultimate consumption. The meat-chopping scene implies that instead of the bread of life being divided, what we witness in Little Italy's streets is the actual stuff of life--raw, human meat, as in the street knife fight--being chopped up. The woman and the butcher are emblems of life in New York's Italian community; the activities of each, despite the ideas with which we would normally associate them (the woman as protector, the butch-

er as friendly merchant), represent a feeding of the spirit
that allows the continued existence of destructive impulses.
Ironically, while the bread-breaking scene would traditionally
connote the distribution of peace and satisfaction, it here
suggests just the opposite: the passing on as a heritage of
a violence akin to that perpetrated on animals who, like the
street-fighting youths, are routinely slaughtered. Even at
this early point in Knocking, then, we see that conflict, not
harmony, is going to be the reigning force in this film universe. [2]

   J. R. and Joey are next seen walking down a street
and entering Joey's establishment, the 8th Ward Pleasure
Club, where their mutual friend, Sally Gaga (Michael Scala),
is playing poker. Gaga is in debt to Joey, and is thus
strictly speaking gambling with some of Joey's money. Joey
therefore breaks up the game by slapping Gaga around. The
youngster apologizes, but Joey replies, "Your priest you say
you're sorry to," suggesting thereby that confession is cheap,
and that what counts is not the spiritual coin (in this case,
penance) in which the church deals but the concrete and material things in life, like the money that Gaga owes Joey. [3]

   In the aftermath of this clash we are given glimpses
into J. R. 's mind that introduce one of the film's main concerns: the relationship between J. R. and a female character
referred to only as "the girl" (Zina Bethune). In this early
flashback scene between the two characters, J. R. and the
girl are seen sitting on the wooden, virtually pew-like benches
of the Staten Island ferry sitting room, where they are waiting for the ferry back to New York. The girl is reading a
magazine, occasionally sniffling into a handkerchief; J. R. ,
carrying a parcel (containing the stuff-of-death bread; he
mentions having visited his mother), is drawn to a magazine
photo of John Wayne, at which he keeps staring. The girl
notes his attentiveness; consequently, their conversation at
first centers on the film from which the photo is culled:
John Ford's The Searchers. [4]

   Although the conversation between J. R. and the girl
initially seems innocent and sweet, Scorsese works assidu-
ously to undermine what appears to be the essential purity
of their blossoming relationship. The conversational opener
about The Searchers may seem a relatively benign way to begin talking until one recalls Wayne's attitude towards the only
female character from The Searchers that J. R. mentions:
Natalie Wood's Debbie Edwards.

In the Ford film, Wayne's Ethan Edwards clearly hates
the mature Debbie, whom he views as sullied because she
has lived with (and, the suggestion is made, had sex with)
the Indians who kidnapped her.   Additionally, in mentioning
The Searchers' Martin Pawley (Jeffrey Hunter), J. R. brings
in by allusion the polarized attitudes towards women that he
himself will exhibit.   Like Hunter's Martin, J. R. believes
in female purity: Martin appreciates the innocence of Vera
Miles' Laurie Jorgensen, and even seems to think that the
grown-up Debbie still enjoys the same quality.   Yet like Ethan,
who believes in Debbie's corruption (although he does keep
his promise to bring her back home), J. R. also realizes
how easily women can be debased.   As we shall see, throughout Knocking J. R. swings wildly between these two attitudes
in his behavior towards the girl.   This essentially unrealistic,
polarized view of women--which divides them into two classes, the redeemed and the damned, the virgins and the whores--
reflects the church-influenced attitude toward existence that,
along with other elements of their Catholic upbringing, poi-
sons the minds and lives of Knocking's male characters, all
of whom are trapped by their circumstances and world view.

Three friends--trapped.   Lennard Kuras, Michael Scala and
Harvey Keitel in Who's That Knocking at My Door?

While the conversation between J. R. and the girl continues, Scorsese undermines our sense of time and our desire to wish J. R. and the girl well by cutting back to the present. No sooner does the scene of J. R. and the girl talking on the ferry end than we see Joey (in the present) closing the pleasure club's padlock (an action depicted in giant close-up), then J. R. buttoning his overcoat, then J. R. slamming closed the door of Joey's car. While these three shots may be regarded as merely advancing the film's action, they can also--given Knocking's emblematic bent--be read as symbols of the claustrophobic, insular attitude towards life that J. R. , Joey, and Sally Gaga all share. Locked up, buttoned into, shut inside their religiously polluted view of life, the three friends are trapped in an existence within which they find reaching out and establishing a forthright relationship with a woman to be simply impossible.

With the next scene, in Joey's car, the conversation has somehow turned to the topic of women. J. R. tells Joey, "I'd like to see you get a girl without paying five dollars for her." Joey assures J. R. that he can, but Scorsese quickly contradicts this assertion. Instead, we see the third representative of the trio, Sally Gaga, back at the club, kissing a young woman who later complains that forty dollars is missing from her purse. In flashback, we see that Gaga stole the money from her while they were kissing. The woman complains that she can't get home without money, so Sally separates a bill from his pocket and gives it to her for cab-fare. Significantly, it is a five dollar note. As Gaga's example makes clear, none of the friends gets something for nothing; indeed, the spiritual price that J. R. is to pay for his association with "the girl" is considerable.

J. R. , Joey, and Gaga are next seen riding up a garage elevator. The lift's machinery gives out a harsh, annoying, grinding noise similar to the noise on the soundtrack during the bread-baking and breaking sequence, thus reminding us of the cruel religious mechanism that keeps these characters trapped in their lives. Scorsese then employs an implied match-cut: the upward-moving elevator leads us to anticipate a later scene in a high place; Scorsese satisfies this expectation by showing us J. R. and the girl on a roof during daytime, where J. R. is holding forth about Lee Marvin's essential nastiness in The Man Who Shot Liberty Valance, a film in which, significantly, Marvin's Liberty Valance threatens the identity of Jimmy Stewart's naive tenderfoot, Ransom Stoddard. Again, then, as in the reference to The Searchers,

we are exposed to a film character who represents a point
of view which, if adopted, could sabotage a young man's social and sexual development. It is difficult to avoid the conclusion that J. R. is obsessed with these cinematic characters
because he himself feels somehow threatened, and that the
person who threatens him is, ironically, the girl.

Scorsese then cuts back to the elevator sequence (the
roof top episode with the girl, as is true of all of her appearances in the film until its end, has been a flashback memory), with J. R. and Joey staring at the elevator shaft's blank
wall from their extremely limited environs (an emblem of
their entire existence), and then back again to a shot of the
club, which is littered with filled ashtrays and dirty dishes,
within which Gaga has just stolen the aforementioned forty
dollars. The effect of these scenes is blatant: there is no
escape from the confines of one's crude existence; love, when
it occurs at all, takes place in essentially grimy, unattractive
surroundings (the dirty club; during the soon-to-occur love
scene between J. R. and the girl, street noises continually
intrude). In any case, love never affords a release from
one's trapped existence. Gaga is a compulsive thief, stealing even from someone with whom he is acting romantic (thus
the harsh-sounding slammed door as Gaga's girlfriend walks
out of the club figuratively shuts him into his destructive mode
of behavior); and there is no reason to believe that either
Joey or J. R. would be liberated from their own obsessive
actions, regardless of their emotional attachments.

To affirm the sense of entrapment, Scorsese then
returns us to still another enclosed place, this time the car
again. The claustrophobia thus created is further accentuated
by the repetition of action; the reversion to the car creates
a sensation of dull, inescapable sameness. From the car
interior Scorsese cuts to a brief shot of J. R. and the girl
on the roof, reminding us of two things: the unrealized possibility of open spaces (even up on the roof, the couple seem
hemmed in by the surrounding buildings) and the fact that
though what we are witnessing is a developing mutual affection, in truth the relationship is already over. All we see
until the very end of Knocking are J. R. 's memories of the
girl; throughout the majority of the film, the relationship is
a fait accompli locked inside J.R. 's mind.

The following shot once again returns us to the car,
whose destination is either indeterminate ("Where should we
go tonight?" "Uptown." "How about the village?" "I want

to go uptown. ") or annoyingly repetitious (back to the dead-
end destination of the club). It is to the latter place that
J. R. , Joey, and Gaga are now headed. No sooner do they
arrive than entrapment once again sets in. Joey says, "Close
the [car] windows" and we are given tight close-up shots of
the electric windows shutting. Then the car doors are slammed, the club is opened (an action that leads the three principals back into a confined space), and we are given three
successive shots of closure: a car window closing again (another throwback in time, further frustrating our desire for
progress) and two identical shots of the club door closing--
a total of three shots of dead ends, one for each of the friends.

    With such a dead-end mood thus created, we are pre-
pared for a return to the past tense and another memory
scene between J. R. and the girl. This time they are in the
bedroom of J. R. 's mother's apartment. It is in this sequence
that one can for the first time fully appreciate Scorsese's
choice of Bethune for the character of "the girl. "

    Although Knocking is shot in black-and-white, one can
see that in the film Bethune is a blonde; if anything, her
blondness is more striking in black-and-white given the film
stock's greater contrast possibilities over color. The girl's
long straight hair is attractive; she appears quite beautiful
and pristine--meek, shy, polite, albeit perhaps just a little
bit too pure.

    Appropriately, the girl in this scene is quite a com-
plement to the religious artefacts (which traditionally, along
with other associations, connote purity) that are scattered
throughout the room. There is a cross over the bed; a statue
of the Virgin stands on the bureau. The scene is not without its worldly taint, though, since throughout it the street
sounds--reminding us of the Catholic-influenced but nonetheless corrupt milieu in which the film takes place--can easily
be heard.

    As a result of his upbringing, which apparently taught
him that good girls don't engage in sex,[5] J. R. feels reluctant
to make love to the girl. Although she seems perfectly (one
might say innocently) willing, and we see that her skirt's
being brushed up and her breasts' being caressed elicit no
objections from her, J. R. cannot go through with it.

    During the sequence the following exchange takes place:

An ultimately unreal vision of unrealized purity.   Zina Bethune
in Knocking.

J. R. : I love you but ...

The girl: What is it?

Scorsese then provides the visual answer: we are
given a mirror shot that shows the statue of the Virgin on
the bureau.   "It" is religion, the Catholic attitude toward sex
that unrealistically divides people into two mutually exclusive
categories (sinners and saints), that makes it impossible for
J. R. to accept this woman's love.   In essence, J. R. himself
is the mirror image of the statue Virgin; unyielding, always
watching, always judging, he is never seen participating in
and sharing the very human love that all of the film's characters need.

Of course, the situation here is wildly paradoxical.
J. R. 's apparently sincere love for the girl cannot be expressed

physically.   As we see later, though, J. R. has absolutely
no trouble making love to women about whom he doesn't care:
the prostitutes whom he frequents.

J. R. finds it impossible to realize the truth of his
situation.   His explanation of why he cannot make love to
the girl falls as far short of satisfaction as the church's unrealistic injunction to either "marry or burn."   J. R. states,
"Just not now--old-fashioned--call it anything you want--I
love you first--as you--to me--if you love me you'll understand what I mean."

We are immediately given a contrast to this scene's
seriousness in the following sequence, which depicts a party.
Significantly, where J. R. in the company of a romantically
associated woman was quite moody and withdrawn, in the party
sequence, among his male friends, he is happy and jovial
again.   The party's frivolity, though, is purchased at a rather
high price, since its main source of entertainment is a scene
between Gaga and a gun-wielding young man who, after pointing his weapon at everyone in the room (with resultant laughs
from all concerned), grabs Gaga around the neck and repeatedly thrusts the gun against his temple as though he were
going to shoot him.   (Cf. the gun threats in Mean Streets [p.
79] and Taxi Driver [pp. 105-107 and Note 12].)   The fact
that the sequence is shot in slow motion, and is accompanied
on the soundtrack by the insistent refrain from the rock song
"Watusi,"[6] only lends an anxious sameness to the scene.   The
slow motion not only draws out the horrifying action but also
subtly duplicates the slightly torpid, drunken state of the party-
goers, while throughout, the song repeats over and over.

Complementing this sense of entrapped repetition is
Scorsese's use of repeated 360-degree pans during the scene,
with each dissolving effortlessly, almost dreamily, into the
next.   The gun, and its eventual discharge (a bottle is shot
off the kitchen table), is, given the sequence's juxtaposition
with the bedroom scene in J. R. 's home, an obvious substitute
for the potency (suggested by the hard metal gun) and ejaculation (the shot) that J. R. fails to achieve with his girlfriend.
To heighten this contrast, in a reprise of the film's three-
related-sequences opening, Scorsese once again employs a
tripartite construction to communicate his film's meanings.
First we have the scene with J. R. and the girl, then the
party sequence.   The third sequence brings us back to J. R.
and the girl, thus suggesting that, as in previous sequences
that doubled back on themselves, progress (movement beyond

one's limitations) in <u>Knocking</u>'s universe is impossible. No
sooner does the gunshot at the party sound than Scorsese trans-
ports us to the outside of a movie theatre where, with repeated shots on the soundtrack, we are given successive stills
of John Wayne in <u>Rio Bravo</u> and Dean Martin in <u>Scaramouche</u>,
films in which both actors play potent gunmen whose firearms
are symbolic emblems of their prowess.

As Junior Walker's "Shotgun" appropriately plays on
the soundtrack, J. R. and the girl are seen leaving the theatre while J. R. tells his date about the two kinds of women
of which the western mythos (like the Catholic dogma) conceives.

> J. R. : That girl [Angie Dickinson] in that picture
> was a broad.

> The girl: What do you mean, a broad?

After an awkward pause, the girl finally states, rather
uncertainly, "You don't mean that." Scorsese then concretizes
J. R. 's response, choosing to let the visuals once again provide the answer. The immediately following scene shows
J. R. in an emptily sterile, rundown loft, in the middle of
which is situated a bed where he copulates with a number of
women who, if we are to judge by their lurid attire and make-
up and J. R. 's obvious willingness to frolic with them, would
indeed qualify as (to use J. R. 's term) "broads" (or, to adopt
a more potent and later-used term, whores). With The
Doors' "The End" (a song about death and forbidden sex) playing on the soundtrack, the scene takes on a truly morbid
quality. This sensation is affirmed when at one point J. R. ,
standing over a reclining nude woman, spews a deck of cards
over her body; the mock ejaculation only serves to heighten
the scene's death-like tone. [7]

We then return to J. R. and the girl and J. R. 's fuller
explanation of what a broad--like the women with whom we
have just seen him--really is. "There are girls and then
there are broads," he says. [8]

As though to suggest that there exists a possible al-
ternative to the dead-end male relationships that are all that
J. R. , Joey, and Gaga seem capable of, Scorsese's next scene
shows us J. R. , Joey, and an unnamed third young man in
Joey's car as the young man ferries them to upstate New York.
At first, it seems that perhaps in escaping from the city's

The death/loft sequence. In a symbolic move, J. R. is about
to flip the pack of cards over the woman's body.

confining and unproductive atmosphere something positive will
occur. Gaga's replacement by an older male also hints that
we may finally see J. R. and Joey acting maturely. Instead,
the first thing that the three are seen doing in the upstate
town of Copake is sitting in a bar. The idea to do so is
Joey's and the event's significance is clear: Joey is merely
repeating what he does in his Manhattan pleasure club; it is
as though he has never left home. The new male now says,
"I want to show you something beautiful," but Joey quickly
reduces this hopeful suggestion to the basest physical and
sexual terms: "OK, what's her name?"

However, the young man does have his way, convincing
Joey and J. R. to climb a mountain with him. At one point
in the climb, Joey refuses to go on. Only J. R. 's goading
(he implicitly affirms Joey's masculinity--but then only at
someone else's expense, just as the gun-wielding man at the

party did when he victimized Gaga--by saying to Joey, "Don't
let this fag scare us; come on") induces Joey to continue.
Ironically, it is fear of snakes, a traditional animal phallic
symbol, that almost deters Joey, indicating that like J. R.
he is probably incapable of dealing with sexuality in a direct
and forthright way.

When they reach the mountain top, Joey fails to see
the significance of the beautiful view. "So what's up here?"
he asks. "Big deal." His last remark, though, is the most
telling. "I don't understand," he says, and while this is
probably true for him, we may wonder what J. R. is thinking
as he thoughtfully gazes into the setting sun. Is he, in fact,
on the verge of realizing what a (Catholic-influenced) orientation towards death (as symbolized by the sunset) and enclosure
represents?

As in much else of Knocking, the answer is provided
in visual form. J. R. and the girl are once again in J. R. 's
mother's apartment; the girl lights a votive candle and places
it on the table. "Now what are you doing with a holy candle
on the table?" J. R. asks. Apparently, the girl does not conceive of religion as J. R. does; for her, religion is not so
sacrosanct that it cannot be integrated along with normal daily
activities. J. R. , though--trapped at the level of the restric-
tive word (not the benevolent spirit) of Catholicism--cannot
tolerate such sacrilegious disobedience. Ironically, he is
about to demonstrate that when it comes to an essential religious quality--compassion--he is incapable of expressing or
understanding it.

The girl relates how she was raped by a former boyfriend. She describes the "boy" as always having been a
perfect gentleman--that is, until the last fateful night. Thus
the boy, like J. R. , exhibited two polarized, antithetical types
of behavior: one sweet, kind, and basically asexual; one
cold, ruthless, aggressive, and sexual. As with the concep-
tion of women held by J. R. , there is no middle ground of
perception or behavior for the film's men: a woman is either
a virgin or a slut; a man either acts tenderly or as a beast.

With the soundtrack playing "Don't Ask Me to Be
Lonely" (ironic in that both the past encounter with the boy
and the present encounter with J. R. will leave the girl quite
alone), the girl relates the rape. As the rape nears culmina-
tion, the images Scorsese gives us of it come faster and faster
and the music on the soundtrack becomes first double, then

triple-tracked, reflecting the growing confusion and anxiety of the scene as it is recalled. The fact that along with the rape scene (many of whose frozen memory images Scorsese presents in stills, and which ends when the boy is seen pulling up the girl's skirt, at which point she screams) Scorsese also inserts flash shots from J. R. and the girl's love scene here, suggests a tragic connection between the two relationships that in purely visual terms seems to doom the later one to failure.

In pitifully predictable fashion, J. R. is unable to accept the girl in what he obviously considers is her sullied state. Although the girl touchingly states that "with you it'll be the first time," J. R. cannot share this view of things. Having known her as essentially "chaste," J. R. cannot now accept her as sullied.

Bluntly and viciously, he reacts.

> How can I believe you? How can I believe that story? It just doesn't make any sense. How do I know you didn't go through the same story with him? You go out with a guy and you don't even know what he's like?

The result is that the girl leaves; Scorsese gives us the shot of her slamming the apartment door three times. The number suggestively leads us into the next sequence, in which our three male principals, reunited, enter a bar and order three scotch and waters. Once again, we see J. R. returning gladly to the company of his male friends, displaying an ease he never seems capable of when he is with the girl. The soundtrack cruelly rings with "ain't that just like me cracking up over you?" and on the repeated words "don't you want to love me, too?" the laughter from the bar blends into the screams emanating from the girl's mouth during the rape scene (which is again depicted in freeze frames), thus drawing a painful connection between the girl's past distress and J. R.'s present pleasure. It is almost as though the two qualities were reciprocal, and in a certain sense they are, since J. R.'s preference for homophilic over heterosexual love allows him to get along with his male friends while simultaneously making it impossible for him to consummate his relationship with the girl.

There is no doubt that J. R. misses the girl. Joey earlier accuses him of thinking about her, although J. R.'s

hostile reaction to this remark suggests that he considers
his yearning for her as a sign of weakness.   Still, after the
bar sequence, when J. R. is left alone in his apartment house
lobby, drunk and tired, he reaches out his left hand for the
girl and Scorsese intercuts a tender flashback shot of the
girl, allowing J. R. , at least in his memory, to caress her
hair.

Yet no sooner does this remembered lyricism end
than J. R. is back with his friends, at another party in another woefully dingy apartment.   This time, Gaga is depu-
tized to bring back some girls (as Joey puts it, "This is the
party you promised us?   Where are the broads?").   Two
young women do eventually arrive (one of whom, like Joey,
fears phallic-like things that crawl), yet it's clear that dalliance with "the broads" is less important to J. R. , Joey,
and Gaga than their relationships with each other.   J. R. breaks
up the simultaneous make-out scenes and the girls depart
screaming, yet the manner in which Joey and J. R. endear-
ingly laugh over this turn of events indicates that they derive
more pleasure from each other's company than they do from
associating with women.

Scorsese still provides J. R. with one more chance at
a productive heterosexual relationship.   Drunk and missing
the girl (just as he was earlier in his hallway), he goes to
the girl's apartment early one morning.   At first, it seems
that they may be reconciled.   Then J. R. says, "I forgive
you and I'm gonna marry you anyway."   Probably the most
painful word to the girl is "anyway," since her circumstances
hardly merit a dismissal of this sort.   What's more, J. R. 's
statement seems to offer some sort of moral absolution, dem-
onstrating that he is still trapped in his Catholic-infected
mentality.

When his inappropriate offer is refused, J. R. becomes
hostile, attempting with words to relegate the girl to Hell.

> You can't marry me anyway ... if that's the
> kind of broad you are ... who do you think you
> are, the Virgin Mary or something?   Who else is
> gonna marry you, you whore?

J. R. refuses to be reasonable since, in his distorted
view, to accept the girl as flawed would be tantamount to
admitting that she was his equal, a situation that would en-
tail his loss of power over her, something he could not toler-

The final meeting in <u>Knocking</u>.   J. R. :   "Who else is gonna marry you, you whore?"

ate.   As he states, "you want me to crawl back to you."
For J. R. , he either has to walk tall like a great western
hero (thus the film's references to male-dominated westerns)
or "crawl"; there is no middle ground of reasonable activity.

J. R. goes on to intimate that the girl somehow en-
ticed him by letting him enter her apartment, and compounds
his offense by again (as he did in the previous quotation)
placing her in the category he reserves for fallen women.
"Leading me on like that, letting me in here at this hour of
the morning ... what kind of <u>broad</u> does that make you?"
(emphasis added).

Significantly, after being asked to leave the girl's
apartment, J. R. goes to church.   The girl, though, told
J. R. to "go home."   But for J. R. , the church is home, an
enclosed place where he may reaffirm his tragically limited
perspective (Cf. Charlie's literal and figurative returns to
the church in <u>Mean Streets</u>; see especially pp. 68-72).   We
see J. R. enter the confessional (although exactly what he has
to confess at this point is unclear, since he obviously feels
he has acted justly).   Then, in a powerful montage sequence

whose structure anticipates the end of <u>Mean Streets</u>, we see
J. R. in the confessional, shots of statues of the Virgin, and
numerous views of stigmata-adorned Christs.   The juxtapositions are instructive.   Immediately after J. R. enters the
confession booth we see a shot of J. R. kissing the girl in
his apartment; a cross on the wall is in the background.   Obviously, J. R. 's true confessor should be this sweet, devoted
woman, but he's too strongly influenced by his homophilic
obsession and his Catholic upbringing to be honest with her.
We see J. R. leaving the confessional and then a shot of J. R.
kissing the girl as church bells sound in the background,
signaling the holy union, the desired wedding, that will never
take place.

J. R. in church, looking for the unattainable redemption.   See
the strikingly similar shot from <u>Mean Streets</u> (page 69).

        More shots of statues follow, with an especial concen-
tration on their stigmata, followed by a shot of the girl's
upper thigh as though, in J. R. 's tainted view, the vaginal
opening is the ultimate wound; bleeding not salvation but corruption into the world.

A shot of the letters INRI follows, then the thigh again to underscore the point about stigmata. The bread-breaking scene then reappears, followed by the rape scene. The suggestion here is striking: the breaking of the bread, the passing on of the Catholic doctrine of polarized good and evil, not only signifies the sharing of a philosophy of death, but condemns one to a self-righteous, lonely, and violent existence (the latter characteristic emanating from the first two qualities).

The film's last scene gives us a mirror image of Knocking's opening (which showed us Joey and J. R. walking down the street together); it depicts Joey and J. R. parting, passing into the shadows as the camera pulls back from the street, thereby declaring that all of these male characters are condemned to pass into the darkness of ignorance, isolation, and death. The soundtrack may flaunt forth "I Love You So" over the end credits, but this song is clearly an ironic counterpoint to Knocking's message about the failure of love and compassion. At Knocking's end, the film's opening symbols and allusions achieve their full resonance. The bread being broken is not the staff of life but the stuff of death, and the answer to the question posed by the film's title and the song that plays during the church montage sequence ("Who's That Knocking At My Door?") is clear: it is the Catholic-corrupted, Catholic-appropriated Jesus, the God of pain and destruction (thus the blood coming out of J. R. 's mouth after he kisses the dead God's feet) who is knocking at the door; it is the God of morbidity who demands entrance.

NOTES

1. The film's credits identify this woman as "J. R. 's mother," as does a short allusive comment made later by J. R. Regardless of her actual identity, her function in the film as a matriarchal figure of the Italian community remains in force.

2. It must be remembered, though, that what we are here watching is a stylized representation of the Italian-American heritage. The loving, supportive aspects of this lifestyle are communicated in Scorsese's short film, Italian American, in which Scorsese's parents, Charles and Catherine (the latter appears not only in Knocking as the grandmother figure but also in Mean Streets' epileptic fit stairway scene and as the

off-screen voice of Rupert Pupkin's mother in King of Comedy),
demonstrate how kind and understanding Italian parents can
be. Of course, given any film's inevitable stylization, Italian
American's point of view is also necessarily limited and, to
that extent, suspect.

3. The statement strongly anticipates what Charlie says to
Johnny Boy in Mean Streets when the latter starts making
excuses about why he hasn't made his weekly loan payment
to Michael: "Michael doesn't care if you're depressed; what
is he, your priest?"

4. The reference here to The Searchers anticipates Scorsese's
use of a clip from the Ford film in Mean Streets. In both
Knocking and Mean Streets, The Searchers is extracted to
underscore the violent tendencies that are soon to surface in
the film we are watching.

5. Some of the promotional ad slicks for Knocking quite
successfully appropriated this theme. Alluding to J. R. 's
obsession, one advertisement for the film stated, "You're a
virgin or a broad; he wants a first-time girl."

6. In addition to establishing a milieu evoking the youth
culture of the Fifties and Sixties, music in Knocking (and, as
we shall see, in Mean Streets as well) plays an integral part
in communicating the film's meanings. The hard-rocking
sounds of "Ginny" provide an aural complement to the tumul-
tous streetfight at the film's beginning. When J. R. and the
girl meet on the roof, the soundtrack's "I've Had It," and with its
theme of disappointment in love, complements the scene's
tragic ambiance. Music is only alluded to in J. R. 's question
in the girl's apartment about her Percy Sledge record; Sledge's
"When a Man Loves a Woman" represents the idealized version of what J. R. thinks he feels towards the girl. Part of
the song's lyric ("When a man loves a woman, don't need no
one else") is in sharp contrast to J. R. 's ever-present need
for his male friends.

7. It is tempting to speculate that Martin Sheen's Saigon
hotel room sequence in Francis Coppola's Apocalypse Now
(a sequence which is also orchestrated to "The End") derives
much of its imagery and sense of insularity from this scene.
        A review of Knocking in the British Film Institute's
Monthly Film Bulletin (43:512; September, 1976, p. 203) claims
that this loft sequence is "a nude fantasy scene" which Scorsese added to Knocking in order "to increase the film's chances

of distribution." Indeed, the film's credits list the sequence's
female participants as "dream girls." The review's author,
Tom Milne, goes on to assert that "this interpolation of an
undoubted fantasy in a film which is already playing tentatively
with time and memory, raises totally unnecessary doubts and
hesitations ... (whether, for instance, the perfectly straight-
forward flashback to the rape might not rather be J.R.'s
fantasy--in which case the girl could be lying)."

Milne tends to miss the point here. Although he claims
that the sequence's inclusion obscures the meaning of the
forthcoming mountain-climbing scene, Milne fails to note that
the "fantasy" sequence occurs, not immediately before the
mountain-climbing scene but before a return to J.R. and the
girl leaving the movie theatre, where they have just seen
Rio Bravo and Scaramouche. The mountain-climbing scene
occurs after the second scene showing J.R. and the girl talking about these two Westerns. Sandwiched as it is between
two essentially same-time, same-place sequences involving
J.R. (who is reacting to the films) telling the girl about the
differences between "girls" and "broads," the loft sequence
acts as a reinforcement and exemplification of the absurd
distinction J.R. insists on making.

Milne is correct when he claims that we may treat
the loft sequence as a fantasy or dream, just as we may
also treat the rape scene as unreal. But to worry about
whether the scenes are "true" (as Milne does in suggesting
that the girl might by "lying" to J.R.) is to raise an irrele-
vant issue. Real or not, these two sequences clearly belong
to the speakers in each sequence's starting-off point: J.R.
(outside the movie theatre) in the earlier threesome, the girl
in the later triumvirate of scenes (in which we see the girl
and J.R. in the kitchen; the flashback occurs; then we are
back in the kitchen). Whether these inserted sequences are
"real" or not is beside the point; what counts here is that
the character visually experiencing these scenes believes
them to be true, that the scenes are accurate representations
of each character's state of mind at the time. That they
undoubtedly are, and that these insertions fit exactly into the
tripartite schema of assertion-exemplification-assertion that
Scorsese has already established in Knocking (e.g., the bread
baking/street fight-butcher/bread baking opening; the can't-
get-a-woman-without-paying-for-her/Gaga's theft/enclosure-
elevator sequence; the elevator/rooftop/return to elevator
sequence, etc.) affirms their essential validity regardless of
the scenes' real versus fantasy status.

8. J.R.'s Manichean view of women strongly anticipates the

attitude evidenced by <u>Taxi Driver</u>'s Travis Bickle, for whom
all women are either virgins or whores. (See Chapter Five.)
      An earlier statement of J. R.'s makes the distinction
he draws quite clear. "A broad isn't exactly a virgin. You
play around with them; you don't marry them." In his ignorance, J. R. believes that by offering to marry this girl, whom
someone has "play(ed) around with," he is doing her a favor.

Chapter Two

RADICALS ON THE RAILS

Boxcar Bertha is the earliest of the two films directed
by Scorsese that center on a female protagonist, predating
Alice Doesn't Live Here Anymore by two years. But while
Alice leaves the viewer with a sense of loss and fulfillment
unachieved, Boxcar Bertha concentrates on a character who
at the film's end has fully realized her aspirations. Like
Alice, Bertha Thompson (Barbara Hershey) progresses from
innocence to experience, but in the process, through affiliation with the labor movement and the oppressed proletariat,
she achieves an identification with moral and spiritual forces
that provide a more satisfying direction and structure to her
life than anything that Alice Hyatt could ever hope to attain.

Actually, Boxcar Bertha presents Bertha with two representative characters on whom she may model her behavior:
the head of the big-moneyed Reader Railroad, Sartoris, and
her labor movement lover, Bill Shelley. In a sly bit of casting, Scorsese has these roles played by the father and son
team of John and David Carradine. [1] Drawing on our simultaneous fascination with the elder Carradine's well-modulated
voice and the inherently alienating upper-class bearing and
baronial presence that he brings to the part (a bearing strongly
at odds with the way that the workers with whom Bertha and
Bill are allied comport themselves) as opposed to the young
Carradine's unstylized actions and speech, Scorsese compels
us, if only through the casting, to sympathize with the working class characters that the film presents.

In fact, Boxcar Bertha's beginning makes it virtually
impossible for us to sympathize with any other group. What
viewer would not be outraged by the manner in which the man
in the film's opening sequence (who pays Bertha's father's
wages) insists that Mr. Thompson return to the air in his

faulty crop-dusting plane even though Mr. Thompson is warned
by Bertha's mechanic companion, Von Morton, that the plane's
engine is in poor condition?   In essence, with the death of
Mr. Thompson in a plane crash, the viewer's sympathies are
determined for the remainder of the film, as is Bertha's future, which is destined to have her side with the poor.

It is this distinction between the haves and the have
nots, and the inherent injustice of the arrangement (a situation exacerbated by the Great Depression, during which the
film takes place), that determines Boxcar Bertha's thematic
course.   The film is quite obviously partisan, somewhat un-
fairly stacking the deck against the rich (all of whom are depicted as greedy, smug, and--through the activities of their
hired minions[2]--murderous), whereas the poor are seen as
predominantly warm, accessible, and thereby attractive to
the viewer.   In essence, Boxcar Bertha is a study in exaggerated contrasts, an exaggeration reflecting the gap between
rich and poor that widened during the depression.[3]   Those
with property or capital seem compelled in the film to protect
and increase their investments; in fact, we never see
the rich doing anything other than attempting to make more
money or discussing ways of doing so.   The railroad owners,
like Sartoris, who kill off union opponents in order to guard
their property; the overfed, unctuous, high-rolling gambler,
(a man who is, significantly, accompanied by a railroad lawyer) who covets Bertha as though she were a piece of dry
goods; even the madam[4] who sells her women like marketable
commodities, and is always on the lookout for more salable
items--all of these people testify to the reprehensible activities in which the rich will engage in order to remain rich.
These well-to-do characters can be seen as perverted embodiments of the self-protective impulse, affirming through
their actions the exploitative and morbid (by virtue of being
blindly acquisitive and thereby death-oriented; cf. Note 3)
essence of the capitalist system while doing things that they
apparently view as nothing more than exercising their rights
to freedom of action.

Through the power of its images; through our appreciation of the loving relationship that even during the worst
times remains strong for Bertha and Bill; through the en-
dearing qualities of its supporting characters (Barry Primus'
Rake Brown and Bernie Casey's Von Morton) and the engaging nature of its depression-era music,[5] Boxcar Bertha not
only ably takes the populist, union side but successfully converts the viewer to its radical philosophy.

Troubled, but together.   Barbara Hershey and David Carradine in Boxcar Bertha.

One can say that the film's entire thematic thrust is
determined by the period in which it is situated, a time when
the poor never seemed poorer, and the rich never seemed
better off.   Unfortunately, when Bertha, Bill, Von, and Rake
band together and begin systematically to steal from the organization that they have apparently identified as the most
visible oppressor (the Reader Railroad), we cannot view their
actions as those of spirited, fun-loving revolutionists and
progressives (although the robbery sequences usually produce
an appreciable amount of pleasure, derived from seeing the
railroad's money more equitably distributed, while the gang
at the Sartoris party show up the rich for the stuffy fools
that they are).   Rather, by deciding to express their opposition to the capitalist system through theft, the gang have thereby (by participating in the desire for wealth and by exposing
themselves to the legal penalties that the system applies to
its most visible opponents) been co-opted by capitalism in a
way more insidious than they apparently realize.

Essentially, the gang turn into nothing more than cheap
criminals, morbidly bent on acquiring the death-oriented ac-
couterments (money, material goods) of the rich (cf. the
stockgrowers club sequence in Heaven's Gate, p. 204).   The
implicit point is made by the union official to whom Bill gives
some of the money he has stolen, when he tells Bill that the
union, its finances and activities, must be above reproach if
the organization is to be effective.

Thus, Bill is incorrect when (in response to Rake's
reading out loud an article about them) he states, "I ain't
a criminal; I'm a union man."   Rake looks askance at him
here, doubtless expressing the audience's suspicion that Bill
is wrong; by this point he is indeed more thief than unionist.

Bill is the film's central political figure, a character
whom we initially encounter speaking to a group of men near
the train tracks, inspiring them with his rhetoric.   Seeing
him for the first time, Bertha immediately recognizes a kindred spirit in this man who talks about refusing to knuckle
under to the power of the moneyed interests.   Indeed, as
Bertha probably realizes, it was her father's need for money
to purchase food and clothing for his family that compelled
him to go back up in his faulty plane.   One should note,
though, that after the crowd which Bill addresses is infiltrated
by a couple of policemen and two of Sartoris' thugs, Bill
quickly incites the gathered men to riot, not for any political
purpose but merely to provide an escape for himself and Bertha, whom he grabs on his dash through the crowd.

Despite Bertha's assessment of him, Bill is correct
when he claims that he is not really such a "straight shooter."
Aside from the allusion to sexual penetration and ejaculation
involved in the statement, if we take the reference as an
evaluation of Bill's political activities, one must agree with
his comment, since his motives in working for "the cause"
are as self-serving as Sartoris' are in working to increase
his wealth.   Unlike the union official to whom he gives his
three thousand dollars in stolen money, Bill is unable to see
that the source of the funds is equally as important as the
money itself, that there is a necessity for capitalism's opponents to act within the legalities of the prevailing social
order.

Of course, in one sense this restriction on the actions
of protesters is grossly unfair, since it compels the radicals
and unionists to obey the law even while the powered elite,
in the persons of their goon squads, can engage in murder,
arson, and torture, secure in the knowledge that money will
buy them protection from prosecution.   For example, as Boxcar Bertha demonstrates, if a working men's insurrection occurs in the jail, why, even there, within a supposed strong-
hold of legality, muder may easily be done.   In fact, it is
the murderers who are seen in this part of the film to be
the ones in command; Sartoris's thugs shoot to death a number of prisoners and then order the sheriff to clean up the
mess that they tell him he has made.

Bill's character is redeemed through his affection for
Bertha, whom he constantly tries to protect throughout the
film.   We may question Bill's becoming a robber (even if,
in Robin Hood fashion, he channels the money back to the
poor), but we must sympathize with his apolitical devotion
to his lover.   The irony here is that in a film whose basic
concern appears to be depicting the inequities in the American
capitalist system during the Depression, it is only the personal relationships that really seem to be worthwhile.   We
may admire Bill's gang's daring but their actions are not,
for all of their rationalizations, laudable.

This is not to imply that the gang willingly become
thieves; they do not.   In fact, the first robbery happens purely
by chance.   The train that the four friends stop is carrying
money, but the gang doesn't know that when they hop aboard.
It is only when the mail car attendant asks, "We get robbed?"
that Bertha inquires, "Why, you got something to rob?"   Only
then does Von come up beside the railroad man and level his
shotgun at him.   Even at this point, it's clear that a robbery

will not occur without the approval of all four friends, so
Scorsese shows them voting.   One by one they gesture with
the tool appropriate in such an election: a gun.   Bertha votes
affirmatively by raising her gun.   Rake, the man who formerly lived through deception (trying to pass as a Northerner),
reluctantly joins in, having traded in his symbols of chance
(the dice, which nonetheless turn against him) and foresaken
his cards (which, when he plays, are always rigged, although
he gets caught) for what he considers a surer thing: a firearm.   We have already seen Von vote. Finally, with great
reluctance, Bill raises his pistol, and the gang's conversion
to totally illegal means is complete.

        The group has thus been changed into robbers (as op-
posed to the robber baron Sartoris, who makes money from
the efforts of the working man) and has thereby passed beyond integrity into corruption, the corruption of money. This
change is most evident later when Bertha and Rake visit Sartoris's party in order to rob him and his pompous, half-
dead guests.   The two are decked out as members of the upper class.   Rake first appears, looking awkward and over-
dressed in a tuxedo, while Bertha is seen bedecked in a fancy
gown (symbol of an upper class allure to which she is un-
accustomed, thus the poor fit of the dress on the proletarian-
minded Bertha) and jewels appropriated in a previous train
robbery.   Nor are these trappings worn only to gain admit-
tance to the party.   Indeed, admission is secured by Von,
who subdues the front-door guard with a rifle.   The clothes'
real purposes are two-fold: to flaunt affectation in the face
of the guests as well as to gain pleasure from dressing up
this way.

        This latter characteristic is regrettable, since it tends
to compromise the last remnant of the gang's integrity: their
vital allegiance to the working class.   The money that the
gang secures through its robberies seems morally to degrade
them.   This effect is symbolized most strikingly in a later
scene.   We are already familiar with the affection that all
of the friends have for each other; this emotion is tainted,
though, as we see at one point when Bertha and Bill make
love in the gang's hideout.   The lovers sit on a red velvet
cloth, perhaps stolen from one of Sartoris's plush club cars;
Bertha's arms are garishly adorned with rings and bracelets
culled from their previous robbery.   The opulent jewelry
seems not only misplaced but objectionable, symbols of a
lifestyle which the film (in the persons of the wily Sartoris
and his friends) encourages us to reject. [6]

The gang in <u>Boxcar Bertha</u> during an evanescent happy moment.

From this point on, <u>Boxcar Bertha</u> becomes more and more violent as it moves towards some kind of tragic conclusion for Bertha and Bill's love.   Rake is freed from the gang's increasing corruption through his shotgun death; the blood on his chest signals the release of his always troubled soul from the gang's dangerous round.   Von also gains absolution through blood.   Avenging Bill's crucifixion by shotgunning Bill's murderers to death, he emerges after the shooting spattered with blood, but at peace.

Significantly, Bertha and Bill do not engage in ritualistic bloodletting, although this does not mean that they will turn the other cheek when wronged.   Nevertheless, in a film in which a great many people are killed--from squatters in tent cities to poor men in jail, to the railroad thugs who kill Bill--it is important to note that not only are none of the murders committed by Bertha or Bill, but that neither of them ever attempts to use a gun (as Rake does before he is shot). Apparently, this reticent attitude towards violence is a screenwriter's ploy to keep the two characters basically sympathetic.

The fact that Bertha never directly causes any violence (even
when it might be warranted), while the only fight which Bill
starts and in which he participates is against the business-
man who hired Mr. Thompson, leads us to conclude that
neither of them really has much of a taste for hostility.

The question remains: are Bertha and Bill, as the
moral and intellectual leaders of the gang, suited to their
revolutionary roles? One must conclude that they are not.
We can only surmise that Bill's crucifixion possibly signals
for Bertha a deliverance from sentimentalism that may presage her ability to deal ruthlessly with the type of men who
victimize her and the gang throughout the film.

Is there the suggestion here that the audience, too,
is to purge itself of traditional emotional and socially ap-
proved ideas concerning the place of violence in social and
political evolution if any change in the working man's status
in America is to be effected? Perhaps so. Again, the viewer
is thrown back to the recurring question that Boxcar Bertha
raises: is violence perpetrated against the violent, and performed in the name of a just cause (as Von's is towards the
film's end), justifiable? Certainly, during the highly emotional moments depicting Bill's crucifixion[7] and its aftermath
(we must remember that although he has escaped from jail
and is strictly speaking a fugitive, Bill is at this point rather
old and feeble), the audience is virtually forced to demand
vengeance for the act's cruelty. We want to see justice done,
and it is done: Von murders all of the thugs, with Scorsese
sparing us none of the details of their murders.

How this moral question is to be resolved is left open
at the film's end. Throughout Boxcar Bertha, the railroad
line has acted as symbol of both life (Bertha and Bill's tender,
affectionate moments in boxcars) and death (present in the
Reader corporation's ruthlessness and exemplified by the many
injuries and deaths perpetrated on or near railroad lines: in
tent cities, at the meetings Bill addresses on the trains themselves, by the beating Bill receives in his shack on a side-
line, and his final death). At the film's end, though, the
railroad ironically becomes a catalyst of transcendence. Having literally and figuratively "lived by" the railroad, Bill now
dies by it as well--at the hands of railroad man Sartoris's
thugs, who beat him and then nail him to a boxcar.

Although Bill's absence will be perceived as a grievous
loss by Bertha, his sacrifice may, like that of Jesus, be an

Live by the train, die by the train: Bill's crucifixion at the
end of Boxcar Bertha.

inspiration to others, who will perhaps be encouraged to emulate Bill's best qualities: his dedication, fervency, and life-
oriented belief in the cause of the disadvantaged.   Moreover,
Bill's crucifixion quite possibly creates a martyr for the labor movement.   For the majority of Boxcar Bertha's last
shots, Scorsese positions the camera behind the door of the

car to which Bill has been nailed, so that all one sees are
the four outstretched fingers of his left hand and, below on
the ground, Bertha staring up at him. As the train begins
to pull away, Bertha follows Bill and then loses him (all the
while screaming "Don't take him, don't take him," as though
he is not only being delivered away from her and unto his
people but is also somehow being elevated to some form of
lasting enshrinement--as in "the angels took him up"). Bill's
fingers point screen left, possibly suggesting that the left-
leaning radicalization of the labor movement should (and, as
we know, will) continue until a proper balance between the
right-wing factionalism of the country's Sartorises and the
revolutionary demands of the working class is achieved. Although we lose Bertha in the film's last few seconds, it is
visually implied that instead of merely disappearing she is
somehow, like Bill, on the brink of apotheosis herself, since
she is not only lost to view near the frame's top, but becomes virtually invisible as the color film stock's graininess
can no longer adequately resolve her diminishing figure, which
in a populist-suggesting fashion seems to blend in with the
surrounding countryside. The manner of presentation of Bill's
death and Bertha's figurative "disappearance" signal eventual
symbolic ascension for them both, thus leaving us with a
powerful feeling of future possibilities that brands the film
as one of hope, not despair, and its message as one of lively
renewal, not deadly destruction.

NOTES

1. One might almost view the characters of Sartoris and
Bill as a father and son pair, the elder bitterly passed beyond his youth's idealism into a pessimistic maturity in which
only money matters. Bill, though, quite possibly represents
Sartoris as a young man, rich with ideas and desires.

2. The animal stupidity of Sartoris' two main killers (referred to in the film's credits as "McIver #1" and "McIver
#2") is aptly demonstrated when, after Bertha--who is hold-
ing a gun on them--tells the men to first "sit down," then
"stand up," then "sit down ... ," the film moves on to the
next scene in which Sartoris, as though he were talking to
a pair of trained dogs, tells the men to "sit ... sit down."

3. For a film with such a hellfire and damnation attitude
about the polarization of rich versus poor, it is surprising
that Boxcar Bertha contains only one biblical reference, which

occurs during an exchange between Bill and Sartoris. Still, this exchange is sufficiently strong to characterize the two men.

During a robbery, as Bill is gathering Sartoris's dinner guests' valuables, which he places in a silver vase (Sartoris, with characteristic upper class disdain, says, "You probably think [that] is a cuspidor"), Sartoris remarks, "Lay not up treasure on the earth," an ironic comment given his own wealth. Bill essays to finish the reference for him: " ... where thieves break through and steal." However, as Sartoris points out, Bill's quote is not only incomplete but incorrect, since it omits the reference to the deadly, corrupting, natural erosions of wealth ("moths and rust") and the injunction instead to "lay up treasures in heaven." This latter rejoinder is a part of the quote Bill would characteristically be expected to forget, since it encourages ignoring one's poverty on earth in favor of some pleasure-denying "pie in the sky" reward in the afterlife. Through the omissions, then, Bill indicates that he relies, not on salvation in another, supposedly better world, but on some form of deliverance through direct action in this one.

Thus, referring to his gun during this sequence, Bill tells Sartoris, "This here's my Bible," thereby giving voice to a sentiment whose justification seems hard to avoid, since we have already seen how necessary the use of guns to counter the forces of the rich seems to be (as when Bertha saves Rake from harm by shooting the fat gambler). However, further consideration indicates that the use of firearms in the film can also be condemned. In the gambling sequence Rake was, after all, cheating, and therefore deserved to be caught; while the use of guns by the gang can simultaneously be viewed as a proper response to the excesses of Sartoris and his thugs, as well as a deplorable fall from grace. For more on the double bind in which Boxcar Bertha's disadvantaged are placed, cf. pp. 54-55, 58.

4. When Bill is in jail, Bertha turns to prostitution for money. In one scene, intending to take a client to her room, Bertha accidentally opens the door to another room in which Scorsese and Gayne Rescher are occupied with a nude woman. The woman is standing up, with her back to Rescher; Scorsese, sitting on the bed, faces her front. When Bertha opens the door, Scorsese says in a friendly way, "Come on in." One can only guess what the two "clients" are doing, although the director's invitation to join in anticipates his appearance in the back of Travis's cab in Taxi Driver, when he has the helpless Travis participate in his spying on a woman whom the character played by Scorsese refers to as his "wife".

5. The music in the film complements and, to a certain
extent, determines our emotional reactions to the scenes in
which it is employed. Harmonica music is used for its evocative effect. This type of accompaniment first appears during the film's opening sequence, in which Bertha and Von
watch Bertha's father piloting his plane. The music reappears when Bertha has taken up residence in Miss Mailer's
whorehouse and is doubtless recalling the days when, in stark
contrast to her present situation, she was still notably innocent (a quality communicated when, in the first scene, she
absentmindedly lifts her skirt to scratch her thigh, a gesture
that Bill, working on a nearby railroad gang, is quick to appreciate; the contrast between Bertha's sexual naiveté and
Bill's experience appears once again when they take refuge
in a boxcar after the riot). Indeed, it is the sound of harmonica music coming from a cafe that causes Bertha in a
later scene (by which point she is already an experienced
prostitute) to look in and discover Von, with whom she is
touchingly reunited.

Bluegrass music is the film's predominant accompaniment, used to complement the enthusiastic, idealistic feelings
of ecstasy and freedom engendered during the gang's daring
robberies and getaways. The music first appears in modified
form as simple fiddle music during the fight involving Bill,
the man who hired Mr. Thompson, the man's black chauf-
feur, and Von. With its conflict between rich and poor, the
scene contains in seminal form the germ of the gang's later
revolt. As a consequence, when the gang begins methodically
robbing the railroad, the bluegrass music reappears; this
time, though, in keeping with the gang's self-conscious behavior, the music is more developed. It is now played by
a fiddle, banjo, and harmonica, the latter instrument introducing a slight evocative effect that recalls the gang's innocent days before they became thieves.

6. This sequence between Bertha and Bill ends with the
sound of a gunshot (either Von or Rake has fired his gun)
which, through juxtaposition of sound and image, links the
personal and public lives that the lovers unsuccessfully attempt to keep separate; the moral compromise involved with
the gang's turning to crime inevitably infects their private
relationships. The unsuccessful separation of the two spheres
has been implied earlier in the film during the sequence in
which Rake, presumably safe in a boxcar, lights his cigar
at the same time as Sartoris's thugs are setting fire to a
camp inhabited by a number of itinerants, Bill among them.

7. Bill's comparison to Jesus (and, thereby, Jesus' eventual crucifixion) is anticipated earlier when Bill, alone among the gang members (all of whom have taken refuge in a church named "Nazarene"), is seen standing where the church's altar would have been located and posed in front of a mural depicting Jesus.

Chapter Three

THE NEIGHBORHOOD

Viewers familiar with Who's That Knocking at My
Door? will realize from Mean Streets' first few minutes that
the latter film is in many ways a continuation of the earlier
work's thematic concerns. What they may not be prepared
for, though, is the striking manner in which Scorsese has
developed his directorial skills in the intervening four years,
enabling him to produce a film whose structural integrity and
emotional impact is greater than anything he has ever done
before.

Mean Streets begins with a disturbing dream (experienced by Harvey Keitel's Charlie) and ends with an outburst
of violence that easily qualifies as a nightmare. Yet even
Charlie's dream has something of a nightmarish anxiety about
it. Instead of opening with titles, the film begins in total
blackness--the blackness of Charlie's sleep, devoid of images, a realm empty of everything but words. "You don't
make up for your sins in church; you do it in the street, you
do it at home. The rest is bullshit and you know it." After
this internalized pronouncement, Charlie wakes up.

In the conflict between the desire for church-sanctioned
and church-dispensed absolution and the kind of redemption (if
indeed one is available) that may be obtained in the streets,
Charlie's statement demonstrates that its speaker is clearly
the philosophical heir to Knocking's J.R. The difference,
though, is that where in Knocking J.R. exemplified the antagonism between the secular and religious spheres (resorting
to the latter to compensate for his shortcomings in the former), no voice in the film was given to the inevitable conflict that such a bifurcated view of reality entails. In Mean
Streets, this conflict is expressly acknowledged in Charlie's
statement, although the film shows us that this problem has

by no means been resolved. The determined, self-assured
voice that offers the above statement is not that of the Charlie
who acts in the film but that of his inner self, the conscience
that gnaws at him throughout Mean Streets as he attempts to
resolve the contradictions between the things that he does
(missing appointments with his uncle; trying to break up with
his girlfriend, Teresa; acting as a protective cover for his
friend Johnny Boy; making a date with the black dancer, Diane)
and the things that he inwardly knows he should do (be punc-
tual; pay attention to his uncle; try to stand by Teresa; realize that Johnny Boy is just using him; stay away from Diane). [1]

   One of the shocking things about Mean Streets is that
the crude justice meted out at the film's end seems somehow
deserved, and this in spite of the fact that we also hope Charlie will continue to do the precise things that precipitate the
attack: protect Johnny Boy and, at the same time, remain
true to Teresa. Yet to hope that Charlie would somehow
act differently is to believe in the possibility of alternative
modes of behavior. Instead, Mean Streets makes clear that
the characters (and, by extension, the audience during the
film's viewing time) are trapped by the film's claustrophobic
atmosphere. If Mean Streets' characters are to survive, they
must act in definite ways; there simply are no choices if one
is to prosper. One must conform to the Italian community's
prevailing (even if objectionable) values or court disaster.
The film's streets are mean because they are all dead ends. [2]

   Waking from the anxious dream, Charlie gets out of
bed and passes a cross on the wall, omnipresent sign of the
church's influence and ironic symbol of the kind of selfless
sacrifice which the surviving characters in the film realize
is impossible if one is to endure. As in Knocking, Scorsese
then employs the film's soundtrack to communicate and suggest themes and meanings. Here, as Charlie traverses the
room, traffic sounds and police sirens can be heard invading
the relative calm, blunt reminders of the noisy, cluttered,
hazardous street life of which Charlie is, as we are to see,
such an integral part.

   Scorsese then cuts to a shot of an eight-millimeter
projector; as it whirrs, we are shown the film it is project-
ing (as in Alice's opening, the included film is framed smaller
than the full size of the 35mm frame, thus making us doubly
aware of both the 8mm movie within a 35mm movie and alternatively, the movie within which the smaller-sized movie
takes place). In essence, the effect of the home movie's in-

clusion is to remind us that the entirety of what we are watching is a crafted representation, an artefact that demands attention to the manner in which it is constructed if we are to
appreciate its significance.

The home movie begins with a piece of leader; a viewer
who is either visually astute or has access to a print of Mean
Streets can divine the writing that appears on this short strip
of film. Although some of the written words are obscured by
thick black divisions between the frames, enough of the writing can be read to determine that the leader labels the following home movie (and by extension the entirety of the feature
film that follows) as the "Scorsese baptism." Literally, of
course, these words refer to the baby whose baptism is celebrated in part of the home movie footage, but the words may
apply as well to the baptism into the doctrines of growing up
Italian in New York's Little Italy that is visited upon three
different groups: the characters in Mean Streets who have
already been successfully baptized into the manner of pros-
pering in Little Italy (Michael, Tony); those who, while literally baptized, must go through another baptism (this time a
blood baptism) if they are truly to appreciate the community's
moral code (Charlie, Johnny Boy, and Teresa); and finally,
the audience itself which, exposed to the film's events, is
baptized into knowledge of the assumptions and beliefs that
underlie the Italian-American experience.

I have already noted some of these assumptions in the
discussion of Who's That Knocking At My Door? In Mean
Streets, the consequences of unsuccessfully resolving antithetical desires are much more harmful than in the earlier film.
It is no longer a question, as it was for J.R., of merely deciding whether one prefers the company of one's male friends
over the love and companionship of a woman (the fact that
such a polarized, absurd choice is even seriously considered
is itself evidence of J.R.'s unnatural situation). Instead, the
price paid in Mean Streets for failing properly to balance the
values and demands of the community with one's personal
frustrations and desires is either banishment from the community (as happens with the young assassin from Tony's bar)
or near-lethal injury (the fate visited on Charlie, Johnny Boy,
and Teresa). In effect, Mean Streets significantly raises
Knocking's stakes from personal and romantic set-back to
life-threatening tragedy. The earlier film's death of emotion
here becomes the possible literal death of one's self.

After the home movie's end, the main action of Mean

Streets begins.   First we see Little Italy's annual San Gennaro feast.   Immediately after this establishing shot, Scorsese cuts to a shot inside the bathroom of Tony's bar, the
first of four such sequences that are used to introduce the
film's central male characters.   Tony (David Proval) discovers a junkie in the bathroom and throws him out of the
bar (judging by the fact that he wears a splint on one of his
fingers for the film's remainder, he apparently breaks his
finger in doing so).   Scorsese then superimposes the name
"Tony" as a subtitle.

This attempt to clean things up is clearly a characteristic pose for Tony.   Yet, as we see from Mean Streets' ensuing action, his efforts are in vain.   The bar is host to
fights, drunkenness, disagreements, even a murder.   There
is no conceivable way that Tony can keep the pollution of the
neighborhood street life from infecting his place of business.
Like the young man sticking the needle into his arm, Tony
and his friends are addicts, not to drugs but to an equally
potent force: their corrupt milieu, which creates an habitual
addiction so powerful that it can never be broken.

Next seen is Michael (Richard Romanus), the neighborhood hustler, who loans money and deals in stolen goods--
camera accessories, cigarettes, even toilet paper that has
been stolen from an army PX.   Michael attempts to sell what
he claims are "German lenses, the best kind ... telescopic."
As the man to whom he is speaking tells him, though, all
he has taken receipt of are "adapters ... Jap adapters."
The foul-up is cruelly comic; Michael adopts a pained look
and stares off into space, while Scorsese flashes his name
on the screen.   The situation aptly sums Michael up as a
cheap, ignorant hustler, one who will, judging from his vignette, never amount to very much.   Michael is a young man
destined to be taken advantage of in stupid deals (even the
kids from Riverdale who are looking for fireworks short-
change him), a characteristic which prepares us for the way
that Johnny Boy continually fails to make his loan payments
to him.   Until Mean Streets' end (when, through violence, he
legitimizes his claim to being serious about collecting the
money owed to him), Michael is seen as incapable of adeptly
handling his business affairs.

The following sequence introduces us to Johnny Boy
(Robert De Niro), the rebel aberrant whose recklessness and
disregard for prescribed behavior label him as Charlie's opposite.   Where Charlie is always officious and polite, trying

whenever possible to placate offended parties, always playing
by the rules, exercising verbal and physical restraint to accomplish his ends (characteristics for which Johnny despises
him, as we learn later in the film when Johnny says of Charlie, "Charlie likes everybody, everybody likes Charlie, a
fucking politician"), Johnny Boy is reckless in both word and
deed. He will not keep quiet when the billiard parlor owner,
fat Joey, offers payment on a bet; even after the pool hall
fight, Johnny risks another violent confrontation by calling
Joey a "scum bag." For Johnny, frankness is preferable to
seeing people get the money they deserve.

Johnny is also given to random, pointless acts of violence, another activity frowned upon in the neighborhood. As
Charlie's mafioso Uncle Giovanni (Cesare Danova) makes
clear, violence is a tool to be used only when necessary, and
then in the proper way. One does not pressure or threaten
a restaurant owner if he cannot meet his loan payment; one
shows restraint. [3] One does not shoot a man merely to avenge
someone else's honor (as the assassin does in Tony's bar);
such techniques are not practical in the contemporary world;
a low profile must be maintained. As the prevailing voice
of the community, Giovanni would doubtless condemn Johnny's
wanton acts of destruction (such as his firing a pistol off a
roof one night in a playful attempt to shatter the light on the
top of the Empire State building). Thus, Johnny Boy's characteristic act in his vignette introduction is to blow up a
mailbox and then run away. This reckless act followed by
flight portrays for us the paradigmatic behavior he exhibits
throughout the film (in which he is often seen fleeing across
rooftops and down fire escapes, running at various times
through the streets) until, at Mean Streets' end, his recklessness catches up with him.

The sirens heard after the mailbox explosion carry
over into the next scene, which finds Charlie in church; the
identity of sound establishes a simultaneity of time. Characteristically, while Johnny Boy is causing trouble, Charlie
is looking for a redemptive, penitential way out of dilemmas.
The casually dressed and coiffed Johnny Boy views excessive
actions as expressions of his freedom; Charlie--the more
repressed of the two (as evidenced by his impeccable dress
and conservative haircut)--goes to church seeking a release
from his anxieties.

He does not find it, though. Unlike Knocking's J.R.,
Charlie clearly realizes the contradictions between a redemp-

Charlie (Harvey Keitel) in church, contemplating the tempting
fires of Hell, in Mean Streets.

tion limited in scope and application (it does not speak to
situations involving physical desire and cannot be applied to
the problems one encounters in street life) and the kind of
saving grace that may be derived from the support of one's
friends.   Charlie knows that his life and the lives of his
friends are not blameless; he acknowledges the need for some
form of restitution.   But he also realizes that the church
cannot make such restitution available to him.   As he says
of the confessional and the penance that the priest routinely
doles out to him, "Those things (the Hail Marys and Our
Fathers) don't mean anything to me; they're just words." It
is at the end of this church sequence that Charlie's name is
flashed onto the screen.   Only Charlie has been afforded two
characterizing vignettes, one at the film's beginning, one here
at the end of its introductory section.   His two vignettes
bracket the others (as the bread-breaking sequence brackets
the straitened universe of Who's That Knocking At My Door?),
enclosing the characters in a structure whose form reflects the

The pool hall scene, just before the fight. Robert De Niro,
Harvey Keitel, Lenny Scaletta and George Memmoli in Mean
Streets.

limitations of the strongly prescribed, restricted lives they lead.

Charlie's realization that salvation cannot be attained
in church is purely intellectual, though, not spiritual. Charlie knows that the church can offer him nothing, yet he returns there nonetheless--either literally (as when we see
him kneeling in prayer before the altar) or allusively, as in
the repeated references associated with him to blessings.
For example, before the pool hall fight, fat Joey, calling
Charlie "Saint Charles," asks him to "bless my balls," a
mocking, playful statement which reaffirms the film's serious relationship between religion and sexuality and the conflict, especially in Charlie, between the two realms. (Cf.
Chapters One, Five and Seven.) There is also the scene in
Tony's bar during which Charlie states, "I've come to create
order: may God be with you."

Charlie may attempt to make a joke out of his spiritual
obsession, may try to minimize the part that his inner voice

plays in his life, but he cannot. His obsession with damnation clearly indicates this. Damnation--present in his discussion about the two kinds of Hell-fire ("the kind you can feel with your hand ... the kind you can feel with your soul")--is one of his constant concerns. Throughout the film--at the bar, at a table, in the kitchen of Oscar's restaurant--Charlie is seen thrusting his fingers into fire. This literal playing with purgation symbolizes both Charlie's reckless and foolhardy "playing with fire by continuing to associate with Johnny Boy (as Giovanni tells Charlie, "Watch yourself; don't spoil anything; honorable men go with honorable men") and Teresa, as well as his anticipation of the painful Hell-fires (comically represented by a scene he watches from Roger Corman's The Tomb of Ligeia) that he expects await him in the after-life.

Charlie clearly expresses this fixation on damnation: "If I do something wrong I want to pay for it my way, so I do my own penance for my own sins, and it's all bullshit except the pain, the pain of Hell." This is a convenient philosophy, since it means that Charlie does not necessarily have to do any penance in this life. Charlie goes on to talk about the two kinds of Hell-fire pain, "the physical" and the worst kind, "the spiritual." On this last word, Scorsese cuts to a slow motion tracking shot inside Tony's bar, suggesting that it is there in this secular church where much of Mean Streets' action takes place, and which is bathed throughout the film in a Hellish red light (red like fire, red like the body's insides)[4]--that a significant amount of Charlie's earthly torment occurs.

As Charlie states, though, the worst agony is "the spiritual"; on the final word, Scorsese cuts to a shot of Diane, the bar's dancer with whom Charlie is fascinated (perhaps predominantly because, being black and therefore unacceptable in his Uncle's eyes, she is as forbidden as Johnny Boy and Teresa and thus appeals to Charlie's perverse desires). It is ironic that we see Diane as Charlie pronounces the word "spiritual," since her appeal for Charlie is purely physical (as he puts it, "She's really good looking, really good looking"). The sequence's juxtaposition of the spiritual and physical suggests that the confusion about what to do, to which we are here being exposed, is in Charlie's mind (as he observes at the above statement's end, "But she's black," cf. Note 1). Indeed, throughout the film Charlie behaves as though he is two different people: one who knows how he should act, one who feels he should do just the opposite. Ultimately, though,

Charlie is weak. Unlike Johnny Boy, Teresa, Michael, and
Tony, Charlie does not really know what he wants; throughout Mean Streets he stands at the crossroads of intellectual
resolve and physical and emotional desire without being able
to decide what to do. He is in turn sympathetic with Michael,
then sympathetic with Michael's adversary, Johnny; he rejects
Teresa on his Uncle's advice and then regrets the decision.

If Johnny Boy represents Charlie's impulsive side,
the part of him that goes ahead and makes a date with Diane,
then Giovanni represents the cold, judgmental part of Charlie's personality, the part that Charlie thinks should not predominate because it is in gross conflict with his major emotional priorities: his attachment to Johnny Boy and Teresa
(although it is unclear whether Charlie would really be concerned about Johnny Boy were he not involved with Teresa,
who is Johnny's cousin. Of course, the reverse may also
be true).

For Giovanni, Teresa is not an epileptic; she is "sick
in the head." We may infer that he feels the same way about
Johnny who is, ironically, named after him. Similarly, commenting on restaurant owner Oscar's partner, Groppi, who
one evening puts a gun in his mouth and pulls the trigger
(the bullet's discharge is depicted in a completely white flash
frame; Mean Streets gives us virtually no blood until its final
cataclysm), Giovanni comments, "That Groppi was always
half crazy, half crazy to say the least." For Giovanni, then,
any individual who exhibits behavior different from the norm
(Johnny's recklessness; Teresa's desire--which Giovanni views
as consistent with her physical aberration--that, contrary to
her parents' wishes, she have her own apartment; Groppi's
disappearance and suicide) is "sick in the head." One either
behaves according to Giovanni's expectations or one is summarily dismissed as an aberrant.

Charlie is continually provided with examples of the
recklessness of his decision to remain sympathetic with
Johnny and Teresa. Thus, the first time that Johnny appears
in the film after the opening vignettes, he walks into Tony's
bar without any pants on. Charlie realizes how absurd
Johnny's entrance makes him, his protector, look, and recognizes how ridiculous it is to continue his allegiance to his
friend. Yet his internal monologue during Johnny's slow-
motion entrance suggests that he views Johnny's behavior as
a form of humiliation that he must bear in order to improve
himself. "Thanks a lot, Lord, we talk about penance and

this walks through the door; well, we play by your rules, don't we?" he says, thereby speaking to God in the bar, the church of the streets, just as directly as he addressed religious questions to himself while he was in the actual church earlier. In this secular church, though, one does not aspire to and desire Paradise; here, one contacts and toys with the notion of Hell.

Charlie apparently sees Johnny as the cross he must bear as a necessary prelude to his redemption. Teresa, too, becomes for Charlie not only a source of pleasure (like her cousin, with whom Charlie kids around at various points) but pain as well, as in his anxious arguments with her. Just as Charlie sacrifices some of his credibility for Johnny's sake (he pledges to Michael that Johnny will make his loan payment, although Johnny doesn't), so too is Charlie seen in a sacrificial position with Teresa (as when, making love to her, he stretches out both of his arms, adopting the posture of someone being crucified). This sacrificial aspect is later reflected in the cross-shaped fleur de lys patterns of the wallpaper outside a hotel room in which he makes love to Teresa (cf. Note 4).

However, neither Johnny nor Teresa is a totally sympathetic character. Johnny takes advantage of Charlie's intercessions on his behalf, while Teresa is at times portrayed as extremely rude. This aspect is apparent when she tells Michael to "fuck off," and especially when she is cruel to the cleaning woman in the hall outside the hotel room where she and Charlie meet. Johnny and Teresa's nastiness not only adds depth to their characters but relieves us of the burden of believing that Charlie is indeed martyring himself for the sake of supposedly admirable people.

Scorsese employs a number of techniques in Mean Streets to both embody and prefigure the film's actions and meanings. As in Who's That Knocking At My Door?, music plays an important role. Mean Streets opens with "Be My Baby," a song that accompanies the baptismal film. We may infer from this juxtaposition of song and image that the "baby" referred to is as much the child being baptised as the entire community and its values, values affirmed for the participants and observers in the baptismal ceremony. In this sense, "Be My Baby" is a request, not for emotional fulfillment but--given the film's claustrophobic setting--for spiritual and moral entrapment.

When Charlie enters Tony's bar toward the film's beginning, The Rolling Stones' "Tell Me" is employed. The
lyric, "Tell me you're coming back to me," takes on the
suggested meaning of a return to a loved one (in this case,
the bar, which represents the neighborhood that Charlie loves),
a tragic desire when we consider that the precise manner in
which Charlie takes the neighborhood to heart initiates the
downward spiral of events which culminate in the film's final
blowout.

Johnny Boy's entrance is appropriately accompanied
by "Jumping Jack Flash." The song not only mirrors Johnny's
neighborhood nickname (Michael at one point asks, "Where's
Flash?") but also suggests explosions, a number of which
(the blown-up mailbox, the gunfire off the roof, the home-
made bomb that he tosses, as well as the flashes from Michael's hired killer's gun) Johnny occasions. The word "flash"
may also be taken as referring to a transitory spark of bright-
ness, a quicksilver gleam, apt metaphors for the behavior
of this emotionally volatile, fast-talking character. And, as
we might expect, the song sums up Johnny's entire attitude
about his reckless actions; rather than regretting them we
see that he indeed does, in the song's words, think them
"a gas."

More classic rock songs begin to appear, evoking the
milieu of the past in which the characters, enslaved by the
community's established values, seem condemned to live.
"Those Oldies But Goodies" plays on the jukebox in Joey's
pool hall; while during the free-for-all melee in the pool
hall, "Please Mr. Postman" puns on the telegraphed punches
that the fight's participants deliver.

When Charlie makes his date with Diane,[5] "Please
Come Back To Me" plays on the soundtrack as an ironic
anticipation of Charlie's failure to return from his day's
rounds to keep his appointment. Preparing for a party,
Charlie's affection for the neighborhood is affirmed in "I Love
You So." At the party, Charlie is dancing with a drunk young
woman and at the precise moment that she passes out in his
arms, the background music trumpets forth the comical lyric,
"I'll Never Part From You and Your Loving Ways."

When, in half-hearted compliance with Giovanni's wishes, Charlie tells Teresa that he cannot see her any more,
The Shirelles' "It's In His Kiss" plays on the soundtrack; the
song's lyrics about "If you wanna know if he loves you so it's

in his kiss" aptly point up Charlie's withdrawal of affection from his girlfriend.

Finally, towards Mean Streets' end, Scorsese once again uses music as an ironic counterpoint to the film's action. When Charlie and Johnny are about to leave the city in Tony's car, "Mickey's Monkey" plays on the soundtrack. The song's title acts as an accurate indication of Johnny Boy's present condition. Having just humiliated Michael in the bar, Johnny apparently thinks that he has "made a monkey" out of the loan shark. In truth, the opposite is the case. Johnny is the monkey who belongs to Michael (Mickey). At this point, Johnny is nothing more than a skittish beast at the end of a chain whose slack Michael will soon pull in.

Traditional music is employed to complement characters and settings viewed as more conventional (and well-adjusted) than those belonging to the film's rock-saturated youth milieu. Giovanni's musical accompaniment is either opera or old-style Italian songs. Both types of music are sung in Italian, the language that Giovanni, as the representative of the status quo, usually speaks when he is talking business (even when in conversation with his Uncle, though, Charlie slips back into using English). One can see Charlie and Giovanni, then, as representing the new and the old ways of life. One of the tragedies that Mean Streets depicts is that the old ways are, apparently, the only ways. It is only the traditionally-oriented characters--those like Giovanni and Michael--who survive and prosper. In a petty way, Michael mirrors Giovanni's big money concerns; his entrance into the bar towards Mean Streets' end to collect his money in old-style fashion is appropriately accompanied by an Italian language song, a type of song whose association with revenge was presaged when it played during Johnny's immediately preceding flight, and which continues on into part of the assassination sequence. Tony also may be considered a survivor, a young man who has somehow learned to prosper, to live successfully with the perennial, oppressive beast of the past (thus his ability to safely enter the cage with his pet lion cub while all that his friends can do is cower in the corners of the room). [6]

The conclusion to be drawn from this schema is clear: there is no real future for the next generation in Little Italy, only the promise of the past's repetition. The film's characters must conform to the old ways. One does not flaunt tradition. One pays the loan shark, even if it is only a token

amount (but not the insultingly meager ten dollars that Johnny
Boy offers Michael). One does not, as Teresa tries to, dis-
obey one's parents; and one stays, as Charlie should have,
only "with honorable men."

True, Charlie's emotional loyalty to Johnny and Teresa
is admirable, but as Mean Streets demonstrates, the death of
such emotions is necessary if one is to survive. One must
be cold, cold like Giovanni (as Giovanni characteristically
says to Charlie about Teresa, "You live next door; keep an
eye opened but don't get involved") or cold like Giovanni's
counterpart, Michael (even when splattered with cake and ic-
ing at the party, Michael sits quietly, cool and detached).
To be lukewarm like the wavering Charlie, or volatile like
Johnny Boy, is simply not smart. Unfortunately, Charlie is
unable to achieve such emotional distance from events.[7]

While Mean Streets exhibits an impressive sense of
energy, the film's action is strikingly restrained. Predominantly, the action is not only limited to the neighborhood but
takes place for the most part in dark rooms, cramped corners, cluttered, smoky bars. This sense of enclosure carries
over to the type of camerawork that Scorsese employs. Rarely
does the camera open up the action. Instead, complementing
and increasing the already created sense of containment, the
camera is pushed right up against the characters, accentuating their facial characteristics (pores, sweat, anxious expressions) and also thereby giving the audience very little breath-
ing room between them and what they are watching.

This is not to suggest that Mean Streets' camera is
always stationary. One immediately thinks of the numerous
handheld tracking shots in the film, from Johnny's slow-motion
barroom entrance to the photography during the pool room
fight, during which the hand-held camera follows the action
around the room.

In the midst of the party at Tony's bar the camera,
in the slow-motion mode, is slaved to a dolly; riding along
on the dolly with the camera, Charlie is thereby maintained
at a constant distance from it as it loops its way through the
bar. Although the effect of the antagonism between Charlie's
rigidly stationary position and the careening background is
vertiginous (thus expressing his drunken state), no sense of
freedom is created. Instead, Charlie's physical enslavement
to the camera's point of view reaffirms the feeling of claustrophobia that the film has already occasioned.

The sense of entrapment that characterizes Mean Streets is complemented by the number of fateful foreshadowings that the film employs as reminders that the future of all the characters is already written. Before Robert Carradine (the assassin) enters Tony's bathroom, where he intends to murder a drunk (played by his brother David) who (we later learn) has insulted a local resident, Charlie asks Carradine if he'd like to play "a little blackjack." The game of chance and the death-symbolic color black provide a rude announcement of the deadly action that is to follow. Later, after Tony and Michael have conned a couple of suburbanite kids out of some money, they pick up Charlie and go to the movies. The scene from The Searchers that we see them watching shows us the fight between two friends (Martin Pawley and Charlie McCorry) over a woman, an action that prefigures the fight between two other cinematic friends,[8] Charlie and Johnny, which occurs partially as a result of their disagreement over the extent of Charlie's involvement with Teresa.

But perhaps the most frightening anticipations are those that prefigure the shooting of Charlie and Johnny at the film's end. A glimpse of a wheel of chance at the San Gennaro feast (a festival celebrating the bloody martyrdom of Saint Januarius, Sicily's patron saint) reminds us of how, having virtually repudiated the certainty of his future with Giovanni, Charlie is now a victim of fate. Later, as he stands outside the movie theatre where he saw The Tomb of Ligeia (itself a precursor, referred to earlier), Charlie is bordered by posters for two significant films: X: The Man with the X-Ray Eyes (whose protagonist's tragically acute vision contrasts with Charlie's self-imposed blindness) and Point Blank, a film about a shadow world of threat and aggression where, as in Mean Streets, no perceptible enemy may be identified and isolated. Significantly, the gun held by Lee Marvin (cf. the Liberty Valance reference in Knocking) in the Point Blank poster points towards Charlie, just as the gun wielded by Michael's assassin will soon be directed at him, Johnny, and Teresa.

Repeatedly throughout Mean Streets, Charlie and Johnny draw attention to their hands and their necks, the two parts of the body (Charlie in the hand, Johnny in the neck) in which they are shot;[9] these innocent gestures thus take on fateful overtones. Charlie's obsession with putting his fingers in fire has already been noted. When he has Johnny stay over with him, Charlie at one point gets out of bed and rubs the side of his neck. Later, when he is talking to Giovanni in

Charlie, with his uncle, Giovanni (Cesare Danova), unwittingly
exhibits the fateful hand-to-neck gesture.

a restaurant, he scratches the side of his neck, as though
somehow anticipating the precise location where his friend
will be shot.

        After the barroom assassination sequence, Charlie
and Johnny enter a graveyard and sit on the tombstones. The
scene's morbidity is complemented by the sound of a woman's
scream which comes from a nearby party, a sound that anticipates Teresa's scream in the car after Charlie and Johnny
have been shot. Later, walking along with Charlie after leaving the graveyard, Johnny stops to admire a small gun (possibly similar to the one Michael's assassin will use) in a
store window and, as he does so, brings his hands up to his
neck to adjust his collar.

        Incredibly, three more instances of this type of gesture
occur. In the bar after Michael has arrived for the pay-off,
Johnny calls Michael "a fucking jerk-off," at which point Tony
rubs his neck, unconsciously anticipating (as Charlie has done)
Johnny's fate. Charlie and Johnny then get into an argument
about Johnny's behavior, after which Charlie once again touches
his neck. Even after the argument ends and Charlie and Johnny

have left the bar, the foreshadowings continue. This time,
after Johnny's manic outburst Charlie hits his friend in the
neck to sober him up, an effect that Johnny's being shot in
the same place will undoubtedly have on him.

Perhaps the most shocking presentiment of danger,
though, occurs while Giovanni discusses with two of the assassin's relatives the shooting of the drunk in Tony's bar.
At a decisive point in their talk, Giovanni states that the
young assassin will have to leave New York for a while. Then,
in a dictatorial pronouncement delivered in the kind of decisive, cold voice that one could easily imagine Giovanni using to pronounce a death sentence, Giovanni says, "Get rid
of him." On these words, Scorsese cuts to a tight shot of
Giovanni's right hand. Giovanni's omnipresent small cigar
is thrust between his second and third fingers; his hand passes horizontally over the table's upright sugar pourer. The
conjunction of the death-like pronouncement with the upright
dispenser and the phallic cigar establishes a linkage between
death and potency that appears three other times in the film.

When the drunk is shot in the bathroom, he is leaning against the wall, holding his penis in his hands. Just
before he fires, the assassin unfurls his long, feminine-
length black hair: the deadly confrontation thus takes on a
sexual suggestiveness. In another scene, Charlie and Teresa, the film's major heterosexual couple, are in bed together:[10] at one point, Charlie makes believe his hand is a
gun and shoots her (cf. Knocking [p. 39] and Taxi Driver
[pp. 105-107 and Note 12]), while on the soundtrack a gunshot is heard. This deadly game between lovers not only
anticipates the later shooting of Charlie, Johnny, and Teresa[11] but its juxtaposition of morbidity (the pretend gun) and
sexuality (the intimate setting, the phallic finger-as-gun-
barrel) reappears in Charlie's dream about Teresa, whose
most powerful image is Charlie's penis coming blood: the
organ of reproductive life here connotes death. Finally,
after Johnny has taunted Michael in Tony's bar by refusing
to pay him enough, Johnny offers two gestures: a threat with
an empty gun (in contrast to the loaded gun that Michael will
soon have his hired killer use) and, as Michael is leaving,
a dry-hump motion to communicate to Michael that in screw-
ing him out of the money Johnny has, in effect, fucked him
up the ass. In each case, the traditional symbols of male
potency (the cigar, the hand-as-gun, the penis in the dream,
Johnny's gun and penis gestures) accompany a gesture and/or
a piece of dialogue that, instead of connoting productive life,

suggests sterility, finality, figurative death. Apparently, traditional symbols of potency in the film's universe have failed; they have been replaced by symbols of death and impotence. Even Giovanni's power and resolve are implicitly criticized; in contrast to Charlie, Giovanni's coolness makes him appear corpse-like.

In reprising the film's opening vignette technique, Mean Streets' end returns us to the film's beginning as though we have been stuck in the same place for almost two hours (an effect that complements the film's static atmosphere). After the shooting of Charlie, Teresa, and Johnny Boy we see Tony washing his hands. Charlie, too, had wanted (like his friend Tony) to stay clear of the neighborhood's taint by being uninvolved (thus Charlie's symbolic washing of his hands while Giovanni consigned the young assassin to oblivion) but he had failed. Tony had suggested to Charlie that he repudiate his pointless religious view, the one that involves compassion, but Charlie did not take his advice. "Why do you let those guys [the priests, with their patently absurd stories about redemption and retribution] get to you?" he asks Charlie. "You gotta be like me if you're gonna be safe." Even though locked in the neighborhood, Tony has learned how to tame the beast of his surroundings, but Charlie cannot emulate his friend.

We next see Giovanni watching a television film which depicts a young woman being lifted supine out of a wrecked car, an image that shockingly matches our view of Teresa being helped out of Charlie's crashed car after the shooting. Characteristically, Giovanni retains his composure in the face of this violent image. Diane is seen coolly lighting a cigarette; nothing has changed for her; she sits alone. Charlie's promise of a hostess job in his pipe-dream club has, as she probably expected it would, come to naught; consequently, she wears the same ironic expression she displayed when Charlie first mentioned the idea to her. Michael and his gunman recline peacefully in their car; having carried out their homicidal mission, and wreaked revenge as the law of the community dictates, they can sit and relax.

As for Johnny Boy and Charlie, Johnny is seen, no longer running jauntily as usual, but stumbling along the street, holding his neck as he weaves down a fire (the judgment of Hell) lane; Charlie, sunk penitentially onto his knees outside the wrecked car, stares ahead blankly, uncomprehendingly, as a police siren (reprising a sound from Mean Streets'

The pay-off in Mean Streets: Charlie, injured in a shoot-
out; Johnny has already stumbled away.   Note Teresa's hand
protruding through the car's broken windshield.

beginning) is heard in the distance, after which a patrol car
pulls up.

        Scorsese ends the film with two symbols of tragic
closure.   He takes us back to the San Gennaro feast (a festival that goes on routinely while people are being systematically slaughtered) and gives us a song from the feast ("There's
No Place Like Home") whose bitter aptness needs no comment.
While a shockingly blithe "Thank you, thank you" from a television show blares on the soundtrack, followed by a depress-
ingly joyous-sounding "buona notte" from one of the feast's
participants, Mean Streets winds down to a close.   The film
ends with a street-side shot of a woman in a brightly lit
apartment pulling down a window shade, thus figuratively shutting out the light of hope and redemption and, in the process,
closing the all-seeing eye of the film on this claustrophobic,
death-oriented neighborhood and the tragically limited individuals trapped within its morbid confines.

NOTES

1. This inner voice continues to hound Charlie throughout the film. It is this voice that delivers the pronouncements about the two kinds of pain in Hell. Addressing itself to Charlie's ego, the voice again appears while Charlie is appreciatively watching Diane, and comments, "She's really good looking ... but she's black, you can see that," as though attempting to teach Charlie's active side how wrong he would be to go out with her. Consequently, when Charlie is on his way to meet Diane, the inner voice asks him, "Hey, are you crazy?" and Charlie tells the cab driver to drive past their destination.

Charlie's conscience is aware of the destructive power he is tempting by his actions in the film; it identifies the flames in the restaurant grill into which Charlie thrusts his hand as "fire." Unfortunately, the presence of this voice, which speaks in contradiction of everything that Charlie does, brands him as an unintegrated, doubtful misfit, a condition that appears ludicrous to self-assured characters like Johnny Boy and Teresa when, towards the film's end, Charlie allows the voice external expression for the only time in the film. When he says, "I think you could safely say that things haven't gone so well tonight but I'm trying, Lord, I'm trying," all Johnny and Teresa can do is laugh at him.

2. Mean Streets' title derives from a passage in Raymond Chandler's essay "The Simple Art of Murder," which appears in The Simple Art of Murder (New York: Ballantine Books, 1972, p. 20). Alluding to someone we may assume to be his ironic private eye, Philip Marlowe, Chandler wrote,

> In everything that can be called art there is a quality of redemption. It may be pure tragedy, if it is high tragedy, and it may be the raucous laughter of the strong man. But down these mean streets a man must go who is not himself mean, who is neither tarnished nor afraid. The detective in this kind of story must be such a man. He is the hero; he is everything. He must be a complete man and a common man and yet an unusual man. He must be, to use a rather weathered phrase, a man of honor--by instinct, by inevitability, without thought of it, and certainly without saying it.

Clearly, given Mean Streets' concern with redemption, and Charlie's lack of meanness, Charlie could qualify as such a man. Yet his continual doubt about his actions, and his trepidation over the choices he is compelled to make, unfor-

tunately brand him as both "tarnished" and "afraid." Charlie
desires honor, but not the kind of honor his Uncle talks about;
he wants an honor that surpasses individual circumstances,
one beyond any judgment, one that is, thereby, essentially
unrealistic and unattainable.

3.   As Giovanni puts it, "You can help by waiting; don't be
impatient." Then, Charlie's uncle goes on elliptically to fore-
tell who will gain control of the restaurant as long as Charlie
behaves. "You like restaurants? he asks.

4.   The bar's color is red, like the carpeting in the corridor
outside the hotel room where Charlie and Teresa meet to
make love; it thereby suggests a vaginal recess in contrast
to the corridor's cream-colored walls (which are, in a reminder of the Catholic dogma that pervades the film, em-
blazoned with cross-like fleur-de-lys patterns) and the light-
ness of the film's characters' skin tones.   Truly, inside the
bar we are exposed to the inner characteristics of most of
the film's principals.   It is therefore no surprise that virtually all of the film's key events (the murder of the drunk;
Charlie's agonizing over his actions and his attraction to
Diane; the drunken welcome home party; the conflicts between
Michael and Johnny and, at one point, Charlie and Teresa;
the scene with Tony and his lion) occur in the bar.

5.   Two shots in the sequence involving Charlie's cab ride
on his way to meet Diane strongly anticipate Taxi Driver's
camerawork and milieu.   One shot is comprised of a slow
point-of-view pan along the street where Diane is waiting.
The nighttime lighting (both cinematographers, Mean Streets'
Kent Wakeford and Taxi Driver's Michael Chapman, intentionally overexpose these respective shots to give them a nightmare garishness), the gaudily-lit stores, the street people
silently drifting along--all reappear in Taxi Driver's shot in
which Travis, looking out from his cab, scans a similar scene.
Similarly, the shot from the top of Charlie's cab, which includes the street scene as an out-of-focus background, also
reappears virtually verbatim in the later film.

6.   In this respect Charlie is just the opposite of the adaptive
Tony; their polarized counterpart status is affirmed in their
dress for the party at Tony's bar.   Tony wears a white tie
against a red collar; Charlie wears a red tie against a white
collar.

7.   Of course, such coolness has its disadvantages as well.

Michael and Giovanni are the least sympathetic and human of
all the film's characters. Indeed, Michael's and Giovanni's
detachment makes them seem more dead than alive.

8. We have seen the use of a film within a film in Knocking,
in which references to Rio Bravo, Scaramouche, The Man
Who Shot Liberty Valance, and The Searchers not only com-
mented on the film's action (as The Searchers and other film
references do in Mean Streets) but also reminded us that the
"frame" which contains the references is itself a film and
thereby demands careful attention if all of its referential language is to be successfully deciphered.

9. Johnny's neck wound also strongly anticipates the neck
wound that Travis receives from Iris's apartment building
caretaker during Taxi Driver's extended "blowout" sequence
(cf. the photo on page 109).

10. During this sequence, Teresa asks Charlie why he never
tells her he loves her, to which Charlie replies, "Because
you're a cunt." Even though something of a bad jest, the
statement contains enough serious meaning to establish a link
between Charlie and Knocking's J. R. , who would consider
any non-virginal woman a "whore."

11. Notably, this precise hand-as-gun gesture resurfaces
at various points in Taxi Driver, where it has a similar figurative and fateful effect.

Chapter Four

SHE'S LEAVING HOME

Alice Doesn't Live Here Anymore represents Scorsese's attempt to produce what might generally be referred
to as a woman's film. Alice Hyatt (Ellen Burstyn) is a character who possesses a great deal of the director's sympathy,
as is clear from her being placed in situations in which it
is people other than herself who seem obsessed, greedy, or
vengeful. For all of her foul-mouthed wise-cracking, Alice
seems for the majority of the film to be a relatively compliant person (perhaps too compliant, as in her servile attitude towards her husband at the film's beginning). Essentially, she is an innocent abroad in a corrupt world, with
only the support of her sarcastic son and an occasional friend
to sustain her.

One can see the genesis of New York, New York's
period look in Alice's intentionally stylized beginning. After
the film's opening display of the contemporary Warner Bros.
logo (a large W superimposed on a black and red background),
the film proper begins, immediately reverting to the old Warner Bros. shield logo. This nostalgic recreation is complemented by the significant amount of masking at the frame's
edges, as though to suggest that what we are watching here
is a film within a film, a dramatization within the drama. 1
Indeed, given the opening scene's exaggerated, stylized set--
which includes a garish red sunset in back of a model house--
one can assume that what we are seeing is a representation
of Alice's memory of her childhood.

This peek into the past is not all sweetness and light,
since when the young Alice responds to Alice Faye's "You'll
Never Know" by singing a few lines from the song and then
commenting, "I could do better, and if anybody doesn't like
it they can blow it out their ass," we can see the seeds of

the present-day Alice's defensive vulgarity (a trait mimicked
by her son).

The transition to the present is slickly accomplished
through an echo chamber repetition of the word "now" from
the song lyric, a telescoping of the image into the dim recesses of the past, followed by an abrupt plunge into the present.
The inset frame is replaced with a full frame, and the Alice
Faye song yields to the loud music of Mott The Hoople.

Unlike the young, aggressive Alice, the present-day
Alice is woefully worried if anybody (in this case her husband
Donald, played by Billy Green Bush) does not approve of what
she does.   Alice is solicitously concerned about whether or
not Donald likes the dinner she has prepared for him (he
wolfs it down without tasting it) and tries, unsuccessfully, to
engage him in conversation.

What is intriguing about Alice's present-tense opening
scene (which includes her son Tommy at the dinner table) is
that what we watch at work does not appear to be a family
unit.   Although we may infer a link between Alice's comic
inventiveness (she herself answers the questions she poses
to her sullen husband) and her son's prankishness (he substitutes salt for the sugar), there seems to be no cohesive-
ness among the three people who are sharing dinner.   In
fact, in his indifference to both Alice and her son, Mr. Hyatt
seems less like a true husband and parent than a cruel step-
father.

It is essential to note the distinctive ways in which
Alice and Tommy (Alfred Lutter) deal with Donald Hyatt.
Tommy's response is one of either selfish unconcern (as
when he plays his loud music) or barely concealed hostility
(the substitution of the salt for the sugar; he knows his mother
does not sweeten her drinks, so the joke is solely on Mr.
Hyatt).   Despite her husband's coolness towards her, though,
Alice is extremely deferential.   Her son may try to ignore
his father, but Alice is totally dependent on Donald for emotional support.   Failing to receive such support, the best she
can do is either affect nonchalance (exemplified through her
kidding) or, like the film's other women (with the notable exception of Flo), resort to tears to get what she wants.

Thus, when Donald later favors the television over
Alice, Alice turns away and begins to cry.   The tears bring
the desired response: Donald turns toward Alice and begins

First of three steps toward liberation: Alice (Ellen Burstyn)
with husband Donald (Billy Green Bush) in Alice Doesn't
Live Here Anymore.

to caress her.   We can assume that no matter how genuine
her crying is, Alice also knows through experience that such
a technique brings her what she desires.   Even the barest
degree of preconception brands her as a manipulator.

Similarly, although later in the film Alice is obviously
weary and depressed after a fruitless job search, understand-
ably breaking down in front of a bar owner (with the result
that he buys her a drink and offers her a job), we can again
assume that her crying is employed as a manipulative tool.
At this point in her life, it is the only way she knows to get
what she wants.   (Later, Ben's wife will use the device on
Alice with similar results.)

Ostensibly opposed to this type of deplorable female
manipulation is the character who embodies an alternate form
of female behavior: Flo, the waitress in Mel's diner.   As
portrayed by Diane Ladd, Flo is, quite simply, one of the
gang.   Her language not only easily exceeds the mild scatolo-

Step two: Alice with violent boyfriend Ben (Harvey Keitel) ...

gies that Alice and Tommy employ, but even surpasses the
kind of speech of which the diner's clientele seem capable.
However, Flo resembles her new co-worker in that she uses
her femininity for personal gain. Alice cries to get what
she wants; to increase the size of her tips, Flo unbuttons
her blouse an extra button down, a strategy she recommends
to Alice.

By the time she goes to work at Mel's, Alice is in
limbo. Donald's death has thrust her into the world, which
she first confronts using the same tools (crying, and an attitude of compliance, which she exhibits with Harvey Keitel's
Ben) she employed in her marriage. Having realized soon
after beginning work at Mel's that such strategies are no
longer useful, she is left adrift, without an alternative model
of behavior. Certainly, Flo is sympathetic to Alice, and
after their initial hostility passes Alice appreciates her friendship. Yet Flo is really nothing more than a replacement for
the female friend Alice left behind in her old neighborhood.
Moreover, both women are still involved in manipulating men
to satisfy their needs.

... And step three, Alice with the supposedly "new man,"
David (Kris Kristofferson).

The question arises whether the new character who
enters Alice's life at this point (Kris Kristofferson's David)
actually represents a change from the kind of behavior patterns that Alice has formerly exhibited and the kind of men
with whom she has been associated.   David is clearly the
third member of the dialectical progress in male relationships that the film shows us (Donald and Ben are the first
two parts of the equation).   But does he represent (for Alice
and for us) a change which would indicate that in some significant way, Alice has improved in the film?

The answer to this question is crucial, because on
it depends our reading of the film's resolution.   Certainly,
Alice's relationship with David is different from anything she
has known before; their affection is openly and reciprocally
expressed.   Alice becomes insistent about her own needs;
at one point, with the relationship at a crisis, Alice demands
and wins from David a concession related to her desire to
move on to Monterey.   David agrees that if she wishes to
leave, he will sell his ranch and accompany her.   Yet there
is also the annoying suspicion that Alice is the same person
she has always been.   She is still strongly dependent on a

man for emotional support, regardless of how liberated in
attitude that man might be. What's more, it is important
to note that as her relationship with David develops, Alice
progressively gives up the idea of working on her own as a
singer. Granted that her voice is rather poor, and that a
repudiation of this aspiration may reflect a mature evaluation of her talents, yet we can also view her abandonment
of her wish as a sacrifice of her ambition.

The essential problem with Alice Doesn't Live Here
Anymore is that the film communicates a semblance of moral
and spiritual progress while what it actually catalogues is a
story of spiritual inertia. Strictly speaking, Alice has merely
substituted one life, meaningless without a man, for another
in which she is as emotionally dependent as before. In this
respect, the film invites comparison with Paul Mazursky's
An Unmarried Woman. The Mazursky film's female protagonist, Erica, is similarly uprooted by a cataclysmic event:
her husband leaves her, and she graduates from a flawed
marriage to a relationship with a man (Alan Bates's Saul)
who seems to treat her (as David treats Alice) as an equal.
Both Alice and Erica are portrayed as having important relationships with strong-minded children who create conflicts
with their mothers' new love interests.

At both films' ends, we are left with images of these
women which suggest, not freedom, but an ambiguous struggle,
one characterized by neither independence nor bondage. Erica
is last seen maneuvering Saul's large painting down the street;
she seems at once both decisive (her attempt to steer the
painting along the street) and powerless (the way that the wind
buffets her about). Alice is last seen walking towards the
Monterey that after Donald's death she stated was her goal.
Yet the mythical destination she set for herself earlier is
now only a sign for the Monterey filling station. To further
undermine the sense of Alice's progress, Alice's moving away
from the camera is photographed with a telephoto lens which
collapses the perspective, making it seem as if Alice is getting nowhere.

Ultimately, despite the feeling of satisfactory closure
that the ends of these films engender, neither An Unmarried
Woman nor Alice leaves us with a picture of a woman in control of her life. While both films chart a pilgrim's progress
from oppression towards something better, neither shows its
heroine getting what she really wants. Consequently, both
An Unmarried Woman and its complement, Alice Doesn't Live

<u>Here Anymore</u>, must be viewed as representations of the
period in which they were filmed, a time of change characterized by a searching for new goals but, unfortunately, not
necessarily an attainment of them. [2]

NOTES

1. Scorsese previously used this frame-within-a-frame technique in <u>Italian American</u>.   At the end of this short film, the
director freeze-frames a shot of his mother, reduces it in
size, has the shot change to a nostalgic sepia tone, and in-
sets it within the film's full-sized frame.   Given <u>Italian Amer-
ican</u>'s wonderful evocation of the Scorsese family's past, which
is visually captured in family stills, this metamorphosis of
Catherine Scorsese into yet another family portrait brilliantly
situates her in the familial context as a chromo of Italian-
American life.

2. The fact that Alice has set for herself a goal which she
never reaches suggests a structural and thematic linkage between <u>Alice</u> and <u>Raging Bull.</u>   Although in the latter film the
protagonist's goal is not consciously defined (nor is his inability to reach it a willing act, as it partially is for Alice),
the notion of frustrated expectations is nonetheless similarly
expressed in both films (cf. pp. 129-130 for the significance of
<u>Raging Bull</u>'s end).   This notion of delayed achievement as-
sumes additional form in <u>Raging Bull</u>'s scene involving post-
poned ejaculation (cf. p. 125).
      One other notable similarity between <u>Alice</u> and <u>Raging
Bull</u> is that in each film the central character moves from
one heterosexual relationship to another, thinking that some
form of progress is being made when, as is made clear to
the audience, no substantial difference in the central character's consciousness exists as a result of the change.   Instead, as we discover, both Alice and Jake merely repeat
with their new partners virtually all of the patterns of behavior they manifested with their original mates.

Chapter Five

GOD'S LONELY MAN

Of the five Scorsese films that feature Robert De Niro, it is <u>Taxi Driver</u> that commands the most attention and respect. <u>Mean Streets</u> features De Niro in an interesting role, but we do not see as much of him as we would like to. None of the other De Niro/Scorsese films partakes of the strange inner logic and ineluctability that make <u>Taxi Driver</u> a true classic. De Niro's Travis Bickle is on a far greater and more profound journey (through the city's Hellish landscape) than any of the other characters that he has portrayed.

Essentially, Travis is in search of total moral and spiritual redemption, which the film shows as capable of achievement only through violence. What distinguishes Travis from Johnny Boy, Jimmy Doyle, Jake La Motta, and Rupert Pupkin is his desire to express verbally and understand intellectually exactly what is driving him. In attempting to reach such answers (which he does partially through keeping a diary, the only De Niro/Scorsese character self-conscious enough to do so), he becomes not only the mythic individual on a symbolic quest that the film makes him out to be, but a self-reflective figure whose thoughtfulness wins him more audience identification and sympathy than those Scorsese characters who are merely interesting (Johnny Boy, Jimmy Doyle, Rupert Pupkin) or pitiable (Jake La Motta).

This achievement of sympathy is especially interesting because it occurs despite the normal reactions one might expect from an audience. After all, Travis is a seriously disturbed man who performs acts of gross physical violence in answer to some nameless and barely expressed calling. <u>Taxi Driver</u>'s black joke ending has Travis elevated to the status of cultural hero; he is depicted by the media as a valiant crusader--the lone taxi driver battling the bad gangsters. This

resolution is both ironic and improbable, since it seems doubtful that the police--given Travis' outlandish outfit and over-
stocked arsenal--would have found acceptable the newspaper-
touted notion of Travis as a simple do-gooder engaged in a
vendetta against evil. Nor does it seem probable that the
Secret Service agent at the Palantine rally whom Travis belittles would not have recognized in the newspaper photos of
Travis the aberrant individual he had encountered earlier.

     Taxi Driver's ending is given a further twist when we
realize that Travis' initial target for violence is presidential
candidate Charles Palantine, who bears the brunt of the hostility to his campaign worker, Betsy (Cybill Shepherd), which
Travis transfers to Palantine after Betsy refuses to see him
again. Had Travis been successful in carrying out his original plan, he would have been an assassin, not a hero.

     Unlike similarly structured blow-out films such as
Straw Dogs and The Wild Bunch, Taxi Driver is unique in
that a number of the film's victims do not seem to deserve
their ends. Certainly, we can fairly easily dismiss the deaths
of two men involved in Iris's prostitution: the Mafioso and
the sleazy apartment caretaker; these are, after all, character types who traditionally earn their usually horrible deaths.
But the shooting of Harvey Keitel's Sport, and the apparent
killing of the black youth who holds up a delicatessen (a murder jointly carried out by Travis and the delicatessen's owner)
seem brutal and excessive reactions to these characters' of-
fenses. As Iris points out, Sport is not detaining her against
her will, while the murder of the youth in response to a petty
theft seems out of proportion to his offense.

     In fact, Taxi Driver's entire attitude towards non-
whites consists of a curious fascination with cultural "out-
siders" along with a dread and anxiety that both attracts and
repels us at the same time. The film's sympathetic black
taxi driver is (to us as viewers) surely a benign character,
as are the black youths seen on the American Bandstand television show that Travis watches at home. Yet countering
these impressions are the tough-looking blacks who frequent
the Belmore Cafeteria (where the cab drivers meet), and the
chain-bedecked black youth who brazenly struts past Travis
outside the cafeteria.

     Can we also ignore our ambiguous feelings about Sport
a reprehensible character to be sure, but a figure who despite his pimping and unctuous mannerisms elicits (for what

Iris (Jody Foster) with Sport (Harvey Keitel) in Taxi Driver.
He's oily, and slimy--but, for us, enjoyable, too.

must be described as basically comic reasons, given his out-
rageous clothes and haircut and the apparent glee with which
Keitel attacks the part) an appreciable amount of sympathy
as well?

An essential point to remember is that Sport and Travis
are quite similar characters.   Each one exploits Iris (Jodie
Foster) for his own purposes.   Sport tries to keep Iris docile
and submissive so that he can continue to derive money from
her prostitution, while Travis uses her as the excuse for giving in to his homicidal tendencies.   Under the guise of saving
her from a life he views as corrupt and debased (although
there is no reason to believe that the deaths of Sport, the
caretaker, and the Mafioso were necessary to effect Iris's
release), Travis goes on a murderous spree.

It would appear that Travis needs to achieve some form
of moral and psychological blindness to his "enemies' " essential harmlessness in order to perform his violent acts.

The imaginary opponents to whom he speaks when practicing his gunmanship ("You talking to me; well who the Hell else are you talking to?") and the painted-on figures at which he shoots on the rifle range are inhuman targets that he must treat as adversaries simply because there is no real, recognizable human enemy in the film on whom he can blame the city's essential corruption.[1] Like Charles Palantine, who misrepresents politics' true operations (his "We are the people" slogan seems to suggest that people can directly influence politics when in fact his entire campaign, which sells him like a consumer product, only points up the deceptions inherent in the political process),[2] Travis oversimplifies the life that he sees in the city. Admittedly, much of what Travis views is sordid and objectionable; the city does seem to be (in Travis's words) "an open sewer," but its basic nastiness does not derive from any one source.

Through a process of narrowing, by means of which his goals become more and more modest (saving the city is reduced to saving voters from Palantine, which finally becomes saving Iris from her captors), Travis works hard at creating objectionable windmills to tilt at in order to justify his own directionless existence. What is most tragic in Taxi Driver is not New York's corruption but the corruption of a rather typical man who can only find peace through violence, and who feels compelled continually to seek out search-and-destroy missions (a pattern of behavior doubtless stemming from his Marine training) in order to give meaning to his life. The only difference that really exists between Travis and ourselves is that Travis acts on his compulsions instead of suffering in silence.

Travis conceives of himself as being on a divine mission; as he puts it, he wants to see "a real rain come and wash all this scum off the streets." By this point in the film we have already heard Travis mention that at the end of his work shift he has to "clean the come off the back seat; some nights, I clean off the blood." In his concern with what he considers necessary cleansings, one can see how Travis has already to a degree prepared himself for the role of the city's deliverer from evil.[3] The fact that throughout the film, despite the garishly lit shots that characterize it, Travis's cab is often covered with glistening droplets of water suggests that its occupant--inside his chariot, within which like a dutiful Charon he ferries his passengers across New York's death-like streets--is a man suited to the role of liberator from corruption.

Yet Travis is in no sense represented as a totally divine deliverer. The shots towards the film's beginning of his cab slowly emerging from sewer steam[4] suggest that he is, additionally, a messenger from Hell. However, since Travis (along with all of New York's occupants) is himself in Hell, it seems appropriate that it be one of the underworld's inhabitants who, in rebellion, attempts to effect a change.[5]

On his initial appearance at Iris's apartment, Travis arrives, not in the guise of a knight in shining armor (a role that the impeccably coiffed and dressed, white-maned Palantine/paladin affects), but casually dressed. He offers Iris financial help if she will leave the city, thereby attempting to use the spoils of corruption--the money he earns from driving the "spooks, whores, and junkies" that he ferries around--to fight corruption.

Like all of the other characters that De Niro has played in Scorsese films, Travis is a loner. "I'm God's lonely man," he writes in his diary. He is a man not only incapable of establishing and maintaining relations with other people but one who, for indecipherable reasons, is constituted differently from those around him. Because he is alone and left to his own devices, Travis must construct and live by his own moral code. Much like the lone cowboys in America's Old West, where every man with a gun was a law unto himself, Travis is a solitary man riding shotgun through the night, a self-appointed marshal cruising the streets for trouble and righting wrongs (e. g. , the grocery store holdup, the supposed oppression of Iris) wherever he sees them.[6]

Taxi Driver leads us to identify isolation as the catalyst for Travis' destructive impulses.[7] In essence, because he is unable effectively to establish relations and communicate with other people, Travis is left without the guidance of human experience. As a consequence, his already-distorted notions about life (he derives his knowledge of love from the pornographic movies he attends, his knowledge of human interaction from the soap operas he watches) are allowed to develop untempered by the attitudes and opinions of others. The film may in one sense be read as a didactic tract warning us of the dangers involved when communication among people fails. There is evidence of this in the non sequitur discussions among the cab drivers; the cliché-ridden dialogues Travis has with Betsy and Iris; and Travis's pointless talk with Wizard, in which the only clear statement Travis can make about his condition is, "I got some bad ideas in my

"I'm God's lonely man." Robert De Niro in <u>Taxi Driver.</u>

head." Wizard's offered rejoinder? "Get drunk ... get laid ... you're all right." Travis' tag name tells it all: Travis Bickle is a man whose travail is to travel towards argumentative (bickle/bicker) confrontations. Although as a cab driver Travis takes people everywhere, the only location towards which he is himself heading is a place where he can play out his self-styled Armageddon.

Our reactions to Travis are highly ambiguous. The self-justified loner, the man who not only carries out the law but <u>is</u> the law, has a revered place in our national mythology.

Often, as in films like High Noon, the lawman becomes the
law's last representative, with the rest of the supposedly God-
fearing townspeople cowed into submission to tyrannical out-
laws whose self-assurance brands them as superior to the
equivocal citizens. Only the man who is upright and pure
(thus Travis' purification rites before attempting to shoot
Palantine: "No more pills, no more bad food, no more de-
stroyers of my body," no more sentimentality--Betsy's roses
are burned) can hope successfully to oppose urban corruption.

Correlative to his belief in God ("I'm God's lonely
man," emphasis added) is Travis's belief in the Hellish judgment that he thinks awaits him in response to his planned
homicidal actions. In this respect Travis is like Mean Streets'
Charlie, a comparison which highlights essential points in the
taxi driver's character. Charlie prepares for the Hell towards
which he believes he is heading by thrusting his fingers into
fire, as though he were already damned. Travis, though,
conceives of fire not as the stuff of damnation but as a puri-
fier, which he uses to prepare for his divine mission; he
holds his fist in a flame to steel himself for the pain of his
mission, and burns Betsy's flowers to free himself from emotional attachments. Charlie sees Hell as the place where he
will spend eternity; Travis views Hell as a purgatorial prerequisite to salvation, a prelude to the peace that awaits him
after he passes through the trials of the murder (or, as it
turns out, murders) that he plans to commit. Like Jesus,
he is ready to die--his note to Iris states in part, "When
you read this I will be dead"--and spend a few days in Hell
so that he can eventually attain Paradise. Charlie's indecisiveness consigns him to a Hell on earth; Travis believes
that his decisive actions will allow him to transcend the city's
Hell, which he apparently conceives of as reserved only for
weak individuals. Thus, between Mean Streets and Taxi
Driver, Scorsese's view of violence has subtly changed; earlier, violence (e. g. , Charlie's shooting) was a divine judge-
ment on those who wavered; now it is a divine act that delivers one beyond judgment.

In setting Travis against the forces of evil, Scorsese
places the audience in a moral double bind. Shall we applaud Travis's desire to do something about all of the filth
in New York? After all, as Taxi Driver demonstrates, the
traditional enforcers of the law, the police, seem relatively
ineffective in dealing with crime and violence (they only arrive on the scene after a crime has been committed). Or
should we condemn him for his essentially pointless, pre-

cipitous acts? The fact that De Niro makes Travis a very
attractive character only makes our ability to achieve a resolution of these contrary impulses more difficult.

As a subtle prelude to the film's twist ending, scriptwriter Paul Schrader inserts a mild twist into the events preceding the blowout. We have seen Travis approach Iris's
apartment in relatively traditional garb; Travis's jeans and
boots are part of the cowboy's familiar attire (indeed, Sport
and the apartment building caretaker refer to him as "cowboy"). When Travis returns to mete out his own form of
western-style justice, he appears with a mohawk-style haircut and, in the guise of an Indian, hands out vengeance to
the cowboy (in a sexual sense) types who have appropriated
from him the land of essential innocence. [8]

Travis has been witness to both Hell (the city's corruption) and Heaven (embodied in his vision of Betsy, who is
seen dressed all in white: he views her as an angel of purity
in the midst of corruption and writes of her, "She is alone,
they cannot touch her"). Yet since in his present state he
exists totally in neither realm, dwelling instead in a moral
and spiritual limbo, he finds it impossible to make mature
contact with a woman (as opposed to a young girl, like Iris)
from either sphere. In the midst of debauchery, at a pornographic movie house, he tries to make a date with the woman
behind the candy counter and, when rebuffed, childishly asks
for "Jujubes, they last longer." Ultimately, he is just as
unsuccessful with Betsy; his intention in taking Betsy to an
X-rated movie merely reflects his lack of experience with
women.

Spurned by two women--one who works in a font of
corruption, one who is initially conceived of in terms of her
purity--and repelled by the "whores, scum, and pussy" that
he sees on the streets, Travis finds to his good fortune a
street angel, part hooker, part (at least to him) virgin (as
Travis says to Iris at one point, "This is nothing for a person to do ... you're a young girl. You should be home now,
you should be dressed up, you should be going out with boys")
on whom he can concentrate his efforts. That the murders
in the tenement apartment house, and not the money he offers
her to get out of the city, result in Iris's safe return to
hearth and home is only a further, minor twist to the film's
ironic ending. In essence, Taxi Driver demonstrates that
only violence, not money, will help Iris escape. In any case,
the money that Travis sends her in the mail is tainted: it

comes from his shepherding many disturbed people--the busi-
nessman with the hooker, the man with the gun--around the
city. The twenty dollar bill that Sport tosses him, which
Travis views as essentially more polluted than all of his other
money, only gains Travis entrance to the tenement for the
final blowout, but does not effect Iris's release (although its
employment is a fine example of corruption being used against
itself); whereas the shoot-out does directly result in her being
returned to her parents. The film makes it clear that in contrast to debased money, violence, judging by its positive effect, is something pure.

Taxi Driver presents Travis as a rather pitiable figure.
Although Travis writes in his diary, "Listen you fuckers, you
screwheads, here is a man who would not take it anymore,
a man who stood up against the scum, the cunts, the dogs,
the shit--here is someone who stood up," Scorsese immediately
follows this entry with a shot of Travis lying on his bunk,
first in an unnaturally stiff, corpse-like position on his back,
then on his side, curled into a regressive foetal attitude. [9]
He hardly qualifies as a self-assured champion of justice.
Again, the film's double bind emerges. In spite of ourselves,
we must admire Travis's ability to act on his beliefs, yet
Scorsese continually provides us with visual images that contradict this tendency. Thus, the message derived from seeing Travis--in full battle gear--foetally-coiled is that violence
is an immature act. Such intentional ambiguity only adds to
our admiration of the film's moral and psychological complexity.

Travis is similarly undeveloped when it comes to sexual
matters. The only way he can interact with Betsy is by trying to impress her with his perceptiveness by telling her how
lonely he knows she really is. It is a testament to Betsy's
basic naivete that she is influenced by this absurdly conventional, tired rhetoric. Rejected by Betsy and shocked by his
isolation (even when associating with the cabbies he seems
distant and removed), Travis becomes a mytho-maniac. He
embarks on a quest to revitalize the sterile New York City
wasteland.

Travis' view of women is also mythical; he conceives
of only two kinds of women: virgins and whores. Interestingly, Betsy and Iris each assume both roles. Originally a
vision of purity, Betsy is later viewed by Travis as a fallen
woman deserving damnation both in this life ("You're in Hell")
and the one to come "(You'll burn in Hell"). In a comple-

Originally a vision of purity, Betsy (Cybill Shepherd), in white, is the woman through whom Travis (De Niro) seeks redemption.

mentary fashion, Iris is first whore then, when she rejoins
her family, virgin once again. The complementarity of roles
extends to Travis himself. When he first sees Betsy, Travis
is the sullied man seeking redemption through a pure woman.
With Iris, though, the woman is the one who is tainted, and
the man assumes the role of the savior. Not at all interested in either a sexual or platonic relationship with Iris,
Travis remains throughout the film on the periphery of male/
female relations, always observing and desiring but never
(not even in fantasies, like those expressed by Wizard) participating.

Of course, one should not discount the appreciable
sublimation in which Travis indulges during his preparation
for his mission. Cinematographer Michael Chapman's camera
lingers over the phallic length of the .44 magnum that Travis
purchases from Andy (Steven Prince),[10] and there is clearly
a significant degree of narcissism present in Travis's prepa-
rations for his upcoming encounter. Additionally, his conversations with his imaginary opponent (the mirror image
whom he challenges, asking, "You talking to me?"), clashes
from which he always emerges triumphant, doubtless appeal
to Travis' sense of egotism.

The film's fateful foreshadowings (a trademark of
Scorsese films with dark undercurrents, like Who's That
Knocking At My Door? and Mean Streets, and present here
in the twenty dollar bill that Travis seems to be saving for
some special event; the purchase of firearms; the ritualistic
burning of the flowers bought for Betsy) work to create an
atmosphere of oppression. Particularly noteworthy is the
feeling of ineluctability communicated in two crucial scenes.
Immediately preceding the scene in which Travis purchases
guns from Andy, the film's soundtrack gives forth with repeated snare drum rolls, suggesting the militaristic, kamikaze-
like aspects of Travis' impending mission (as his note to
Iris indicates, he does not expect to return alive). Additionally, the drum rolls suggest the march to an execution, their
repetition hinting that the unstoppable mechanism of fate has
already been set in motion. This fateful aspect reappears in
the subsequent scene in which Travis prepares to meet Palantine. Throughout this sequence, a clock is heard in the background, an emblem of fate, ominously ticking off the minutes
that remain until the planned assassination. Complementing

Opposite: Travis, finally ready for the "You talking to me?"
game to become a reality.

the sense of unease here created is the work of Michael Chapman, who has the camera restlessly pace back and forth past a corner of the table on which Travis is intently constructing his quick-draw device and converting his regular bullets into dum-dums.

The viewer should also note that Travis seems virtually destined to become involved in Iris's life. Indeed, she is twice accidentally thrust into his path before he seeks her out, thereby indicating that more than mere chance appears to be bringing them together. Travis first sees Iris when she enters his cab during an argument with Sport; later in the company of a female friend, she steps in front of the moving cab and is almost run over. During her brunch with Travis, Iris entertains the notion of leaving New York for a commune (that is if Travis will accompany her), which suggests that in an important sense, Travis represents for her a catalytic, curative force; this role precisely reflects the way that he views himself. Travis tries to save Betsy from boredom, to liberate Iris from oppression. The two women's equivalent status in his life is only further affirmed by Bernard Herrmann's astute use of the same romantic love theme to accompany many of the scenes in which they appear.

In response to Travis's failed attempt to verbalize his anxiety, Wizard (Peter Boyle)--speaking more perceptively than he knows--points up the fact that man's fate, despite his efforts, is sealed. "You got no choice anyway," he says. Travis appropriates this notion of fate; in doing so, he attempts to lend teleological purpose to his plans. Incorrectly attributing his anxiety solely to seclusion, he writes, "Loneliness has followed me everywhere ... there's no escape," thereby suggesting to us that his homicidal quest, which is a new idea to him, will possibly release him from his alienation. However, as Taxi Driver's end makes clear, there is not only no deviation from fate but no change in Travis as a result of his actions. He is destined to be alienated.

Narrating an entry into his diary, Travis states, "The days move along with regularity, over and over, one day indistinguishable from the next, a long, continuous chain. Then suddenly, there is change." Immediately after the word "change" we see Travis meeting Andy. The "change" for which Travis has been waiting (which is really less a change than the fulfillment of his fate) is the accessibility to the weapons that he needs to carry out his plans. What Travis represents as an implicit change for the better is actually an

explicit turn for the worse: the purchase of weapons by a
man who has severe psychological problems.

When Andy first appears he is referred to as "easy
Andy, a traveling salesman." Andy's nickname links him
with Iris, who initially tells Travis that her name is "Easy,"
and who, like Andy, travels the streets meeting people to
whom she sells her "goods." Sex (Iris) and death (the weapons Andy sells) are here verbally linked.

The substitution of death-connoting objects (in particular, weapons) for acts of love (symbolized by the penis) is
one of Taxi Driver's most important aspects, a quality that
that can be seen to derive from similar attitudes in Mean
Streets. In the present film, the replacement of the penis
by the gun is initially established when one of Travis's fares
(played by Scorsese) talks about what a .44 magnum "can do
to a woman's pussy." The speaker is a man whose wife is
cheating on him (appropriately, given the film's expression
of fear of dark-skinned characters, with a black man; the
fare refers to him as "a nigger"). It is therefore entirely
fitting that Travis, who cannot successfully express himself
sexually, first asks Andy if he has a .44 magnum. Given
the absence in Taxi Driver of normal heterosexual relationships (the only film characters who exhibit closeness are
Sport and Iris in their dance together, yet the dance seems
suspiciously like a ploy of Sport's to keep Iris in his stable;
Wizard talks about having sex in the back seat of his cab
with one of his customers--almost certainly a fantasy), we
must conclude that the men in the film who use guns--the
hold-up man; Sport; the caretaker; Travis; even the Secret
Service man at the Palantine rally?--do so because they cannot express themselves heterosexually in any other way.

The gun takes the place of the penis; and violence
takes the place of tenderness and communication. Overt
aggression is thus depicted as the response of individuals
who not only are incapable of achieving human closeness, but
cannot tolerate seeing it enjoyed by others. Consequently,
when Travis evaluates the .25 Colt automatic that Andy is
showing him, he sights it out the window at a couple seated
on a park bench. Later, Travis will again thrust his way
into the middle of other people's relationships and fantasize
breaking up their interaction, as when he aims the magnum
at a black couple whom he watches dancing together on American Bandstand,[11] and when he uses his hand as a pretend
gun to shoot a couple in a pornographic movie he attends.[12]

Travis shoots the stick-up man during the delicatessen hold-
up in Taxi Driver.

        Even after the film's final murders, when Travis's
deadly passions are supposedly (at least for a time) quelled,
he still cannot jettison this hostile attitude, reinvoking the
hand-as-gun gesture (to which he resorts after finding that
all of his guns are empty and that he cannot therefore really

shoot himself) by bringing his right hand to his temple and, index finger extended, firing three imaginary shots (one for each of his victims: Sport, the caretaker, and the mafioso) into his brain. By this point in the film, having accomplished his task, Travis is apparently ready to commit seppuku by turning some of his formerly externalized aggressions against himself.

Interestingly, the only dark character in the film to whom Travis is not openly hostile (the black cabdriver) also uses his hand as a gun to "shoot" Travis (Sport performs the same gesture--once inadvertently, when innocently pointing, once intentionally, in a hand-as-gun movement--but he suffers for it). There is a strong hint in this sequence of something most viewers have probably suspected throughout the film: that Travis implicitly hates this man because of his color. Perhaps the black cabdriver realizes that Travis feels this way, and is--in a morbid fashion--kiddingly dramatizing the fact.

Additionally, we should note that the black cabdriver and Wizard inadvertently recognize Travis's potential for violence. Both characters call Travis "killer," references that occur within two minutes of each other and which bracket the sequence in which Travis directs an angry, hostile stare at a black, chain-bedecked youth who struts past the Belmore Cafeteria. Travis's already-noted hostile attitude towards blacks--affirmed in the "killer" reference, exemplified in his stare, and soon to take initial concrete form in the delicatessen shooting--is eventually given full expression when, at the film's end, he takes vengeance against the three "dark" characters (the swarthy Sport, the dark caretaker, the unctuous mafioso) whom he has identified as his enemies. Combined with the film's moody pacing (slow and, in tandem with the plot, ominous), intentionally garish colors (blood-like reds and threatening blacks predominate), and washed-out lighting, these powerful aspects draw the viewer into Taxi Driver's menacing urban milieu.

Even in the midst of humorous interplay, Taxi Driver sets up morose foreshadowings. The game that Betsy's coworker, Tom, plays--which involves trying to light a match one-handed while pretending that three fingers on the left hand are missing--does more than implicate him, also, in the film's hand-as-gun-as-penis schema; the game not only involves an implicit castration wish, thus characterizing the essence of Tom's essential sexuality, but bears homicidal

Tom (Albert Brooks), with Betsy, inadvertantly duplicating
the hand gesture from the mock-castration game he will soon
play in Taxi Driver.

fruit when Travis first shoots three fingers off the tenement
caretaker's right hand.   Then, when the caretaker--having
followed Travis upstairs--attacks him in Iris's room, the incident is, in effect, repeated.   Travis impales the man's
left hand with a knife, an action that causes three of the caretaker's fingers involuntarily to curl inwards, as though they
had disappeared. [13]

Travis repays Sport in kind.   When he is first with
Iris, she unsuccessfully attempts to fellate him (as Sport
earlier promises, "You can come in her mouth ... ").   Travis
figuratively turns this sexual trick against Sport; when he
shoots Sport in the stomach, Travis tells him to "suck on
this," the reference thereby reinvoking for us the gun's substitution for the male organ.

Taxi Driver's music also anticipates its shocking conclusion.   In a rare, self-reflexive homage to his own work,

composer Bernard Herrmann reprises the three-note murder
theme from Psycho (employed in the Hitchcock film when
Norman Bates is on the scene) to anticipate some homicidal
activity. In Taxi Driver, this music appears immediately
before the delicatessen hold-up and shooting (itself visually
anticipated in the hostility Travis shows towards the black
teenagers he watches on American Bandstand) and during the
film's final credit sequence when, accompanying the film's
last image (a washed-out, overexposed shot of a city street
as seen from Travis's cab), the theme is reprised, indicating
that although we are presumably in the safe area beyond the
film's action, the possibility of unpredictable violence still
exists. [14]

The wounded neck gesture from Mean Streets (see photo on
page 78) resurfaces with a vengeance in this scene from
Taxi Driver.

        Taxi Driver's ending clearly indicates whether or not
Travis's violence has delivered him from his anxieties, and
their homicidal effects. While it is true that by the film's
conclusion Travis is no longer obsessed with Betsy or her
damnation, there is no reason to believe that he is free from

his fixation on corruption and evil. After a calm ride with
Betsy, Travis pulls his cab away from the curb and once
again begins to drift though the urban night. The garish city
lights reflect in his rear view mirror; the editing is smooth,
deceptively lulling, until Scorsese introduces a discordant
musical sting and gives us three rapid, alternate-angle shots
of Travis looking at himself in his rear view mirror--an
action/reaction trio (with Travis obviously still playing the
earlier game of "You talking to me?" which was also con-
ducted in front of a mirror) which chillingly indicates that
the homicidal ride is far from being over.

NOTES

1.   A political reading of Travis' obsession is possible, although this aspect of Taxi Driver is undeveloped. As we are
aware, Travis is a Vietnam veteran. His present quest for
recognizable enemies may in part be a function of his past
frustration over not being able to find identifiable villains
among the North Vietnamese, on whom he could have blamed
the war's widely recognized inertia. We may infer that Travis
has carried his emotional imbalance (manifested, for example,
through his sleeplessness) home from Vietnam's jungles to the
jungles of the New York City streets.
      However, Scorsese has addressed the issue of a ten-
dency to violence which, undirected, is ultimately turned
against one's self (present in Taxi Driver in Travis' willingness to commit suicide at the film's end and his apparent,
self-destructive ability to institute new, perilous vendettas
in the future) in his short film The Big Shave, which concerns a young man who can't stop shaving until he cuts his
own throat. The short's soundtrack is highly ironic, since
Scorsese uses Bunny Berrigan's version of "I Can't Get
Started" not only to provide a cutting rhythm for the film
and to act as a romantic/sexual counterpoint to The Big Shave's
violence (the latter characteristic--the yoking of impulses
towards love and death--is present in all of Scorsese's films)
but also ironically to play off against the fact that the problem for the young man in the film is not that "he can't get
started," but that he simply cannot stop. This parable of
overt violence unleashed against one's self (violence which
ultimately ends in one's own destruction) ends with the title
"Viet 67," thus confirming the film's status as a statement
about the self-destructiveness of the United States' big-muscled
military presence in Southeast Asia.

2. Scorsese emphasizes Palantine's essential artificiality by repeatedly giving us shots of the candidate that cut off his head, as though the politician is merely a brainless puppet mechanically and incessantly mouthing platitudes.

It should be noted that Travis's shooting of Palantine would have made far more sense in the context of the film than his assassination of the various individuals at Iris's apartment. After all, Palantine--as a man who, in a transparently artificial manner, sets himself up as a crusader for urban integrity and the restoration of essential purity (in this case, to politics, through his slogan, "We are the people," which smacks of populist jingoism)--obviously invites comparison with Travis, who is himself a lone crusader for urban health and purity, albeit on a personal, rather than political level. One is tempted to assume that Travis's initial attraction to Betsy has as much to do with his view of her as an agent of this purity-espousing politician as it does with the woman's deceptively pristine appearance.

3. Scorsese seems to support the view of the city as essentially corrupt in an interesting shot during a scene at the cafeteria. Travis has just dropped two Alka Seltzers into a glass of water (he probably suffers from indigestion in addition to sleeplessness, although one wonders how the previous condition is affected by his putting cheap liquor over his breakfast cereal). As the tablets begin to fizz, Scorsese zooms in on the contents of the glass, and the camera discovers that within this medicinal potion there is a tiny, but nonetheless recognizable, speck of dirt, as though to suggest that even in curative draughts there are signs of pollution and corruption, aspects of the city that Travis, in his blind quest for some form of revenge against the urban monster, opposes.

4. Appropriately, it is from such steam at the end of the title sequence that Scorsese's name emerges, first in white, then slowly fading into a blood-red color that presages the violence to come.

Scorsese likes to present himself this way, as a lover of violence. Thus, as early as The Big Shave (1967), he employs a fade to red, which occurs after a significant amount of bloodletting and before the end credits, to emphasize the shocking nature of violence. This technique reappears in New York, New York's title sequence, which fades to red after Scorsese's name has appeared.

5. Despite its supposedly laudatory purpose (the newspapers claim that he was trying to save Iris), Travis's homicidal

outburst at the film's end will itself contribute to the view
of New York as a dangerous place to live, a city where violence is often used against violence.   Nevertheless, Travis
does have a solution to the city's filth: "Flush it right down
the fucking toilet."
          Travis's view of the city as essentially debased is,
of course, quite traditional.   Frank Lloyd Wright, quoted in
Susan Sontag's Illness As Metaphor (New York: Vintage Books,
1978), referred to cities as cancers, blights: "To look at
the cross-section of any plan of a big city is to look at the
section of a fibrous tumor" (pp. 72-73).   While Travis's reference to the city as a sewer emulates this view, an even
stronger link with Wright's astute perspective is present in
Travis's statement that he thinks he has "stomach cancer,"
an attitude doubtless reflecting an internalization of the city's
inherent sickness and corruption.   In his dual impulses towards both sickness (taking drugs to work longer hours, gulp-
ing aspirin for recurrent handaches, putting liquor on his
cereal) and health (swearing off all drugs, adopting a rigid
plan of body-building and regeneration), Travis reveals that
he represents a typical city in microcosm.

6.   Of course, it is possible that Travis wants to kill Palantine because he recognizes him as a "wrong," as a hypocrite.
Yet given his endorsement of Palantine's campaign, offered
while he drives Palantine to a hotel, and Travis's hostile
reaction to Betsy's rejecting him, it is likely that he wants
to kill the politician solely as a way of hurting the woman
who hurt him.

7.   Although isolation is clearly a major cause of Travis's
imbalances, we must nevertheless acknowledge that Travis
derives some sort of benefit from acting alone.   His self-
styled vendetta against corruption becomes a satisfying one-
man fight precisely because Travis individually wills it to be
so.   Like an urban guerilla, he actually (in the light of the
film's end) seems to thrive in the big-city environment, whereas removed from the city and its threatening atmosphere, he
would doubtless languish in the suffocating peacefulness of
the commune towards which Iris would steer him.

8.   In this respect, it is almost as though by killing the men
involved in Iris's prostitution, Travis were effecting the Indians' ultimate revenge.

9.   Travis's only rival for Betsy's affections--Betsy's fellow
campaign worker, Tom--is similarly stunted in his personal

growth, a characteristic communicated most clearly when,
in what he means to be a humorous riposte, he tells Betsy
that "I'll play the male in this relationship." (emphasis added)

10. The stand-out performance of Steven Prince in the role
of gun salesman Andy should here be noted. Prince's comically speeded-up verbal delivery, and the way he blandly sells
Travis on the various weapons he shows him ("That's a beauty,"
he says, going on to state with unintentional comic irony,
"I deal high quality goods to the right people") are a pure
delight to watch. Interestingly, despite his unquestioning
willingness to sell the guns to Travis, Andy nevertheless
realizes the weapons' potential for misuse. Referring to a
Colt .25, Andy states, "It's a nice little gun, it's a beautiful
little gun; it [the chamber] holds six rounds, if you're dumb
enough to put a round in."
    Nevertheless, Prince's acting gives the scene a wonder-
ful quality of black comedy. When he and Travis are con-
cluding their deal, Andy not only offers Travis a brand new
Cadillac but some nitrous oxide, at which point Prince flashes
onto his face a priceless comic expression that makes it seem
as if he had himself just taken a considerable dose of laughing gas.
    Prince's portrayal brings up an important considera-
tion: the nature of the humor that Taxi Driver uses. In one
sense the entire film may be taken as a black comedy; Wizard's asinine analysis of Travis' condition, the sequence with
Andy, Travis' luncheonette discussion with Iris about horo-
scope signs and communes, and the film's ironic ending support this view. Still, one must question the employment of
such a comic attitude, which draws upon our ability to respond to the film's deplorably violent events as though they
were somehow amusing, albeit in a grim way. The fact that
many moviegoers (myself included) seem capable of this reaction is a depressing commentary on our capacity for finding
humor in the midst of the most terrible situations. Although
this capability may be understandable as an attempt to rationalize certain aspects of urban life, it is nonetheless objectionable.
    Further insights into Prince's personality may be
gleaned from Scorsese's short film American Boy--A Portrait of Steven Prince, film number two (after Italian American) in what the director planned as a six-film cycle of works
about various nationalities. Oddly enough, Prince chooses in
the film to relate a remark made by his father which has to
do with the kind of attitude towards weaponry exhibited in Taxi

Driver. Prince quotes his father as saying, "Never point a
gun at anyone unless you plan to shoot. Never shoot unless
you plan to kill." The words are strongly applicable to Travis's initial feints with his gun, which Taxi Driver's viewer
soon realizes are practice moves for his later actual use of
the weapon.

11. Significantly, the scene involving the pretend shooting
of the black dancers occurs immediately after the delicatessen
holdup sequence, during which Travis shot a black youth. It
would appear, then, that Travis's appetite for racial vengeance
has been whetted by his first homicidal experience, and that
he is now searching for a new way to appease it.

12. In a daring move, Scorsese later reprises the gun-as-
penis symbology. Watching a television soap opera scene
about a couple's marital difficulties, Travis again reacts
negatively and with violence to heterosexual intimacy, first
sublimating his sexual desire by sitting with the magnum's
barrel jutting out penis-like between his legs, then directly
expressing his hostility and frustration by intentionally knocking over the television set.
     The contrast between Travis's behavior here and that
of certain characters in Who's That Knocking At My Door?
and Mean Streets should be apparent. The earlier films'
empty gun threats (present in Knocking's all-male party sequence and Mean Streets' scene involving Johnny Boy's threat
against Michael) certainly have their corollaries in Taxi
Driver. Unlike the partygoer and Johnny Boy, though, Travis
will eventually actually use his weapons against people, thereby retroactively making of his initial gestures soon-to-be-
fulfilled promises of violence instead of mere empty threats.

13. The sirens heard in the background when Travis and
Iris enter her building during their first encounter reappear--
silently--after the shoot-out when a patrol car pulls up outside the building thus complementing the sense of fulfilled
inevitability created here.

14. However, Herrmann did not intend that his three-note
theme end the film. Instead, as Herrmann's score for Taxi
Driver indicates, the composer wanted the final title sequence
to conclude with a symphony-like musical resolution of the
theme's discordance. Apparently perceiving that such an assertion of order in the face of the film's chaos was inappropriate, Scorsese eliminated this musical conclusion. One
can only speculate about whether the strong-willed Herrmann,

who died before the film's completion, would have sanctioned
such editing of his work. In any case, students of Taxi Driver
can evaluate the film's music by purchasing the long-out-of-
print (and now reissued) soundtrack, which is available on
Sweet Thunder records (distributed by Arista Records, 1776
Broadway, New York, N. Y. 10019).

        Taxi Driver's most notable Hitchcock cross reference,
though, is Scorsese's use of an extended, slow motion backward tracking shot out of the murder room, down the tenement's stairs, and out into the street.   The shot is, apparently, an intentional homage to the virtually identical backward tracing shot (also away from a "murder room") that
occurs approximately midway through Hitchcock's Frenzy
(1972).   Cf. paragraph 2 of Chapter 8's Note 2.

Chapter Six

HELLO TO NEW YORK; GOODBYE TO THE BAND

It should come as little surprise that Scorsese was strongly interested in two musical projects--New York, New York and The Last Waltz--especially when one considers not only his involvement as supervising editor of Michael Wadleigh's Woodstock but his strong reliance on music in Who's That Knocking At My Door?, Boxcar Bertha, Mean Streets, and Taxi Driver. Given the casting of Robert De Niro as Jimmy Doyle, a comically obsessed saxophone player who comes into conflict with authority and a rather conventionally

Music as a source of harmony (above) ... and discord (opposite), in which the argument is over who "counts down the
band." Liza Minnelli and Robert De Niro in New York, New
York.

minded lover (Liza Minnelli's Francine Evans), New York,
New York seems like a logical outgrowth of the approach to
characterization present in Mean Streets and Taxi Driver.
How much difference, after all, is there between Jimmy and
Travis Bickle? Both are intense, single-minded individuals.
Travis would no sooner give up his taxicab, which ferries
him magically through Hell, than Jimmy would give up his
saxophone. As Jimmy says to Francine at one point when
she questions his playing in Harlem every night, "Do you
want me to smash this thing"--his saxophone--" against the
building? Is that what you want me to do?"

Indeed, it is clear that for both characters, music
represents not only harmony (e. g. , in the form of a gratify-
ing profession) but discord (present in the form of their music-
related arguments throughout the film cf. pp. 11-12) as well.
Francine's singing career brings her pleasure, but it also
contributes to her marriage's dissolution. Jimmy's instrument provides him with the means of working out his aggressions therapeutically in the same way that Travis' toying with
(and ultimate expression of) violence provides him with a
means of passage through the underworld of pimps and push-
ers.

New York, New York's opening titles give us a clue
to the violence-prone, nether-world forces beneath the film's
sweet-seeming veneer when we see that, as in Taxi Driver
(which begins with shots of Travis' cab emerging from sub-
terranean steam), the name of the man who gives direction
and shape to the film (Martin Scorsese) appears, not in pink
like New York, New York's other titles, but in red. The
underworld suggestion here--one reflected in the film's Scorsese surrogate, Jimmy Doyle--is most obvious. It is clear
that for all of his kidding and comic patter, Jimmy is like
a drug addict in constant withdrawal, whose only means of
escape from his own excessive behavior and the straight world
around him is through his palliative: music. Like Travis,
Jimmy requires attention and gets it; Travis wins acclaim
through his violence, Jimmy through his playing. Travis and
Jimmy may blow slightly different tunes played on different
instruments, yet each needs some form of acceptance, some
indication that his efforts bear recognizable fruit (Travis
through "saving" Iris; Jimmy through commercial success
with his group) to pour balm on their cruel inner fires.

New York, New York recounts a rite of passage through
the anxiety of artistic anonymity to a relatively calm plateau

where one can sit back and be oneself. What is frightening
about the film is how quickly and easily Jimmy and his music
are accepted by audiences throughout the country. As in Taxi
Driver, the outsider is integrated into the prevailing social
structure, which is shown to be adaptive enough to accommo-
date even the most outlandish forms of aberration.

Jimmy is, in essence, a likable but often annoying
fanatic. The fact that he elicits our sympathy and commands
our respect (regardless of how great a musician he is, he
is still a poor human being) affirms once again the miraculous
manner in which Scorsese can have us sympathize with a character whom we might normally condemn. Equally responsible
for Jimmy's acceptability is his portrayal by Robert De Niro.
By now, students of Scorsese's work, and viewers of film in
general, have come to appreciate De Niro's extraordinary
talents. We love and enjoy his antics, even when he is por-
traying characters who are reprehensible (as Raging Bull's
Jake La Motta often is) or annoyingly vulgar (e.g., King of
Comedy's Rupert Pupkin). Often, it is difficult when watching the people De Niro plays to separate the character's behavior from his acting. I think it is fair to say that Scorsese relies on this resultant confusion, and that when he employs De Niro, he does so partially for this reason.

De Niro's characteristic performance, and the atmosphere of barely repressed, dangerous aggression that he creates around him, would lead one to believe that what we have
in New York, New York is a successful film. Yet New York,
New York seems more like a good idea for a film than a
well-realized production. While there is much to enjoy in
New York, New York--especially the opening thirty minutes,
as the Jimmy Doyle character is given room to develop--the
film's rags-to-riches love story seems for the most part
rather dull and lifeless. Though Scorsese obviously wished
to resurrect this classic formula and give it a new twist by
using strongly contemporary actors like De Niro (whose facial
tic delivery of comic lines is masterful), he detracts from
the production's verve by using Liza Minnelli more for her
Judy Garland-like qualities (the large eyes, the big-voiced
delivery of songs) than for the contemporary appeal the actress commands.

Moreover, the conventional aspects of the production,
especially during its second half, overshadow whatever vi-
brancy De Niro and Minnelli bring to the film. New York,
New York's production mumbers are for the most part en-

joyable, and the title number is especially good, although it amounts to little more than a filmed nightclub rendition of the song. However, in his desire to pay homage to forties musicals, Scorsese allows his usual good judgment to be put in abeyance by including (and restoring to the initially cut release version) the appalling "Happy Endings" number, which appeals neither as an original production sequence nor as a tribute. The number is best summed up by Jimmy Doyle (who sees it in Francine's latest film) when he tells Francine that he has seen "Sappy Endings." Sappy is, indeed, the word for it; the woefully sentimental spirit that the sequence embodies ultimately infects the whole movie, thereby defusing this hopeful and energetic film.

If New York, New York is a well-intentioned failure, by what designation may we refer to The Last Waltz? An interview/concert film focusing on The Band's farewell performance, The Last Waltz fails to distinguish itself from many other concert films. The audience is given technically competent, filmed versions of many Band songs, as well as views of various performers (among them Joni Mitchell, Neil Young, Bob Dylan, Dr. John, and Van Morrison) who stopped by to participate in the proceedings, but the footage is in no sense different from the type of music event coverage to which we have been exposed in films like Woodstock, Monterey Pop, A Film About Jimi Hendrix, etc., except for one small but significant detail: the virtual absence of any shots of the audience.

It is traditional in films of this type for the director to give us views of the appreciative crowd. Perhaps it was in reaction against what has become a cliché that Scorsese decided to show us virtually nothing of the concertgoers. Yet a more comprehensive explanation for this approach suggests itself: namely, that Scorsese was not predominantly interested in the concert as an event for the audience's entertainment, but as a symbolic act which, we may safely assume, had meaning for him as a filmmaker.

Why else would Scorsese have gone to the trouble of making the film at all? Even if he were a fanatical devotee of The Band's music, one would think that he would therefore have concentrated more on the concert and devoted less screen time to the musings of Band lead guitarist (and apparent spokesman) Robbie Robertson.

Robbie Robertson--at center stage, as usual--with Band members Richard Mañuel, Rick Danko, Garth Hudson and Levon Helm in The Last Waltz.

Given the amount of footage devoted to Robertson, the film might just as well have been titled Robbie Robertson Speaks. What with Robertson's self-conscious posturings on stage during the concert, and his less-than-enlightening backstage ramblings, the film constitutes a virtual vehicle for his musical and verbal skills. It is difficult to avoid the negative impression that Robertson makes on the viewer, since little of his lead guitar work in the film is outstanding, while his off-stage reminiscences are not very different from the kinds of stories any veteran musician could tell.

It is likely that what Scorsese saw in Robertson was an eerie reflection of himself. Both Scorsese and Robertson are, in effect, leaders of groups: Robertson encourages cohesion among The Band's members; Scorsese coordinates and directs the activities of various professionals on a film set. Each man is thus involved in preparing others (and sometimes himself) for performances. Moreover, as their groups' leaders, both Scorsese and Robertson expose themselves to the potential negative criticism that a bad performance (be it a concert, a record, or a film) may occasion.

It may be that in allowing Robertson to give in to his
self-aggrandizing impulses, Scorsese somehow exorcises his
own, that through Robertson, Scorsese achieves some temper-
ing of the hubristic power that being the main force behind
million-dollar films may occasion. Perhaps what Scorsese
sees in Robertson's incessant talking, then, is a part of himself he would prefer to tone down.

As the title indicates, The Last Waltz is about endings;
this concert is indeed a last waltz, a goodbye. Here in the
film it is literally The Band that is being dispatched, but
symbolically, what we see in The Last Waltz is a whole era
of rock music that is disappearing. True, The Band's playing is lively, but the same cannot be said for their guest
artists, who seem for the most part to be a rather tired,
uninspired bunch. Joni Mitchell and Muddy Waters escape
this judgment (Dr. John's set is interesting, but we've seen
this identical act numerous times before), but Neil Young,
Paul Butterfield, Van Morrison, and Bob Dylan bring very
little to their performances. Young seems distracted during
the singing of "Helpless"; Paul Butterfield's harmonica playing is dull and uninspired; it is all Van Morrison can do to
work up a bit of energy for his song. As for Dylan, while his
drawn-out vowels and nasal twang delivery may be suitable for
some songs, it is discordantly inappropriate for the beautiful
folk song, "Baby Let Me Follow You Down, " which is further
ruined by the singer's electric guitar back-up.

Dylan's other offering, "Forever Young," is significant only in the choice of song. The Last Waltz is clearly
a film about a group of once-young musicians who have reached
an impasse; one only remains "forever young" in dreams.
Appropriately, the marquee of the Winterland Theatre, where
The Last Waltz was filmed, comments on the whole situation.
Most of the letters in the theatre's sign--like the inspirational
lights of many of the performers we see in the film--have
burned out.

Perhaps there is a warning in The Last Waltz that
ultimately constitutes its basic message. Robertson notes
towards the film's end that music is a hard road. The Band
has had eighteen years of it. "That road killed Elvis; it
killed Hendrix," Robertson says. It may be that in this observation Scorsese sees a parallel with his own work, itself
as emotionally rewarding and spiritually demanding as The
Band's. As Robertson implies, maybe it's time to stop press-
ing one's luck and quit. Perhaps such a fateful conclusion

also expresses Martin Scorsese's fear that if he presses too
hard, the entertainment road will figuratively kill his talents
as well.   Ultimately, then, The Last Waltz is a testimony,
not only to the end of a musical period, but also to the beginning of a grim, melancholy reflectiveness in the work of
its director.

Chapter Seven

THE ANIMAL

Raging Bull presents the viewer with a perplexing dilemma. While the film is clearly Scorsese's most ambitious
work to date, employing stunning black-and-white cinematography and incorporating Robert De Niro's brilliant portrayal
of fighter Jake La Motta, it nevertheless represents the first
time that Scorsese has chosen as his central character an
individual who is predominantly unsympathetic. [1]

Such a situation would not prove so troublesome (after
all, many films have dealt with objectionable protagonists)
were it not that the structure of the film, as well as its tex-
tual epilogue, indicate that what we are supposed to see in
Raging Bull is the progress of an unreflective, unself-conscious
character towards wisdom and self-awareness. [2] Unfortunately,
while this is clearly the film's intention, it is at variance
with its effects.

Raging Bull begins in 1964; Jake La Motta, an ex-
champ, considerably heavier than in his fighting days, is
preparing for his dramatic reading before a cabaret audience.
Always brilliant with filmic transitions, Scorsese cuts from
La Motta's dressing room singing of "That's Entertainment"
to a view of one of his 1941 fights, during which he gets hit
in the face by his opponent. Surely this is entertainment to
some, brutal though it may be; this crass attitude towards
pain prepares us for the brutal coarseness that La Motta exhibits throughout the film. Yet Raging Bull turns this brutality to its own benefit; Michael Chapman's brilliant cinematography pushes us right up against the fighters (and into the
midst of La Motta's domestic battles), exposing all of the
pain that is so much a part of this man's existence.

As a boxer and human being, Jake La Motta is pre-

dominantly bestial. It is no coincidence that his sport nickname is "the raging bull" (despite the amount of punishment
he received, La Motta was never knocked down during the
entirety of his professional career). Moreover, people throughout the film repeatedly refer to Jake as "an animal." Animal-
like as well is the manner in which Jake's masculinity is so
firmly involved with demonstrations of his strength and endurance. La Motta at one point laments the fact that he has
"small hands," which he significantly calls "little girl hands."
Immediately after this speech, when he asks his brother Joey
(Joe Pesci) to hit him in the face (which Joey does), the following exchange takes place.

> Jake: Don't be a faggot.
>
> Joey: I ain't a faggot.
>
> Jake: You throw a punch like you take it up the
> ass.

Later, when he is scheduled to fight an opponent whom
he considers a pretty boy, Jake characteristically comments,
"I don't know whether to fuck him or fight him."

Jake's obsessive equation of male prowess with sexuality, and his inability to define his personality in anything
other than the grossest physical terms, is traditionally ani-
malistic, especially when we consider that in the animal world
it is only the healthy, strong beasts--the ones that seem the
most capable of enduring--that usually engage successfully in
mating. In fact, the courtship rites practiced by many male
animals involve demonstrations of their size and strength.
These facts help to explain why Jake, in the only culminated
(albeit off-screen) sexual encounter we are given in the film,
initially shows Vickie (Cathy Moriarty) a picture of himself
and his younger (and smaller) brother striking boxing poses,
as though to prove his superiority, strength, and virility.
Immediately afterwards, he has intercourse with her for the
first time.

Like many athletes, Jake subscribes to the belief that
there is an antithesis between having sex and being at one's
prime for a physical encounter with an adversary. Consequently, he refuses sexual contact with Vickie at one point
because, as he says, "I gotta fight Robinson; I can't fool
around." The implication here is two-fold: first, sexual
satisfaction with Vickie is delayed in favor of the satisfaction

Before (opposite) and after The Fall.   Jake La Motta (De
Niro), here, in Pauline Kael's words, in the guise of the
"swollen puppet."

that arises from his encounter with Robinson (sex is replaced
by boxing, which must somehow be equally as satisfying); and
second, that unlike fighting, sex is not serious business; it
is only "fooling around. "[3]

If we are to judge by the striking correspondence between his actions in and out of the ring, it is only through
brutal physical encounters that Jake can express himself.
While it is easy to see that he is truly in love with Vickie
and his brother, he nevertheless finds it impossible to communicate with either (with the rare exception of the clowning
around he does in his home movies) except through violence.
Constantly obsessed with what exactly Vickie's sexual activities are ("Did you fuck my brother; are you fucking him?")
but unable to maintain a satisfactory sexual relationship with
her (it is suggested more than once in the film that even
when he's not preparing for a fight Jake hardly ever sleeps
with his wife), he can only relate (in his own way) to Vickie
and Joey (just as he had, apparently, with his first wife,
Irma) by attempting to strike and maim them.

Love may in one sense be regarded as a transcendent
experience sometimes expressed physically; such a view precisely corresponds with the manner in which La Motta in-
teracts with his only formidable opponent, Sugar Ray Robinson. In the brutal fight with Robinson during which La Motta
loses the middleweight title back to Robinson, one can see
in La Motta's insistence on taking more and more punishment
from Robinson--and the manner in which he waits, only half-
conscious, expectantly, for the coup de grace--intimations of
a brutal love/hate relationship being played out. Certainly,
in La Motta's insistence that Robinson "never got me down"
we hear the trumpeting of one's accomplishments before a
revered enemy, and the unexpressed request for some form
of acknowledgement from a person whom one respects. In
many senses, the film depicts Robinson as La Motta's only
truly complete lover.

Regardless of La Motta's pathetic plight--his loss of
the title, his weight gain (turning him, as Pauline Kael said
of the La Motta character's appearance late in the film, into
"a swollen puppet"), [4] the break-up of his marriage, and his
unfortunate conviction on a morals charge--Raging Bull nevertheless makes it difficult to sympathize with La Motta. Here
is a man who beats his wife, almost as part of a daily rou-
tine; a man who constantly badgers his brother; a man who
seems to have no friends.

Eventually, even Joey turns against Jake. La Motta
has already suffered defeat at Ray Robinson's hands.   Robinson and Joey are quite similar characters for Jake; together,
they represent his two potential male lovers. Both men are
physically small.   Both withdraw affection from Jake: one
(Joey) withdraws familial love; by taking back the title from
him, the other (Robinson) robs him of the crowd's adoration.

After the loss to Sugar Ray and his rejection by Joey,
Jake allows his only remaining valued possession--his tre-
mendously resilient fighter's body--to fall apart. As he goes
to fat, his attitudes about himself go to fat as well. His
self-conception and personal habits become more and more
degraded until, overweight and pitiful, he sinks to the level
of a buffoon, becoming a third-rate stand-up comic and master
of ceremonies in barroom dives. Even the routines we see
him performing in his own club involve a kind of self-humilia-
tion that is painful to watch.

The turning point for La Motta presumably comes when
he is thrown in jail on a morals charge. Housed in a dark
and squalid cell, now completely out of the public limelight
(be it the spotlights in the ring or the ones in the club), he
sinks into the cell's screen-right darkness and futilely pounds
his head on the wall screaming, "Why, why?"

It is after this flashback scene that we revert to the
film's present tense, to La Motta rehearsing his act of readings from the works of writers like Paddy Chayefsky (Marty?),
Rod Serling (Requiem for a Heavyweight), Shakespeare, Budd
Schulberg (On the Waterfront, The Harder They Fall), and
Tennessee Williams. The juxtaposition of these two just-
mentioned scenes--the one leaving us with an image of La
Motta frustrated over his stupidity (an underage female was
served liquor in his club), the other showing us La Motta
now decked out in a tuxedo though still overweight--seems
to imply that somehow Jake has achieved peace by attaining
a proper perspective on himself.

The speech that he rehearses in front of his dressing
room mirror--the "I coulda been a contender" piece from On
the Waterfront--might, if taken at face value, suggest that
even in defeat (like Terry Malloy at the appropriate point in
the Kazan film), the speaker nevertheless retains a significant amount of dignity. The view that we are supposed to
have of La Motta as a self-conscious, enlightened man (as
the thoughtful Terry Malloy seems to be throughout the Kazan

film) is reinforced by Raging Bull's two closing titles, one
a quote from John 9:24-26 (about the man who "once was
blind but now ... can see"), the other a dedication to Haig
Manoogian, a co-worker (on Knocking) and friend of the director's who presumably exerted a positive and profound influence on Scorsese.

The problem with Raging Bull's end, though, is that
there is no justifiable reason to assume that La Motta at
this point is any different from the blind, egotistical oddity
he has been throughout the film. Well-dressed in his tuxedo,
he may be delivering passages on the fight game, but these
stylized speeches about fighters' tragedies do not bear any
necessary correspondence to La Motta's case. In fact, given
the halting and unfeeling manner in which La Motta delivers
the On the Waterfront speech, one might be led to believe
that despite the film's end quotation and epigraph, and despite La Motta's change in garb (which, in the vernacular,
would be referred to as "a monkey suit"), La Motta is still
predominantly "an animal," no different from the person we
have known all along.

Some things never change. Opposite, La Motta argues with first wife Irma (Lori Ann Flax); and (above) with second wife Vickie (Cathy Moriarty). Scenes from Raging Bull.

This is undoubtedly a problematic situation for the viewer: what are we to make of the film's sincerely offered ending quotation and dedication? I believe that we may recover the majority of Raging Bull's effect and still not fault Scorsese for the ending's being inconsistent in tone with the rest of the production if we view the quotation and dedication as no more than Scorsese's observations on La Motta's life, with no implication that we are necessarily compelled to view them as strictly apposite to the film's events. After all, it is ultimately up to the viewer to determine whether or not these citations have relevance. We can reject their referential status and still be affected by the sincerity and aptness of the quotations, since even if La Motta is (as I claim) unchanged, the film--in attempting to find some core of meaning (realized or not) in Jake's life--may nevertheless be viewed as the instructive story of a pitiful man who deserves at the very least some of our sympathy.

Relying on the power of Robert De Niro's performance to make La Motta in many senses a fascinating creature despite his human shortcomings, Scorsese manages to evoke an appreciable degree of, if not sympathy, at least non-judgmental interest. The successful creation of such an engaged attitude would itself be sufficient to rescue La Motta (in spite of his many brutalities) from condemnation, and thereby make of the film the story of a man condemned to fall short of success and exist in a moral and spiritual limbo--neither saved nor damned, pitifully poised on the brink of self-awareness without the sensitivity or intelligence to pass over into enlightenment.

NOTES

1. Of course, to a certain extent New York, New York's Jimmy Doyle may seem to fit this category, yet the earlier film's first third shows us Jimmy in such a wide array of engaging poses--joker, lover, impetuous romantic--that we can almost forgive his later callousness and selfishness towards Francine Evans. In contrast, Jake never seems to be anything other than a brute. Even when he is tender with Vickie, the suspicion exists that he is doing so either to seduce her (initially) or to counterbalance his virtually simultaneous brutalities (as during the period after they are married; he plays with her for the benefit of their home movies but slaps her around when the two are "off-camera").

2.   That this didactic sub-text is clearly Scorsese's intention
is further affirmed by a statement the director made during
the film's editing.   Scorsese said that he saw La Motta's
life as the story "of a guy attaining something and losing
everything, and then redeeming himself." (Thomas Wiener,
"Martin Scorsese Fights Back," American Film, November,
1980; p. 31.)

3.   Delayed sex here serves as a metaphor for a never-
reached goal, a corollary for Jake's inability (although it is
unconscious) to reach some form of self-awareness.   Cf.
Note 2 in Chapter 4 for the significance of this type of symbolic movement and the relationship between it and a similar
structure in Alice Doesn't Live Here Anymore.

4.   The New Yorker, December 8, 1980, p. 217.

Chapter Eight

NO LAUGHING MATTER

Astute followers of Scorsese's work may not need to
be told but others should keep it in mind: The King of Comedy is not a comedy. This idiosyncratic, challenging film
finds Scorsese returning seven years later to the same basic
themes and plot of Taxi Driver, with the difference that the
character Travis Bickle jestingly offered as his persona to
one of the Secret Service agents guarding Charles Palantine[1]
has now become an awkward and embarrassing reality, a man
who only superficially seems to be a fool.

The King of Comedy's premise and plot are quite
simple and direct. We meet aspiring comic Rupert Pupkin
(Robert De Niro) and his female friend Masha (Sandra Bernhard), both of whom idolize late-night talk show host Jerry
Langford (Jerry Lewis). [2] Rupert attempts to hold Langford
to his promise to listen to one of his demo tapes; Masha
tries to set up a private meeting with Langford; both fail.
To get what they want, they kidnap Langord and tie him up,
with the result that Rupert appears as the first guest on Langford's show (which that night is hosted by Tony Randall) while
Masha has a secluded rendezvous with the comedian. When
Masha frees Langford from his restraints he slaps her and
escapes. Rupert is sent to jail to serve two years of a six-
year sentence. When he emerges, he writes a best-selling
book about his escapade, sells the movie rights to the story
for a sum in excess of a million dollars, and gets his own
television show.

What we have here is clearly a reprise of Taxi Driver's
basic plot and denouement. The frustrated social misfit employs violence as a means of realizing his ends. [3] Rather
than markedly suffering for his actions, he is rewarded.
Travis becomes a media hero; Rupert not only wins public
acclaim, but garners a great deal of money as well.

Unlike Taxi Driver, though, The King of Comedy yields little if any pleasure during viewing. Instead, what the film-goer experiences is dread, a mounting sense of anxiety about Rupert's activities, and a pronounced feeling of embarrass-ment in reaction to the way that Rupert forces himself on people as though he actually had a talent deserving recogni-tion (when in fact, as his Langford show monologue makes clear, he is a terrible comedian).

One of The King of Comedy's most daring qualities is the manner in which it presents to us characters whose per-sonalities remain rigid and fixed, whose lives seem to take place inside of some great show business void. We know nothing more about Rupert at the film's end than we do at its beginning, and the same may be said for everyone else in the production. Quite possibly, the explanation is that there is nothing more to be learned about these individuals. Everyone appears to be one-dimensional (Rupert's high school acquaintance, Rita--whom he drags along on one of his em-barrassing excursions--may be an exception, but her char-acter is never developed), precisely because there is nothing more to them than what we are allowed to see. Given The King of Comedy's overriding concern with the depersonalizing and dehumanizing aspects of the entertainment business, the unavoidable conclusion is that people in show business (or those enamored of it) are basically shallow. In essence, the only thing that counts for the performers is how they are perceived by the public. Image is all-important; everything else is inconsequential.

Moreover, none of the film's show business characters, especially the ones who are already successful, are interested in seeking out and presenting new talent. This is a highly understandable attitude given the intensely competitive nature of the performing arts. Still, the illusion that entertainers are approachable and concerned with improving the quality of their field by encouraging new talent must be maintained. Again, illusion is more important than reality.

This point is obviously one that Rupert simply cannot appreciate. In one of his fantasied meetings with Langford, Rupert imagines the star telling him how great his material is and how much he admires it. Langford goes on, however, to assure Rupert that he would never think of stealing the material, that he is only interested in Rupert's success. It is clear that this sentimental view of the way that "stars" op-erate could only be spawned by someone like Rupert, who is too naive to know the truth.

Rupert fails to realize that there is more than just
the entertainment side to show business; it is, as its title
denotes, a business as well.   As Langford points out to the
unperceptive Rupert during their brief limousine ride together,
in this business--as in all businesses--you must observe the
rules.   In this case, that means starting at the bottom and
gradually, through hard work and luck, climbing to the top
of one's field.   Rupert, though, continues to believe that he
will be discovered and immediately acclaimed as "the comedy
find of the year" and be crowned as "the new king of comedy"
(words he writes into his introduction on the Langford show).

Rupert's hunger for notoriety and desire for the life
that he thinks celebrities lead overlook the true nature of the
existence into which notoriety thrusts one.   As essayed by
Jerry Lewis (on whose on-stage personality--and that of Johnny Carson--the character seems to be based), Jerry Langford is a singularly unattractive person: haughty, presumptuous, and short-tempered.   What makes Langford doubly unattractive is the job he performs.   The position of talk show
host is in itself quite demeaning.   After all, here is a man
paid large sums of money to orchestrate meandering, meaningless conversation with people only interested in sitting
around and discussing themselves and their accomplishments
(e. g. , the pseudonymous author who, under the guise of idealism, has written a successful best-seller about "the vanishing
Siberian tiger," and who is glimpsed selfishly--and violently--
clawing his way into the Langford show studio when it turns
out he will not be featured on that night's show to talk about
his self-serving campaign).

When Langford is seen at his show's beginning, strut-
ting on stage with the characteristic Lewis swagger (the upper
body held unnaturally stiff, the arms swinging at the sides),
all Scorsese lets us see of his work is Langford making fun
of show announcer Ed Herlihy's apparent inattentiveness, ("Did
I wake you, Ed?"), a lack of attention that may very well be
due to the show's rather boring nature.

Throughout the film, Langford is portrayed as a self-
centered individual whose characteristic emotions are rage,
annoyance, and peevishness.   With the exception of the crowd
scene towards the film's beginning (the crush of the throng
causes him evident distress, although he would doubtless be
disappointed if a crowd had not gathered for him), Langford
never exhibits any sympathetic emotions.   Langford lives
alone in a penthouse apartment, his only company a ridiculous Pekinese, whose sullen face and pampered accouter-

ments subtly mock its owner's situation. The penthouse fur-
nishings are restrained to the point of sterility (although the
apartment does feature four television screens, evidence of
Langford's obsession with media), as are the sparse trappings
at his weekend home.

The tragic irony of The King of Comedy is that Rupert
(whose haircut and manner of dress are crude imitations of
Langford's) aspires to Langford's situation.[4] Nor does Scorsese let us forget what kind of emotional vacuum Rupert desires to enter. Rupert has constructed in his basement a
mock-up of the Langford show set; he sits in the set's middle
chair, flanked by life-size cardboard cut-outs of Langford
and "guest" Liza Minnelli as companions. These dummy figures' two-dimensional lifelessness acts as a mocking reminder
of these superstars' natures. When Rupert sits between these
figures, engages in characteristic show business reciprocal
complimenting ("Liza, I saw your show"; "Jerry you crack

Double, double. Rupert (De Niro) and Langford (Lewis) in
a typical Pupkin fantasy sequence. Note Rupert's cheap imitation of Langford's haircut and his affectation (but on the opposite hand) of a Langford pinky ring.

Rupert's doubled "romantic" interests: top, Rupert with
Masha (Sandra Bernhard) and, below, with Rita (Diahnne Abbott). Note the symbolic barriers between both couples and
each woman's virtually identical skeptical reaction to the ami-
able Pupkin.

me up"), and displays the overtly exaggerated, false sentimentality (kissing so profuse that it becomes meaningless)
that we've come to associate with late-night talk shows, Rupert is indeed a tragic figure, still corporeal and alive, in
contrast to the cardboard figures, but already poised on the
edge of a lifeless, two-dimensional fame.

Later, when Rupert practices his act, he does so in
front of a huge blow-up photo of a smiling studio audience.
He gestures in front of them, tells them jokes (which we do
not hear; our suspicions about the quality of Rupert's act are
not answered until the film's end),[5] while the soundtrack res-
onates with the laughter that Rupert has taped from some of
Langford's television shows. During the monologue, Scorsese
retreats from Rupert, having the camera dolly back down a
silver-colored corridor further and further until, at a pronounced physical distance from Rupert's performance, we
achieve a figurative distance as well, and hear the canned
laughter (supposedly coming from the two-dimensional, "canned" audience)--now reverberating down the corridor as though
processed through an echo chamber--ringing with a mockingly
hollow sound.

Significantly, this view of Rupert is attained from behind him. Instead of being given the audience's point of view,
we are given instead the vantage point of the technician or
performer behind the scenes. This privileged, insider's view
only confirms our initial impression that the vacuity we intuit
in this sequence is an accurate indication of the behind-the-
scenes reality of show business.

Even when Scorsese provides us with the audience's
point of view, we are no closer to an accurate assessment
of what the general reaction to Rupert's performance might
be, since although we do see Rupert on the Langford show,
we are never given audience reaction shots. All we see is
Rupert; and all we hear is the audience's laughter and ap-
plause, reactions that (judging by Rupert's essentially second-
rate material) must undoubtedly have been responses to ap-
plause signs and off-camera prompters employed by the show.
The fact that the audience can be so easily manipulated in
this way only further cheapens the far-from-stellar qualities
of Rupert's television appearance.

If any further confirmation were needed of the markedly
unpleasant aspects of the fame to which Rupert aspires, one
need only point to the speech in which Langford, while a hos-

tage, tells Rupert and Masha about his life.   Langford does
not mention the pleasures of fine food and clothing, comfort-
able surroundings, and freedom from want that the money
derived from fame can bring.   Instead, with his face set into
a virtual death-mask rigor, he talks about all of the terrible
aspects of being a celebrity:

> I'm just a human being, with all of the foibles,
> all the traps, the show of depression, the groupies,
> the autograph hounds, the crew, the incompetents,
> those behind the scenes you think are your friends
> and you're not sure if you'll be there tomorrow be-
> cause of them.   There are wonderful pressures that
> make every day a glowing, radiant day in your life.
> It's terrific.

Characteristically, the meaning of this speech--the
only sincere and impassioned bit of extended dialogue the film
gives Langford--is completely ignored by Rupert, who blithely
proceeds with his plot to appear that night on the Langford
show.

Langford's staff and associates hardly display any more
humanity than their boss.   In fact, The King of Comedy demonstrates that the higher one proceeds up the organizational
ladder of success in show business, the more unsympathetic
and unattractive the people one encounters.   The degree of
humane treatment that Rupert receives is in inverse proportion to the power that the person dealing with him wields.
It is the Langford office receptionist, the person who can do
the least about getting Rupert's demo tape played, who treats
him with the most kindness and sympathy.   Cathy (Shelley
Hack), a Langford aide, while polite to Rupert in an officially
acceptable way, acts so mostly as a matter of course; indeed,
under the guise of such politeness she dismisses Rupert from
the office with a studied kindness that makes her rejection
that much more pronounced and cool.

When the most responsible members of the Langford
organization are finally seen, they are revealed as nothing
more than materialistic opportunists.   While Langford is still
being held prisoner, these men are reduced to squabbling
about who is going to sue whom.   Even when the business of
rescuing Langford is attended to, one is left in doubt as to
whether the comedian's release is being secured for humani-
tarian reasons or simply because he is needed for the continuation of his financially successful show.

To play the most powerful member of the Langford organization (Langford's executive producer), Scorsese uses Fred de Cordova, a veteran television director who currently serves as director of The Tonight Show. De Cordova's actions may be quite correct (he does arrange to have Rupert appear on the show) but his appearance is not in general attractive. Scorsese repeatedly shoots de Cordova from the left side of his face, thereby drawing attention to a rather pronounced, unappealing blemish on his upper cheek that could easily have been eliminated by makeup or a change in camera angle. It is difficult to avoid the conclusion that in this respect (as indeed throughout the whole film), Scorsese is intentionally accentuating the least palatable aspects of the show business milieu.

Like Langford, his replacement, Tony Randall, is only seen performing at one point. When Randall takes over as substitute host he only (like his predecessor) effects laughter by maliciously ridiculing someone standing off camera, in this case the man holding the cue cards from which Randall reads. This is a cruel form of humor, the lowest kind of comedy. By contrast, one must at the very least respect and admire Rupert's approach to comedy; his material may be dated and not very good, but at least he does not resort to cheap insults to garner laughs.

Ultimately, what The King of Comedy leaves us with, despite Rupert's eventual fame and fortune, is an immense sense of vacuity and waste. Rupert is last seen onstage during his own television show. More an oddity and freak than anything else, he is absurdly dressed (in even worse taste than during the rest of the film) in an alienatingly red jacket, caught naked and alone in the glare of two spotlights while an off-screen announcer's introduction is repeated over and over again[6] (cf. the echoes during Rupert's basement performance), resounding absurdly in the lonely and abstracted place where, thanks to his new-won fame, he will be condemned to dwell. [7] Unbeknownst to Rupert, fame's visitation is more a cruel joke than a hoped-for blessing, bringing with it a meaningless form of recognition that will doubtless turn Rupert into the image of the emotional cripple whom he idolizes: Jerry Langford.

By The King of Comedy's end there is nothing to laugh about except morbidity; ruling over the film's ironic black humor is the ultimate comic king, the figure who saves the nastiest joke for last, the ruler plenipotentiary of emptiness and waste. The real king of comedy is death.

America's new King of Comedy: Rupert, triumphant, on the
Langford show.

NOTES

1. Travis told the agent that his name was Henry Krinkle--
obviously the silliest name he could devise at the time.

2.   The precise nature of this idolatry suggests a view of
the film somewhat different from the one I offer.   It is quite
possible to read The King of Comedy as a story of misguided
love.   The "ideal" couple (Rupert and Masha) are, typically,
not interested in each other sexually; instead, their passion
is directed away from sex and towards what at first seems
an unattainable object: Jerry Langford, who for Masha represents romance and for Rupert represents achievement and
power.   The film's title sequence supports this approach.
The sequence runs over a freeze frame of Masha, who is
trapped inside Langford's car.   The camera looks out from
within the car and through its window.   Masha's hands are
pressed against the glass and are "apportioned" to the film's
male doubles (Rupert and Jerry), between whom she mediates.
Masha's left hand blocks out part of Rupert's face, while her
right hand covers the spot where, just before, Langford (who,

like his double, is dressed in a grey suit) had previously
stood.   All the while, Ray Charles' version of "Come Rain
or Come Shine," with its lyric about "I'm gonna love you
like no one has loved you" (a promise fulfilled by Rupert and
Masha's abduction of Langford--violence as an act of love),
plays on the soundtrack.

3.   The viewer should note that while the violence in The
King of Comedy (all of which is perpetrated by people desiring fame) is restrained, there are nonetheless a number
of characteristic Scorsese foreshadowings of ominous events
to come.   The crowd waiting for Langford at the film's beginning displays an enthusiasm that borders on mania.   Most
significant is the manner in which Scorsese photographs Langford's walk from the stage door through the crowd, and to
his limousine.   Shot in slow motion, with Langford moving
toward his car while Rupert is seen advancing towards Langford, the sequence takes on the ominous overtones inherent
in the often-replayed news film of Jack Ruby, in slow motion, advancing on Lee Harvey Oswald to shoot him.   Taxi
Driver, too, cites the Ruby-Oswald shooting in the scene in
which Travis (stationed, like Rupert, in front of and to the
left of his "victim") moves towards Palantine in an attempt
to shoot him.   It would appear that Scorsese modeled both
the Taxi Driver and King of Comedy scenes on that famous
newsreel image, relying on disquieting emotional suggestiveness to create in us an anticipation of the violence that both
films will, in later sequences, display.

4.   Rupert and Langford are not the only doubles in the film;
Rita and Masha (Rupert's two female romantic interests, with
neither of whom he seems to be physically involved) qualify
as counterparts as well.   Moreover, in a Taxi Driver-like
shift, each woman in turn assumes the polarized role of either
virgin or whore: Masha figuratively passes from innocence
to corruption; Rita, from corruption to innocence.
     When Rupert and Masha finally kidnap Langford, the
abduction is thus anti-climactic; we have already experienced
vicariously most of the action's violence in its anticipation.
Since we know that the gun Rupert and Masha hold on Langford is not loaded (cf. the essentially empty threats involving
guns in Knocking and Mean Streets and the realized gun threats
in Taxi Driver), our sense of anxiety is additionally somewhat relieved, although Scorsese then again increases the
tension by using another filmic cross-reference to make us
feel uneasy.   After Rupert and Masha have decided that Langford needs to be bound in his chair, Rupert says, "Sorry,

Jerry," and Scorsese cuts to an overhead God's eye shot that
cites both the prelude to the stairway murder sequence in
Psycho and the overhead shot in Taxi Driver after the final
cataclysm, references that increase the sequence's tension
despite its comic aspects.

5.   However, we do know what an un-self-conscious person
Rupert is, a quality that may account for his inability to evaluate his material. Scorsese underscores this aspect by having a man sit in back of Rupert when he takes Rita out to
dinner.   For an anxious minute and a half, the man--who can
easily be seen by Rita--mocks all of Rupert's wildly exaggerated gestures.

6.   The viewer should note that the audience continues to
applaud Rupert although he never speaks.   Obviously, they
like him for his daring kidnapping of Langford and not necessarily for his comedy (which in this sequence he is never
seen performing).

7.   Rupert's dream has come true; as in his basement fantasy,
he stands before an audience that (if we are to judge by their
knee-jerk laughter to his poor jokes) is as inherently lifeless
as the people in his basement mural.

PART TWO

MICHAEL CIMINO

INTRODUCTION

Although the major thematic concerns of Michael Cimino's films have been covered in this book's introductory chapter, there are a number of observations that should at this point be made about Cimino's work before proceeding to a detailed consideration of his films.

It may appear somewhat unusual that I have decided to devote space to a filmmaker who has thus far produced only three films. However, Cimino occupies an important position in today's cinema. Among contemporary American filmmakers, Michael Cimino is virtually unique in that he qualifies as a true mythmaker, a man whose cinematic obsession it is to extract, represent, and investigate those essential elements in the American psyche (manifested most prevalently in his films through the communal events he depicts) which bond us together as a people but which, despite their integrative effects, are nevertheless powerless against the forces of isolation, fear, existential loneliness, and moral confusion. At best, as in The Deer Hunter's end (with its group sing), myth and ritual can only offer ex post facto solace, not protection from grief.

To chart Cimino's films chronologically in this respect is to reveal his increasing concern with the causes and consequences of moral and spiritual poverty. From film to film, this condition assumes increasingly significant forms. In Thunderbolt and Lightfoot we see it in the emotionally crippled persons of the two lead characters; in The Deer Hunter, it is implicit not only in the doomed relationship of Michael and Nicky but also in the effects on Americans of the Vietnam War, which has rudely shattered the lives of the friends who nevertheless triumph over it to a degree when they gather together in John's bar at the film's end. Cimino's pessimism is to return in full force, though. By the time of Heaven's Gate, the inability of a Cimino film's main character to integrate ritual and myth effectively into his quotidian consciousness is seen by the director as a sickness which has so af-

fected the national psyche that it seems virtually impossible
to root out. As a consequence, through the person of Heaven's
Gate's Jim Averill, we witness America's ethical decay, a
debilitation all the more recognizable by contrast with the
myth-bolstered customs of the film's peasants, who are nevertheless crushed by the country's morbid thrust toward mer-
cantile consolidation (a trait symbolically present in Jim and
his wealthiness).

However, it would not be accurate to say that Cimino
appears to have become increasingly convinced of America's
tendency to thwart its own best impulses. Although the powerful tragic effect of Heaven's Gate's end easily dwarfs that of
Thunderbolt and Lightfoot, and even outdistances the intensity
of The Deer Hunter's conclusion by virtue of its closing a
film of greater scope (which initially suggests that in his
latest film, Cimino's despair is greater than ever), in truth
Heaven's Gate's melancholy outlook is wondrously counterbalanced by the film's depiction of America's beauty, which
is evoked more strongly than in either of Cimino's previous
films. With the exception of the brief river's edge sequence
in Thunderbolt and Lightfoot during which Eastwood and Bridges wait for the boat Idaho Dream (a figurative expression of
the hope that the country's unspoiled regions may revitalize
the utter vacuity of its industrial wastelands) and the two actual deer-stalking sequences in The Deer Hunter (which con-
jure up rustic associations familiar to readers of James Feni-
more Cooper), the viewer of Cimino's first two films is
vouchsafed no visions of America's powerful and, to this date,
still-existent vastnesses.

In Heaven's Gate, on the other hand, we are given
numerous examples of America's beauty. Image: the faint
wisps of smoke arising from Ella's cabin, which is located
in the middle of a great, wide plain, and above which is the
delicately colored evening sky. Image: the Army officers
at their ease, playing baseball in a large open field. Image:
the lovely morning haze that seems to hang in the air when
Jim shows Ella his present of a horse and carriage.

These bittersweet glimpses of a time long gone call
forth feelings of sublime pleasure. To temper this effect,
Cimino, always the melancholy romanticist, has chosen to
situate Heaven's Gate in the precise period in America's history when, through the actions of rich men like Canton, the
destruction of the country's open fields and rich plains was
really just beginning.

Heaven's Gate, then, occasions both pleasure and pain, and it does so, we must note, intentionally, with a great deal of art and design. What Cimino intends by this design is quite clear: the creation, through images of ritualistic activity and both beauty and ugliness (respectively present in the film's celebrations and conflicts), of a true American myth based on a dramatization of a country tottering between sweet innocence and harsh experience. Created thereby is a nationalistic representation that has not been seen in American filmmaking since D. W. Griffith's The Birth of a Nation, a film which Heaven's Gate rivals in its scope, its simplicity, and its purity of feeling.

Some readers may object to my claims about Cimino's status as a mythmaking filmmaker and point to the work of men like Steven Spielberg and George Lucas, supposed mythmakers whom some regard as having revitalized the American filmmaking industry. There is an important distinction, though, between storytelling and mythmaking, a distinction often overlooked when praising the work of Spielberg[1] and Lucas and (as has been popular since the release of Heaven's Gate) denigrating the work of Michael Cimino. What Spielberg (in Close Encounters of the Third Kind, Raiders of the Lost Ark, and E. T.) and Lucas (through the Star Wars trilogy) communicate are not myths but simple adventure stories. Unfortunately, such storytelling is accompanied by a reliance on technical wizardry and the absence of simple human emotional affect (something of which Spielberg and Lucas simply seem incapable). Indeed, Spielberg and Lucas fail to achieve human resonance in their films; they make up for this deficiency by keeping the action moving so fast that, supposedly, the audience will not notice that they are not reacting to people but to special effects and lots of light and noise.

Spielberg's feature film career began with Duel, a story about a ruthless force (embodied by an apparently driverless, and thereby coldly mechanical, truck) out to kill Dennis Weaver; Lucas debuted with THX 1138, a futuristic drama about an unemotional advanced society. These portentous beginnings are highly ironic, since the quality derided in these men's first feature films (the lack of feeling) characterizes all of their work, these initial films included. In essence, Duel and THX 1138 don't portray emotionlessness; they embody it, a situation that is not the result of intentional style but rather a reflection of a simple lack of feeling on the part of the films' directors.

In an attempt to cloak this lack of emotion, Spielberg and Lucas resort to emotional appeals whose coercive aspects border on the mechanical. One thinks immediately of the embarrassingly sloppy, supposed innocence communicated in Close Encounters, and the premeditated grasp for sentimentality at the end of E. T. , the latter tactic an overt, objectionable, and unjustifiable manipulation of the audience that had not been seen in American films since the trick ending of Disney's Lady and the Tramp (which portrayed the "death" and miraculous rebirth of one of Lady and Tramp's canine friends). As for Lucas, a glance at the failed attempt to involve the audience with the Star Wars characters (a shortcoming supposedly masked by these films' special effects) indicates how like Spielberg as a filmmaker he really is.

In contrast to Cimino, Spielberg and Lucas are less filmmakers than technicians; if the viewers of Spielberg's and Lucas's films come away from them thinking that they have in any sense been emotionally entertained, they do so only because the cinematic machines these men have constructed have so cunningly duplicated human attributes. Cimino, though, is a true filmmaker, a man who communicates a grandeur of feeling that may truly be deemed magnificent. It is quite likely that in the annals of filmmaking it is Michael Cimino who will come to be recognized as the director who dramatized the great myths that are truly worth remembering.

NOTE

1. While I don't consider him an admirable filmmaker, Spielberg is nonetheless an occasionally accurate commentator on the moviemaking scene. See Chapter 12, p. 249.

Chapter Nine

TWO FOR THE ROAD

Thunderbolt and Lightfoot, Cimino's directional debut, only seems to represent and co-opt the traditional themes and actions of male bonding adventures that are so traditional in both American literature and American movies. One might be led to deduce from Clint Eastwood's presence in the film that we are to be treated to a violent and action-filled thriller featuring a male character fiercely concerned with the repeated confirmation of his masculinity.

However, Eastwood (who was responsible for giving Cimino his chance at directing) and Cimino (who wrote the film's script) are far too serious about their craft to present such a hackneyed and by-now-traditional theme without also including within the film rhetorical devices (symbol, camera-work, allusive dialogue) which indicate that Thunderbolt and Lightfoot is more a meditation on, than a representation of, the male camaraderie theme.

A number of the film's themes and techniques are evident from its opening shot. We view row upon row of wheat swaying lazily in an expansive field; no fences, boundary markers, or other limiting devices can be seen; just a few tall trees acting as windbreaks dot the background. On the soundtrack only the wind is heard. Eventually, about midway through the film's titles (which are superimposed over the opening shot), the sound of a church congregation's singing fades in, at which point Cimino dissolves to a shot of a simple church situated all alone in the middle of what appears to be another part of the same wheat field. The church is placed slightly to the left of the frame's center; extremely off center, to the right, a car approaches along a dusty road.

The car pulls up; the occupant gets out, looks at the
church bulletin board. The hymn ends; Cimino then cuts to
a shot inside the church, where the Reverend John Doherty
(Eastwood) begins his sermon.

Notable about the film's opening are three factors:
its photography, its pacing, and its thematic suggestiveness.
Notable with respect to the sequence's photography is the
manner in which Cimino employs the Panavision frame to full
effect. The opening shot of the wheat field is static; instead
of panning to create the sensation of a broad vista, Cimino
allows the setting to speak for itself. The following shot is,
with an interesting, short exception, also static. Cimino
thereby establishes an implicit identification between natural
creations (the field, the wheat, the trees) and man-made
creations dedicated to God (the church), all of which seem
inherently to belong just where they are. Therefore, when
a moving object, rudely off center and thereby inappropriate
to the sense of natural order and balance already created,
appears--an object that is man-made and noisy--we must
view it as an intrusion. The car does not belong in this
picture of order; the feeling of dislocation and inappropriate-
ness is quickly transferred to the car's inhabitant, Dunlop,
who has come to kill Doherty.

The pacing of the sequence--up to the point at which
Cimino cuts from a shot of Dunlop staring at the billboard
to an inside view showing Doherty beginning the sermon--
complements the expansiveness of the photography at the opening shots by being extremely (one might almost say unusually)
measured. Neither overt camera movement nor editing in-
trudes upon the feeling of restful repose created by the notable length of the opening two shots. Their length evokes a
sense of undisturbed, natural rhythm that is at odds with the
entrance of Dunlop's car into the picture. Even then, the
feeling of serenity to which we have grown accustomed is
not totally disturbed, since the car's entrance is noted without a cutaway; the static camera allows the car simply to
enter the frame and then merely pans with it very briefly,
finally returning to a view of the church which--in contrast
to the first shot--is now situated in a balanced position at
frame center, with the threatening (because it contains Dunlop) car now totally excluded from our field of view. And
though the car's entrance does signal a discordant intrusion,
its "invasion" of the shot is not totally unexpected, since we
have already seen a present, albeit mild, contradiction between the wheat and the wooden, man-made church.

Given the fact that Dunlop's mission is to kill Doherty for what is assumed to be his betrayal of the other members of a gang that robbed an armored truck company, Dunlop can be viewed not only as a secular outsider, but also as a divine messenger seeking an eye-for-an-eye vengeance that has biblical precedent. Consequently, although Dunlop's entrance into the church in one sense (which ironically occurs at the point when Doherty begins talking about mercy and forgiveness) creates a jarring visual message (he is dressed far more formally than the parishioners), in other senses we feel that he has a perfect right to be there. For one thing, Dunlop's formal attire reflects the prescribed mode of dress that Doherty, in jacket and priestly collar, affects. Additionally important are the images we are given when Dunlop walks into the church.

First, Doherty is seen behind the pulpit, at frame center. When Dunlop enters the church, he passes through the very center of the church doorway. Standing at the opposite end of the aisle from Doherty, Dunlop is therefore positioned in such a way that he seems to belong where he is as much as much as Doherty does.

After Dunlop's unsuccessful handgun attack on Doherty, and Doherty's escape through the back door of the church into the field, Cimino cuts to another static view of the wheat field. The director again employs a non-moving camera, and eschews cutting in favor of an extended take. We start with an unimpeded view of the field. Doherty enters from frame right; just as he passes the frame's mid-point (the precise position in the frame where, in the most striking shot, his church has been located), Dunlop enters from frame right in pursuit, thus once again disturbing, as he did in breaking up the placid church service, a visual composition's serenity and order.

Thunderbolt and Lightfoot's structural paradigm describes a tripartite series of events; natural order followed by disturbance followed by a restoration of natural order. In the present case, the congregational meeting (connoting order) leads to Dunlop's break-in (disturbance), which then leads to Thunderbolt's meeting Lightfoot (a re-establishment of order).[1] It is significant that when they occur, these disturbances are not coaxed into the field of action; they enter naturally under their own power. Thus here, Doherty and Dunlop move into an already-established, static frame (as did Dunlop's car in the film's opening sequence). The breadth

of the Panavision frame complements, but does not exaggerate, the extensive amount of ground that Doherty and Dunlop
cover.

Throughout the film, a series of complementarities
establishes and reaffirms linkages between Doherty and Jeff
Bridges' Lightfoot, who is the next character to appear. Doherty's sermon takes as its text the biblical message, "Remember that we are all imperfect; we see but in part, we
know but in part, as under The Redeemer's gentle reign the
wolf shall dwell with the lamb, the leopard shall lie down
with the kid." On the word "kid," Cimino cuts to a shot of
Lightfoot walking through a wheat field that looks very similar to the one in which Doherty's church is situated.

Doherty represents a return to normalcy, an affinity
with unchanging values which, while fleetingly glimpsed, nonetheless remain constant. Thus, Doherty's nickname, Thunderbolt (derived from his renowned use of an anti-tank cannon
during a previous theft; cf. p. 157), which suggests a flash
of light that, like the man who bears it, moves quickly but
is remembered. Lightfoot, though, unlike a thunderbolt
which is glimpsed in the sky and is thereby, even if only for
a second, physically situated, represents movement itself.
The first syllable of Lightfoot's nickname already establishes
a link with the speed-of-light bolt of electricity suggested by
Doherty's nickname, thus giving us "lightning/bolt." If, in
an appropriately complementary fashion, we drop the first
syllable of Thunderbolt's name and the last syllable of Lightfoot's, we come up with "Thunder and Lightning" as the name
of this pair of characters. Appropriately, then, Lightfoot's
first action in the film is to procure (through robbery; like
Doherty, he is a thief) a means of transportation, in this
case a sports car reputedly as fast (in essence, light-footed)
as his name suggests he himself might be.

Even before these two characters meet, we are given
additional information linking them. We have already seen
how Doherty's sermon's text anticipated "the kid('s)" arrival
on the scene; later, when Doherty dons a shirt appropriated
from a stolen car, the shirt's regular geometric pattern of
squares suggests the spots of a leopard, which is supposed
to "lie down" with the kid.

Yet for all of their immediate kinship, there are important differences between Thunderbolt and Lightfoot. Thunderbolt is introspective and emotionally reserved; Lightfoot is

gregarious and freely expresses his feelings. Thus, when
they are about to part early in the film, Thunderbolt offers
Lightfoot his watch as thanks for helping him escape from
Dunlop. Lightfoot, though, wants more than material things
from Thunderbolt. "I don't want your watch, man; I want
your friendship," he says.

Cimino has the two characters exhibit similar but opposite physical debilities in order to both reflect their opposing (but complementary) personality tendencies and to symbolize the essential emotional frigidity of their relationship,
which is doomed to failure. On his way into the used car
lot to steal a car, Lightfoot affects a limp of the left leg;
later, we see that Doherty is compelled to wear a brace on
his right leg. Nevertheless, he quickly eludes Dunlop; thus,
neither character's apparent handicap in any way detracts
from his abilities.

In another example, Thunderbolt's left arm is temporarily dislocated during the escape from Dunlop. Lightfoot,
attacked by the emotionally repressed Red Leary, eventually
suffers real injuries to his left side. His left arm, like
Thunderbolt's, becomes temporarily useless (soon after his
paralysis he dies), while the left side of his face droops down
leadenly before his death in a manner reminiscent of the way
Thunderbolt's dislocated arm had felt (in Thunderbolt's words,
"like lead"). Appropriately, the injuries which turn out to
be permanent for each character are, respectively, to Thunderbolt's right side (his bad leg) and Lightfoot's left (his paralysis), suggesting that they are an ideal, albeit crippled, couple
who (together) equal one total, undamaged personality.

The mutual attraction between two characters who
seem ordained to meet develops into more than mere ami-
ability, though. The leopard's "[lying] down with the kid"
suggests not only friendship but some sort of sexual relationship as well. Indeed, Thunderbolt and Lightfoot is not just
a film about camaraderie; it is also about the nature of the
sexual relationship between male companions. Throughout,
dialogue and action affirm the view that what we are witnessing in the two central male characters' actions is the growth,
development, and end of a love affair. Yet ironically, both
Thunderbolt and Lightfoot are initially revealed to us affect-
ing roles that mask their sexual potency. Thus, Doherty is
a country preacher (whose sexual activity, if not proscribed,
would at least certainly be expected to be limited), while
Lightfoot, on entering the used car lot, pretends to have a

Remarks about waitress's "tight" asses notwithstanding, <u>Thunderbolt and Lightfoot</u> is about a love affair between two men: Clint Eastwood and Jeff Bridges.

wooden leg, an obvious symbol for a loss of sexual power. This condition is alluded to by the lot's salesman, who asks Lightfoot somewhat cruelly, "Are you man enough to take on a car like this?" Significantly, he replies, "I don't know; I have a wooden leg." The suggestion here is that Lightfoot (at least in a humorous sense) and Thunderbolt (in a somewhat more serious sense, given his leg brace) are somehow deficient sexually.

Such a view is borne out by the film's events. The only direct sexual encounter the two men have with women occurs during the evening when Gloria and Melody spend the night with them. However, the sex between Lightfoot and Melody is never seen, while in the sequence involving Gloria and Thunderbolt, the woman's overt aggression, coupled with Thunderbolt's obvious distaste at the way she pursues her own pleasure (apparently to his exclusion), leads one to conclude that despite Lightfoot's good-natured cracks about waitress's "tight" asses and the like, these men are not particularly demonstrative heterosexually.

Instead, as is traditional in male bonding relationships, the majority of sexual interplay occurs between the
film's real lovers: its male couples. Lightfoot tries to
elicit Thunderbolt's friendship by alluding to their interaction
in terms that usually refer to sexual performance: "We're
good together." After they are briefly separated and then
reunited, Lightfoot's first comment is, ""We gotta stop meeting like this; people will talk ... with a preacher, man, especially." And toward the film's end, with the getaway botched
and Lightfoot near death, the youngster still refers to his
relationship with Thunderbolt in words suggesting that their
entire interaction throughout the film has been one large sexual experience, an experience that--like all of the central,
doomed homophilic and (heterosexual) relationships in The
Deer Hunter (Michael and Nicky, Michael and Linda) and
Heaven's Gate (Jim and Billy, Jim and Nate, Ella and Nate,
Ella and Jim)--only reaches true fruition through death. "We
made it," Lightfoot says towards Thunderbolt and Lightfoot's
end and, appropriately enough, he is soon dead.

Despite the placidity and gentle mode of speech that
Eastwood brings to the characterization, Doherty's Thunderbolt assumes the role of the traditional male figure in the
relationship. He is quiet, powerful, but sullen, whereas
Lightfoot is constantly jabbering and chattering like the teen-
age girls the movies have been giving us for the last forty
years. During the heist in the film's second half, then, it
is entirely appropriate that it is Thunderbolt who, as in the
first heist, operates the anti-tank cannon (the scene with the
armored car company's safe being blown contains a beautiful
shot of Doherty kneeling by the floor-mounted cannon, which
rises up next to him like a powerful erection),[2] while Lightfoot's role in the robbery is to act as a decoy by assuming
feminine garb. Thunderbolt, the aggressive male figure (thus
his identification with the predator/leopard in the film's sermon quotation), is thus paired with the meek, recessive figure,
the kid who, as well shall see, is led like a lamb to the
slaughter.

To affirm this pairing of the two men as lovers, Thunderbolt and Lightfoot gives us two additional wayward thieves,
also a complementary pair. Like the male/female, aggres-
sive/recessive pair of Thunderbolt and Lightfoot, Red Leary
(George Kennedy) and Eddie Goody (Geoffrey Lewis) complement each other. Red is a loud-mouthed, extremely aggressive, physical man with possible misogynist tendencies (he
has been sent to jail for stabbing a woman); Goody, as his

A posed shot, with Eastwood appropriately at the controls of
the phallic cannon.   Surrounding him are Bridges, George
Kennedy and Geoffrey Lewis.

name implies, is good-natured, of a meek demeanor.   Like
Lightfoot, Goody is somewhat repelled by the violent nature
of the planned robbery; he wields guns but does not like to
use them and, again like Lightfoot, is never assertive physically (whereas both Red and Thunderbolt can be seen striking people with their fists).   Moreover, as with Lightfoot,
Goody's male sexuality is somewhat suspect.   Lightfoot may
be seen admiring women but never touching them; Goody is
shown as also sexually immature, an attribute suggested by
his inability to exercise control over his urethral sphincter.
Child-like, he is liable to wet his pants at any moment, especially times of stress.   To Red, this characteristic is
enough to label him "a ding ding" (a comment made, significantly, immediately after Red has implicitly affirmed his
own male potency by firing off his shotgun, which he holds
ramrod straight, pointing it into the sky).

        Yet despite Red's aggressiveness, he is similar to
Goody in that his male sexual identity is flawed.   Despite
his gruff, machismo nature, Red suffers from two debilitat-
ing conditions--asthma and hay fever--that severely hamper
his style when confronting adversaries like Thunderbolt.   Additionally, regardless of his claims to prowess ("It's a good

The archetypical American homophilic couple: Thunderbolt
(Eastwood), still in his leopard-spotted shirt, and his mate
(Bridges).

thing I didn't hit him in the face, he'd be dead now," he says
after striking Lightfoot), Red is out of condition and a poor
fighter (Thunderbolt easily beats him) and has an unfounded
opinion of his physical capabilities. As Thunderbolt tells
him, "You always did exaggerate."

Like Goody, also, Red is extremely child-like. This
characteristic is especially evident in his attitude towards
women's nude bodies. When Lightfoot comments on a woman's
exposing herself to him while he is working (something that
he characteristically does nothing about, which Red uses as
a point of derision), Red asks, "Did you see it ... everything?" Lightfoot asks him to be more specific but Red cannot proceed beyond his infantile euphemistic usages to an accurate statement of precisely what "everything" he is talking
about. Instead, Red can only gawk open-mouthed in response
to Lightfoot's account of the incident, a childish reaction he
duplicates when peering down at the nude body of the daughter of
the armored car company's general manager during part of
the heist.

Red's immediate and continued hostility to Lightfoot appears to derive from a thinly disguised jealousy over Lightfoot's relationship with Doherty's Thunderbolt.   Red and Thunderbolt had both been together in Korea; each had apparently at one time saved the other's life.   Now, looking for the money from the first heist, Red pursues Doherty like a disappointed lover.   When he finally confronts him and Doherty asks him directly, "What do you want?"   Red replies in words that, while colloquially acceptable, also reveal a virtually literal meaning that links up with his desire to possess Doherty in the suggestive way that Lightfoot does (Red, though, cannot compete; Lightfoot is younger and more attractive than he).   "What do I want?   You got balls, I'll say that for you, Johnny.   I want your ass," Red says.   Significantly, Lightfoot's comment at this point discards the statement's colloquial meaning, and instead cuts directly to the sexual allusiveness apparently being verbalized here.   "Flattery's not gonna get you guys anywhere," he says.   Red, stung at having been both exposed and mocked, responds in the only way he knows.   He reasserts his fragile masculinity by punching Lightfoot in the stomach, reducing the upright youth to a groaning, fetally coiled form on the ground.

This jealousy between Red and Lightfoot continues throughout the film.   When Red asks Lightfoot what he did about the naked woman, Lightfoot responds by pretending to kiss Red on the mouth.   Such a blatant affront to Red's supposedly well-established masculinity is more than he can stand, and he attempts unsuccessfully to attack Lightfoot.   Subsequently, though, he pays the kid back in an appropriate way.   Lightfoot's pretended kiss on the mouth cast Red in the role of the woman whom Lightfoot supposedly was kissing.   When plans are later being made for the second heist, Red takes particular pleasure in Lightfoot's having to dress up as a woman, and is careful to note that perhaps the youth should shave, although he thinks it is hardly necessary given "the kid's" light beard, an obvious affront to Lightfoot's masculinity.

Throughout the film, Lightfoot is heard to repeat homilies of proverbial wisdom, such as "Where there's smoke there's fire," "In for a penny," and "The rich get richer."   In response to Thunderbolt's inquiry about his sexual dalliance with Melody, Lightfoot chooses to respond obliquely: "Red-haired women are bad luck."   Later, after the second heist, when the police are pursuing the foursome's getaway car as a result of Red's shirt-tail sticking out of the trunk and his

having sneezed audibly as they entered the drive-in to hide,
Lightfoot repeats his homily. Again, Red assumes a non-
male role, as Lightfoot intimates that Red's old-womanish
clumsiness and allergies have indeed given them away.

The traditional male role of the sexually potent, aggressive individual is shown in the film to be a misconcep-
tion, a notion that simply does not reflect the facts of American culture. Thunderbolt and Lightfoot steal a car from a
married couple; the man is so inept that he cannot even lo-
cate the correct credit card for Dub Taylor's gas station attendant, (who tells the man, "That ain't it"). All the while,
his wife badgers him with questions like "What did he [the
attendant] say?" and "Did he insult you?" A co-worker at
the welding plant where Thunderbolt takes a job tells him a
curious story about a joke he played on the night manager
of the local telegraph office, and how he put his "pecker" in
the man's hand one night for a jest. The humor of the incident is, to say the least, highly elusive (as are most of
the male-oriented bits of comic business that are scattered
throughout the film). [3] In any case, the tale involves a rather
disquieting kind of braggadocio that seems more a result of
overcompensation for some defect in potency than anything
else.

This same telegraph attendant is a fat, unattractive
man who reads Penthouse-type magazines on duty, which he
masks with a newspaper so that passing people will not see
what he is doing. Nevertheless, the truth will come out: Thunderbolt's comment that "he spends a lot of time" in the bathroom suggests that what he does in there is masturbate. It
is appropriate (and ironic) that during the heist this sexually
repressed man is undone by Lightfoot's flirtation with him
when the youth is dressed up as what would only to a des-
perate, repressed individual appear to be a sexy blonde.

The film's other males are similarly shown to be weak
and ineffectual. The night manager of the armored car company is seen asleep in bed while his wife stays up to watch
television; her erect posture next to his recumbent form
brands him as a weakling. Similarly, their daughter, in bed
with her boyfriend, is (like Gloria) portrayed as the dominant
member in her heterosexual relationship. At one point she
is compelled to remind her lover to restrain himself from
premature ejaculation; like Goody, her lover lacks control.
Finally, the tourist couple in the one-room schoolhouse where
Thunderbolt and Lightfoot find the first heist's money also

The impotence of traditional American heterosexuality: the
armored car company's night manager and his wife, both
fittingly bound, with the verbose wife cruelly, if deservedly,
gagged.   George Kennedy wields the gun.

disappoint traditional expectations; the husband suspects that
Thunderbolt and Lightfoot are robbers, and willingly gives
them his car keys and both of his cameras although he is in
no way threatened, while his agonized wife rolls her eyes in
exasperation over her husband's weakness.

The movement of the film's plot itself suggests disappointment, a delayed reward that frustrates fulfillment, as
though in the film's universe neither satisfactory sexual interaction nor fulfilling companionship can be obtained in an
American culture in which heterosexual love has failed and
homophilic relationships cannot endure.   The fruits of the
first robbery are hidden, made unavailable to the original
gang members, and then are lost when their hiding place is
moved.   It takes a second heist, from the same company,
to yield the amount that the first one netted.   Ironically, this
money is not the cash from the second job (which is lost),
though, but from the first.   The obvious conclusion to be drawn
here is that the second job was pointless; tracing the where-

abouts of the schoolhouse where the original heist's money
was hidden would have been a much easier way to get rich.
In essence, then, although three people (Red, Goody, and
Lightfoot) die as a result of the second heist, the second job
leaves Thunderbolt right back where he started at the film's
beginning. The film's entire action has essentially been unproductive. [4]

    Thunderbolt and Lightfoot's two main homophilic lovers
are not destined to enjoy the money together. Lightfoot dies
from the injuries that Red inflicts on him as revenge for all
of his wise-cracking insults. When Thunderbolt--driving in
the male-symbolic long white Cadillac that Lightfoot wanted
to drive but cannot--breaks the phallic symbol cigar after
Lightfoot's death, he is figuratively breaking the easily snapped
bonds of their fragile, death-oriented, unproductive (the dead-
end heist; their inability directly to express their mutual affection) relationship.

    The opening sermon's forecast of "the leopard('s) ly-
ing down with the kid" is thus only an unrealized hope; however, the prophecy of "the kid('s) dwell(ing) with the lamb"
is realized. The mastermind of the first heist was Billy
Lamb, a genius who died of a heart attack before the money
could be split up. In death, both "the kid" and "the lamb"
do indeed lie together, suggesting (with the sexual sense of
the word "lie" in mind) that it is only through death that homophilic relationships come to fruition or, concurrently, that
the very nature of successfully expressed and realized homophilic love is itself death. Free of Lightfoot, Thunderbolt
can disappear down the road with the half-million dollars, but
he must, as at the film's beginning, travel alone. Despite
the film's recurrent images of regeneration (notably the peri-
odic returns to bodies of water, which serve as symbols of
both fertility and replenishment), [5] there is no promise in
Thunderbolt and Lightfoot, nor, for that matter, in the America it portrays, of potency or power. All of the film's men,
Thunderbolt included, are ultimately shown to be ineffectual
and weak. All of its women are aggressive and strong. The
men recoil in the face of such energies and, not knowing what
to do with themselves, compensate by effecting assaults against
supposedly impregnable objects (like the armored car company's vault), conquests they value more highly than sexual
and emotional relations with the opposite sex. Only Thunderbolt remains at the film's end, a lonely man, richer in money
but bankrupt in spirit, driving down an endless highway towards
futility and death.

NOTES

1. Other examples of this schema: Thunderbolt and Lightfoot, an established team (order), are fired upon by Red (disorder), an occurrence that eventually leads to the formation of a new four-man gang (order) which takes the place of Doherty's lost congregation. Significantly, when Red shoots at Thunderbolt and Lightfoot, he initially does so from a fixed (orderly) position, one that the film's continuity has quite definitely established.

Finally, the order-disorder-order dialectic is reinvoked: the four-man gang (order) is decimated by the robbery's aftermath (disorder; all of the gang's plans for escape break down) until the film returns to its beginning with the congregation-free Thunderbolt on his own once more (restoration of order). Given the schema's constant reassertion of order, we must therefore conclude that Thunderbolt's being alone (his situation at the film's beginning and end) is the way things are supposed to be. Indeed, the film's sub-text bears out this conclusion: Thunderbolt's insular homophilic relationship with Lightfoot is fated to fail.

2. This equation of weaponry and sexuality, present also in The Deer Hunter, may be seen as well in the Clint Eastwood-starring Magnum Force (1973), which was co-scripted by Cimino and John Milius. Unlike Thunderbolt and Lightfoot, though, the earlier film repeatedly leavens its violence with a liberal amount of graveyard humor. Where joking in Thunderbolt and Lightfoot virtually disappears once the robbery is committed, it remains in Magnum Force even after the most grisly of crimes. As a former policeman-turned-counterman says to Eastwood and his partner after the pair have just seen the bodies of three men who were shot point blank with a .44 Magnum (a sight that ruins Eastwood's partner's appetite but does not affect Eastwood's at all), "In broad daylight at close range, huh? Musta looked like ripe melons. I'll never forget the Floyd case--got it with an axe during the rush hour. How about some cream pie?" The free-association movement from melons to body fluids (released by the axe) to cream pie is too blithely presented to be anything other than intentionally morbid mirth.

3. However, the surrealistic sequence with the crazed driver who tries to asphyxiate Thunderbolt and Lightfoot, and who is transporting a truck full of white rabbits, is (along with Dub Taylor's bit in the film) an example of a species of successful humor, albeit of a kind that simply defies classification.

4. True, Doherty causes changes at the armored car company; he breaks in there twice, both times blasting open their
safe with a well-aimed thunderbolt from his anti-tank cannon.
Yet all of his actions in the second robbery lead only to the
establishment of what appears to be the natural outcome of
the first heist, namely that the stolen money be recovered,
to be enjoyed by Thunderbolt alone.

5. After Thunderbolt and Lightfoot first meet they drive to
the water's edge; the foursome of Red, Goody, Thunderbolt,
and Lightfoot first meet near water; Thunderbolt and Lightfoot wait for the aptly named boat of desire, the Idaho Dream,
near water; Lightfoot and Red, flushed with enthusiasm, un-
load the cannon parts near water.

Chapter Ten

GOD BLESS AMERICA

The Deer Hunter generated a great deal of press on
its initial release, much of it concentrating on the film's
depiction of the Vietnamese, its approach to the issue of male
bonding, and its attitude towards fate. None of the reviews,
however, attempted to fully explore these themes or reconcile
the film with the artistic stance prevalent in Cimino's previous film. Now, with three films to Cimino's credit and
an end to the Vietnam conflict, The Deer Hunter may be more
comprehensively evaluated.

Many commentators have already drawn passing attention to The Deer Hunter's depiction of the way that men and
women get along. One of the film's major characteristics
is its emphasis on the primacy of homophilic versus heterosexually expressed love. In fact, the word "love" as a direct
expression of a personal feeling is used only twice in the
film's dialogue,[1] both times by Michael (Robert De Niro) in
talking to Nicky (Christopher Walken), whom he is trying to
rescue from the South Vietnam Russian roulette game. Yet
the affection among all of the men in the group (Michael,
Nicky, Steven, Stanley, Axel, and John) is usually expressed
fairly directly through a great deal of play and comradely
touching (embraces, hand-grasps, fake fighting).

By contrast, when these men are with women everything is quite different. Conversations are hesitant, touching
is intermittent, and there is very little eye contact. When
Nicky asks Linda to marry him, and she replies yes, neither
looks at the other; at the film's end, it takes a long time before Michael and Linda can look at each other directly. Indeed, despite the fact that the first third of the film depicts
the events leading up to Steven's (John Savage) wedding, the
ceremony itself, and the wedding's aftermath, the viewer never

A figurative elevation in The Deer Hunter as prelude to an inevitable fall.   The purity of Angela's (Rutanya Alda) white dress can't last.

sees the bride and groom embracing.   Cimino intentionally denies us the usually obligatory shot of the couple kissing after the ceremony is over.   In fact, the only time that Steven and Angela are seen jointly participating in an important activity after the ceremony is when they drink from the dual-siphon wine goblet, an object from which the wine spills blood-like onto Angela's dress in a fateful presentiment of the couple's fate.

As is usual with Cimino, the early portion of his film contains a communal event that obviously has figurative and mythic significance for the members of the community.   In The Deer Hunter, such an event is present in the form of the wedding and reception.   In keeping with the plot structure set up in Thunderbolt and Lightfoot (in which the communal church service leads to a breakdown of the preacher's following) and destined to be repeated in Heaven's Gate (the dance at the film's beginning turns into the slaughter at its end),

The Deer Hunter's celebration acts not only as a unifying
event affirming communally-shared values but also as a di-
visive force which prefigures the destruction of individual
and social bonds through some cataclysmic event. That Cimino intends us to draw this conclusion is made clear by the
fact that the wedding reception/celebration doubles as a going
away party for Michael, Nicky, and Steven, who are soon to
leave for Vietnam. Thus, the party at one and the same
time affirms both life (intentionally, through the wedding) and
death (unintentionally, through the war).

    Early on in the film, there are faint but nonetheless
disturbing foreshadowings of the Vietnam War, an event that
will leave a lasting destructive mark on the film's principals. The opening shot of a steel foundry furnace anticipates
the first glimpse we have of Vietnam, which involves the na-
palming of a Vietnamese village's outskirts. [2] Soon after the
steel plant sequence, we follow five of the friends to John's
bar, where they are destined at the film's end to be reunited
after Nicky's funeral (Nicky's suicide, a further cataclysmic
event, has the ironic effect of bringing the group back together, but only through death). Additionally, when Cimino
cuts to a brief pre-wedding sequence inside the church (during which Steven's mother asks the priest why her son has
to go to Vietnam), the director initiates a backward track
down the pews, leaving the viewer with a visual prefiguration
of the rows of body bags and aluminum coffins that are later
seen outside the United States military hospital where Nicky
waits before encountering the Frenchman and deciding to go
AWOL.

    The film suggests that the church--in the forms of
both the destruction-anticipating wedding ceremony and the
funereal pews--brings death and grief instead of life and solace. Indeed, this view is echoed in the banner draping the
wedding reception hall which reads, "Serving God and Country proudly." The tragic way in which Michael, Nicky, and
Steven are there "served" by their God and country makes
it clear what a terrible sacrificial price a man must sometimes pay to remain a loyal American who truly is proud of
his country.

    Michael's reaction to the statement about the war made
by the Green Beret who drifts in to the reception indicates
that, like his other friends, at this point he is still painfully
naive about the Vietnam conflict. In fact, he--and Nicky--
support Steven's statement to the Green Beret that, "I hope

they send us where the bullets are flying and the fighting's
the worst." In answer to questions about "What's it like
over there," the man only replies, "Fuck it." The friends
not only draw away from this reaction (it appears to annoy
Michael), but fail to intuit the knowledge about the war's
utter pointlessness that this uninvited guest (like the similarly
uninvited precursor of doom in Coleridge's The Ancient Mar-
iner) brings to the party. A celebration traditionally about
life--both secular (the earthly affection shared by Steven and
Angela) and divine (the church-sanctioned and -performed ceremony, which includes wearing the crowns of heaven which
are, significantly, held above their heads by another pledged
couple: Nicky and Linda)--becomes instead a prelude to death,
here present in the form of the taciturn soldier.[3] The soldier's presence suggests that a movement from innocence to
experience, from a yearning for life to an awareness tinged
with knowledge of death, is inevitable (the plethora of fateful
foreshadowings in the first third of the film also suggests
this), thereby indicating that Cimino views the passage from
hope to resignation as unavoidable, a realization which brands
The Deer Hunter as a film predominantly about fate and the
ineluctability of despair.

In this respect, Michael and Nicky (at least at this
point in the film) hold opposite convictions about the role
that predetermination plays in one's life. In response to a
bet with Nicky (which Nicky loses, just as he does in the
barroom pool game with Michael and in the loss, involving
his life, during their second Russian roulette game), Michael
intentionally and dangerously moves his car into the right inside lane to pass a trailer truck. He does so because he is
certain that accomplishing such a feat is "a sure thing," despite Nicky's comment that "There's no such thing as a sure
thing." Yet such beliefs do not totally determine one's actions. Later, Michael does not bet on a football game but
Nicky does. The difference here from the former situation
is important: in the car's driver's seat, Michael was in control of his fate; with the football game, chance is in the hands
of other people. Significantly, Nicky bets (and loses) on the
game, apparently relying on his good luck to see him through.
Later, in the South Vietnamese Russian roulette game his
amazing luck (he has been playing for months) will again, in
Michael's presence, desert him, suggesting that in Nicky's
life Michael represents the personification of his destined
end (cf. p. 177 and Note 19).

Michael is firmly committed to the belief that he can

One symbol in a symbol-rich film: the sun dogs in the sky, here being observed by Stanley (John Cazale), Axel (Chuck Aspegren), Nicky (Christopher Walken), Michael (Robert De Niro), and Steven (John Savage) in The Deer Hunter.

influence his own fate; this attitude may be recognized as that of a man who feels that participation in events is part of the predetermined plan. Michael's attitude, strongly in evidence in the Russian roulette game played while he is a prisoner of the North Vietnamese, is that the time of one's own death is predetermined, but that this does not preclude one from trying to influence the events that control one's destiny. In essence, he is a self-conscious actor playing in a drama whose conclusion has already been written.

There are signs--in heaven and on earth--of what must be. Michael is the only one among the friends who looks for and reads these indications of fate. The "sun dogs" in the sky, which Michael claims mean "a blessing on the hunter sent by the great wolf to his children," are one such sign. [4]

Another fateful factor is the manner in which one's life is lived, as though a serious approach to existence qualified one for an extra-mundane life. Among the friends who go hunting, only Michael takes the ritualistic act of ascending into the mountains (where one can be closer to the great spirits) as an act of grace, one demanding absolute concentration and dedication. As in a sacred rite, one must prepare properly for such an event. Prescribed ritualistic attire is present in the form of the proper hunting outfit, the right gun, the correct stalking technique (in sympathetic magic form, one must walk as quietly as the deer whom one seeks).

The other friends simply do not qualify as seekers of the truth about life that Michael finds in hunting. Stanley's lack of boots and his little gun are the most obvious examples of their shortcomings. Only Nicky, Michael's roommate and homophilic counterpart,\ comes close to Michael's vision of what is necessary if one is to be vouchsafed a look at fate. First with Nicky, then alone, Michael stalks the deer, climbing higher and higher into the mountains (a literal and figurative ascent and additionally--as the film's emotionally positive "high point"--a counterpart to The Deer Hunter's emotional nadir: the funeral, during which, unseen, Nicky's coffin is lowered into the ground. Cf. p. 181 and Note 27 for correlative movements). Nicky's touching mention of his "lik(ing) the way the trees are in the mountains," with their branches reaching up for the light, identifies him as the only other man in the group who expresses a desire to rise above the ordinary into a higher world. Like Michael, his spiritual hunger is strong and well developed. [5]

The vision that Michael achieves is an affirmation of life's significance through an awareness and acceptance of death. After Michael fells his deer, Cimino cuts to a shot of the wounded animal, which loses its footing and falls. The camera then zooms in on the deer's eye as the animal, in fear and ignorance, moves towards death. The difference between this fallen animal and the other fallen animal we have just seen in the film (Steven--who slips in a fall that presages his later fall from grace, the emblem of which is the injury he suffers to his legs--trips and falls during the wedding reception) is that man's ability to reason supposedly gives him some form of ascendant perspective on his life's events. A man's death may, like those of Nicky and the deer, be predetermined, but at least he can attempt to understand (and perhaps justify) the things that happen to him.

Michael and Nicky on the deer hunt, climbing toward their
spiritual goal.

        Yet there is also a similarity between the animal and
man, since some men cannot attain a perspective on their
suffering. Steven, wounded in battle, is shown to be incapable
of understanding why such a thing has happened to him. There
is very little appreciable difference between the wounded, un-
comprehending look in Steven's eyes after he is injured (a
look that remains there for the rest of the film) and the look
in the deer's eyes after Michael has shot it. [6]

   If we view Michael as the ultimate hunter he seems
meant to represent, we are led to the conclusion that Michael,
the deer hunter, the man who killed the animal, is also responsible for Nicky's death as well. Before the hunting trip,
Michael says. "One shot is what it's all about; a deer has to
be taken in one shot."[7] It would seem that Michael hunts
with only one bullet--like the one he holds up for Stanley's
benefit (cf. p. 175) in his gun. If we treat the word "take"
as a euphemism for some form of sexual possession, and the
word "deer" as a pun that refers both to the animal (deer)
and a loved (dear) one, we can see how this "one shot" philosophy[8] destines Michael (and, by extension, his dear friend,
Nicky) for the second, single-shot Russian roulette game they
are fated to play together. Michael hunts his prey, Nicky,
on his return to Vietnam. On this trip, though, instead of
ascending into the mountains, there to meet both his fate and
the animal he stalks, he travels instead to Hell, past the
fires of bombed and burning villages (in shots that prefigure
the nighttime battle scenes from Francis Coppola's Apocalypse
Now), across a river of death ferried by a latter-day Charon:
the Frenchman who introduces Nicky to the civilian version
of the military game of death which Nicky has already encountered. On his journey, Michael travels into the inner
recesses of a cesspool quagmire of filth, darkness, and corruption to a well-lit room where a man's fate is suitable material for betting, and where a decisive "one shot" ends the
life of his latest victim.[9]

   We must recall at this point that Nicky has been AWOL
for months; he has been successfully playing Russian roulette
for a considerable amount of time. It is only when Michael
shows up and enters the game against him that Nicky loses
and dies. What seems suggested here is that Michael is responsible (albeit unconsciously) for Nicky's death. Indeed,
since Michael is the only central character present when virtually all of the film's deaths--those of the deer, the Vietnamese villagers, the North Vietnamese soldier, the torturers,
various individuals killed in Russian roulette games he watches,
as well as Nicky--occur, we could say that in an important
sense, Michael is death. Unable to possess his dear friend
in a way that he would like to (the constant badgering in the
film about "fags" indicates how completely unacceptable a
homosexual affair would be to these men),[10] Michael can only
truly "take" Nicky through the "one shot" that causes the latter's death. Although all of the friends will share their memories of Nicky, only Michael will have the curiously sublime
image of his friend gracefully swooning out of his chair, a

mortal wound in his head, and being cradled in his arms
(their only depicted intimate contact, thus affirming the linkage of death and love), an image that, like Michael's view
of the dying deer, is vouchsafed only to him because he has
killed his intended. And since Nicky refuses to, or simply
cannot recognize Michael until the very last moment (seconds
after Michael has said, "I love you," thus expressing a sentiment upon which he cannot act), [11] when Nicky recalls the "one
shot" notion (although he clearly intends the one shot for himself, and thereby makes of the remembrance not a life-
connoting association with the good times of home but merely
an excuse to free his arm from Michael's grip so that he
can fire the gun), Michael can only fulfill his earlier promise
to Nicky not to "leave (him) over there" by bringing him
home dead: the only state in which he can be pried loose
from the games. [12]

     A recognition of The Deer Hunter's emphasis on fate
should make more understandable the activities of the film's
Vietnamese (both North and South), who employ the game of
Russian roulette[13] as a rather objectionable form of diversion.   Admittedly, the fact that it is the Vietnamese, not the
Americans, who institute the game, [14] taken in tandem with
the film's only scene of armed conflict (during which a North
Vietnamese soldier tosses a grenade into a pit in which women
and children are hiding), indicates that in The Deer Hunter's
view, Southeast Asians apparently place a smaller value on life
than the Americans who (in the person of Michael) deliver the
Vietnamese village from the Northern scourge through a cleans-
ing fire that belches forth in an ejaculatory manner from Michael's flame thrower, a device that, along with the depicted na-
palming of the countryside, recalls the flames of the steel mill
where Michael worked. [15] Yet it is precisely the film's predominant American presence, Michael, who becomes both a passive
and active participant in the South Vietnam Russian roulette
games.

     Michael is, after all, the film's moral center; he is
the strongest and most resolute of the friends, the man to
whom both of the film's love interests (Linda and the finely-
featured Nicky) gravitate as a source of vitality, power, and
comfort, and to whom Nicky and (especially) Steven turn for
assurance and, ultimately, deliverance.   The latter expectation is inadvertently affirmed by Steven when he significantly
exclaims, "Mike, Jesus!" on first encountering his friend in
Vietnam while they are all in captivity.   Yet Michael is voluntarily involved in these games of death.   In fact, even before he enters the game with Nicky, he is seen watching a

game played. Michael is there in the crowd during the game
that Nicky walks in on after initially encountering the Frenchman.   Characteristically, at this point Nicky spurns the view
of life that the game suggests; he grabs the gun out of one
of the participants' hands, thrusts it up against the man's
head and pulls the trigger, then puts the gun to his own temple and pulls the trigger again.   Nicky's act indicates both
his disdain for the game (doubtless derived from his experience with it during the North Vietnamese torture sessions)
and his superiority to it (he is not afraid to pull the trigger).
He is thus branded as a prime candidate for the game, which
he will later dominate as its featured attraction.

Significantly, Michael sees Nicky enter the room and
pursues him into the street.   Nicky gets into the Frenchman's
car, realizes that Michael is following on foot, but ignores
him.   At this point, Nicky tosses away all of his paper money.
Obviously Nicky intends to participate in future games (his
riding with the Frenchman affirms this), yet he is not, despite
the man's assurance that there is plenty of cash to be made,
interested in Russian roulette for fiscal gain.   The fact that
Nicky intentionally ignores Michael here (who earlier, against
Nicky's will, had him participate in the three-cartridge game
with the North Vietnamese) indicates that Nicky somehow
blames Michael for his own casual indifference to life, and
perhaps resents him for coveting Linda's affections.   Although
for Michael Russian roulette may be a confirmation of fate
and life, for Nicky it is a means of playing out his self-
destructiveness (cf. Note 9).

No matter what the motivation for and degree of his
participation, though, Michael actively encourages the game's
continuity by becoming one of the spectators.   Michael apparently sees in the game an affirmation of the attitude that
life is transitory, and that one's fate (like the position of the
single deadly cartridge in the gun--be it a hunter's rifle or
a Russian roulette pistol) is beyond one's control.   He emphasizes the game's important lesson (which is the same point
he makes at the beginning of the first hunting trip) during
the second hunting journey when, responding to Stanley's
threats with the gun, Michael jerks Stanley's partially loaded,
"stupid little gun" (as Axel so aptly refers to it) out of Stanley's hands, thrusts it against Stanley's head, asks, "You
want to play games?" and pulls the trigger.   What Michael
demonstrates here is that the threat of death is not a game;
if one appropriates the artefacts of death one must be prepared to use them, not in bluffs (as Stanley does when point-

ing the gun at Axel) but in earnest (like the Russian roulette
players).

The Russian roulette game is not only (as it might at
first appear) a mere diversion to the Vietnamese; to them,
it communicates and embodies the very essence of fate.   In
truly learning a corollary lesson that it teaches (that life's
fragility makes it precious, and that death in itself is objectionable, points affirmed when Michael intentionally misses
the deer he aims at during the second hunting trip),[16] Michael
underscores its significance.   By doing so, and upholding the
meaning of Russian roulette, he indicates for us that in contrast to those holding Stanley's attitude (a blitheness about
death and destruction that was shared by many supporters of
the Vietnam War, people who--unlike Michael, Nicky, Steven,
and the Green Beret--had no real appreciation of war's hor-
rors), the Vietnamese are in deadly earnest when they play
at death because death, despite the betting and shouting that
attend its invocation, is not a game.   To thus call The Deer
Hunter a pro-war, anti-Vietnamese film, as many reviewers
have done, is totally to miss the film's point.

By this juncture in The Deer Hunter, one should note
the relationship between the Russian roulette game and the
rituals in which the film's Americans engage when they are
home.   Both the wedding ceremony/reception and Russian
roulette games are communal events, celebrations (of sorts)
which mainly involve a limited number of people (Steven,
Angela, Michael, and Nicky in the first instance; the two players in the latter) but are nevertheless shared by the community as a whole.   However, there is a subtle irony that
emerges from comparing these activities.   Where the Russian roulette game is a ritual only apparently about death
but actually involved (through a realization of existence's transitory nature) with an affirmation of the importance of life,
the wedding ceremony (held in the church with the coffin-like
pews, and officiated over by the same priest who--in the
same church--conducts Nicky's funeral service) and reception
farewell party (with the fateful wine-spilling, the essentially
doom-saying Green Beret, etc.) are ostensible celebrations
of life (marriage as a joyous occasion; wishes of good luck
to the departing friends) that through the ominous foreshadowings involved with their depiction really signify dissolution
and death.   The film clearly demonstrates that it is only
through rituals which directly confront death (either hunting
or Russian roulette) that the truth about life's importance
may be learned.

With respect to the fates, there is a foreshadowing
of events in The Deer Hunter that predicts with unerring accuracy what will happen to the principal characters. [17]

   As homophilic friends who share a bond of both affection (to each other; for hunting as a transcendent act)[18] and
allegiance (Michael's pledge to bring Nicky home from Vietnam), Michael's and Nicky's fates are already firmly en-
twined.   Their fateful bonds are further strengthened during
the Russian roulette games in which they participate while
prisoners of the North Vietnamese.   Steven has already taken
part in a game; his breaking under the strain of captivity
and exposure to the shootings, and his missed Russian roulette shot to his head, firmly indicate how weak a character
he is, a shortcoming for which he ultimately pays with the
loss of his potency (symbolized by the amputation of his legs).
When Michael and Nicky enter the game against each other,
we are given a powerful foreshadowing of events to come.
The game starts off with the traditional single bullet in the
chamber, but Michael raises the stakes to three bullets, hoping
that with Nicky's assistance he can kill their captors.   Michael sits at camera left, Nicky at camera right.   The three-
cartridge game begins; on the gun's third pass Michael fires,
initially killing the game's "referee," then shooting two other
captors.   As always, the number of cartridges in the gun
equals the number of men who are to die.

   Later, when Michael reluctantly (it would seem) plays
against Nicky in South Vietnam, the earlier game's conditions
are virtually recreated.   Michael and Nicky again assume
the same physical positions--Michael on the left, Nicky on
the right.   They are surrounded by yelling, cheering onlookers
who, like their predecessors, bet on the game's outcome.
Nicky wears a sweatband on his head, just as he had in the
earlier game.   The pistol is once more passed back and
forth three times.   With the third shot, a man again dies, although this time the victim is Nicky, who shoots himself.
Michael's role in the game as Nicky's deliverer (in both instances through death) is made symbolically obvious this time,
though, in the dark lens of the referee's eyeglasses.   This
lens is located over the man's right eye (Michael's right eye
pained him after his return to the United States, appropriate
since both he and the referee preside over games of death).
Since the referee faces the camera, his right eye is seen on
the screen's left side, the placement thus favoring Michael's
side of the table, from which the figurative, dark force of
death ultimately emanates. [19]

The manner in which The Deer Hunter's two Russian roulette games are photographed is highly portentous and significant.   During the entirety of the first game and the majority of the second, the camera shoots from the vantage point of an outside, invisible fourth wall, never crossing the conceptual 180-degree line (running through each of the games' playing tables) that exists in the two scenes as a traditional precaution, for the purpose of continuity, against violations of established screen direction.   True, during the second game the room in which the major action takes place is "opened up" somewhat by the camera's moving away from the playing table, but this occurs only to reveal the room (also on the audience side of the 180-degree line) from which Nicky emerges and which Michael and the Frenchman enter when Michael attempts to buy his way into the game.

After Nicky shoots himself, though, Cimino immediately has the camera cross the 180-degree line, to the playing table's other side; we see Nicky lying on the floor, his head at camera left being held up by Michael, who is to the right. This change of camera position is more than just the result of the need to give us at this point a shot of these two characters unimpeded by the playing table (indeed, Cimino could conceivably have easily crossed the 180-degree line at any other time in either Russian roulette scene without violating continuity, merely by first giving us an intervening, establishing, head-on shot of some mid-point object or character). Instead, the shift in camera placement has the intended symbolic effect of situating us as viewers on the intimate, formerly inviolate, other side of the magic half circle, allowing us a glimpse of the game's most important moment: the instant of death.

Moreover, this particular moment does not involve just anyone's death (after all, two other participants--one in the first game, one in the second--also die), but that of a character for whom we, and a number of the film's characters, have great affection.   In this instance, Nicky's death, the significant death of a important character, quite clearly acts as the key that admits us to a true view of life's meaning. While the threat of death unlocks the significantly used word of intimacy ("love") from Michael's vocabulary, it is death itself that makes possible the most intimate, and most revealing, contact between Michael and Nicky that The Deer Hunter gives us: Michael's tender cradling of his dying friend.

Since their love is homophilic, we know, even before

the final game, that Michael's and Nicky's relationship is
destined to come to naught. Steven and Angela's (Rutanya
Alda) fates are sealed in the spilling of the wine/blood on
her dress during the reception, the wine signalling both the
wedding night's inevitable loss of innocence (in the form of
the blood from Angela, the virgin soon to be deflowered by
Steven, himself sexually innocent, at least as regards his
bride) and heralding the awesome injury that Steven will suffer to his legs during his Vietnam tenure, an injury that only
in an interpersonal (as opposed to sexual) sense, threatens,
through its devastatingly alienating effect on Steven, the integrity of their marriage. For Stanley (John Cazale), the
slightest and most homely of the group, there is similarly
no possibility for love and fulfillment. In the film's symbolic
language, he lacks maleness: his gun is short and ineffective
compared to Michael's powerful rifle; he avoids confrontations
with men, slugging his date instead of the bandleader who
puts his hand on her behind (although he does say he's going
to get his gun). In essence, the gun is a symbol for his
lack of true potency, as is evident from Axel's unwitting comparison of Stanley's gun to his penis. "Show him [Michael]
that gun, that little pussy thing you carry around," he says.
In a poor imitation of Michael's behavior, Stanley uses his
weapon as a substitute for, instead of complement to, his
aggressiveness. As a result of his recessive behavior, Stanley winds up with no depicted family life, drifting from one
woman (his date at the reception) to a second (the tired-looking
woman whom he brings to the bowling alley) to a third (the
plain-looking wife who accompanies him in the graveyard
burial scene).[20] In Michael, Nicky, and Stanley we have a
curious male triumvirate: the aggressive male (Michael),
the passive male (Nicky), and the ineffective male (Stanley).

Despite Nicky's rather recessive qualities compared
with those of his counterpart, Michael (he is shy and soft-
spoken; Michael is aggressive and usually more talkative),
the two men are nevertheless demonstrative. The Deer Hunter's remaining central male characters, Axel and John, each
take the part of a relaxed presence in the film. As his name
implies, Axel (Chuck Aspegren) is a fixed point around which
other things (in this case, his friends) turn; he is merely
along for the ride, a good-natured, always affirmative man
(thus his constant rejoinder, "fuckin' ay").

John (George Dzundza) also provides a central, fixed
point for the group; he is above all else the bearer of the
group's mythic unities, which are usually expressed through

(or with the aid of) music. John owns and maintains the bar
where the friends traditionally meet, in musically expressed
anticipation of pleasure (e. g. , before the wedding, which is
accompanied by the singing of a choir in which John, in the
view the camera affords us, figures prominently), as when
the men sing along with the bar's juke box; or in the aftermath of sorrow (as after the funeral when, following John's
lead, everyone begins to sing "God Bless America," a song
that seems to reconcile those present to the grievous states
to which life has brought them).   Even after the first hunting
trip, John again uses music to establish a communal mood,
playing a moving piano solo that provides a wondrous conclusion to the just completed outing.

     Like Axel and John, Linda (Meryl Streep) is an emo-
tional center; she is a person who is acted upon, not one
who acts.   She waits for Nicky instead of seeking him out;
and though she suggests that in Nicky's absence she and Michael could "comfort each other," she does not pursue this
idea, instead waiting until (apparently) Michael asks her to
the motel (where, significantly, their liaison is not consum-
mated; Linda and Michael only make love during their second
meeting and even then, as before, Linda initially finds Michael asleep).

     Although both Michael and Nicky carry Linda's photo
in their wallets (a further link between the two men who are
both, as Linda observes when giving Michael Nicky's sweater,
"about the same size," and who seem to be making love to
each other through her),[21] the memory[22] of her serves only
as an emotional, not a physical, rallying point for them.   In
the traditional sense of a place where one lives and where
one's life is figuratively centered (e. g. , the "Clairton, Penn-
sylvania" that Nicky asks for when he makes a long distance
call from Vietnam, an attempt for contact that, significantly,
is never successfully made),[23] there is no literal "home" in
The Deer Hunter.   Although all of the film's principals live
in Clairton, we never feel that they actually belong there in
any permanent sense.   Perhaps for economy, Michael and
Nicky live in a trailer (an ironic symbol of their relationship's impermanence).   Stanley and Axel's homes are never
seen; John's living quarters are also not shown. [24]   The re-
liably permanent meeting places in the film are those halls,
one sacred (the church, although it connotes death), one pro-
fane (the bar, which connotes life) where the principals gather
to reaffirm their sense of belonging.

A final moment of happiness. Stanley, Axel, Michael, Steven, Angela, Nicky, and Linda (Meryl Streep) at the reception.

As is suggested in Steven's remark while in Vietnam ("I want to go home"),[25] home in The Deer Hunter is not a building or city but America, the "Home sweet home" of the song sung at the film's end, the one thing for which affection can be directly expressed ("Land that I love").[26] In The Deer Hunter's last scene, as the shaken, distraught characters reunite in the bar and, upset by the way life has turned out, sing the patriotic song of hope, they affirm, not a blind jingoism, but a desire for poignant reconciliation to the fate their country has dealt them. Despite what has happened to them, it would be as senseless for these people to hate America as it would be for them to hate death. Instead, both concepts--America connoting a sense of place and belonging, death affirming life's significance through its absence--have their own important lessons to teach. True, like its final freeze-frame, virtually oxymoronic image (that of Michael, the film's ultimate representative American and the group's most stable and powerful member and Stanley, the group's weakest individual, falling down at the reception, in only one of the film's numerous falls),[27] The Deer Hunter's last scene has an ambivalent effect. In one respect we feel a sense of loss, an intuition of a figurative fall from grace resulting from the ugly Vietnam War, an event that seems somehow to have

permanently scarred this country. Yet there still remain
the desire to remember those whom one has loved[28] and to
belong to something greater than one's self, impulses that
suggest a symbolic ascent above grief and bereavement. The
ability of these characters finally to comfort each other" successfully signifies a sharing of compassion that transcends
individual and nationalistic allegiances, becoming instead an
emblem of hope and love that points towards what is best in
America's people rather than what is worst in its politics.

NOTES

1. The word does appear in Michael's brief comment about
his friends other than Nicky ("I mean, I love 'em"), although
the remark seems more an expression of camaraderie than
a verbalization of Michael's true feelings.   However, the
word "love" assumes significant form when it appears as
part of "God Bless America" ("Land that I love"), which the
group sings at the film's end.
     With respect to The Deer Hunter's use of pre-recorded
music, the viewer should note that, repeatedly, songs with
lyrics either about going home ("Midnight Train to Georgia,"
which plays in a Saigon bar), satisfactory love ("Can't Take
My Eyes Off of You"), or unsatisfactory relationships ("Good-
hearted Woman in Love with a Two-Timing Man," "Tell-Tale
Eyes") are used to complement many of the film's themes.

2. The film's transition from Clairton to Vietnam is a wonderful study in contrasts and technique.   The rowdy return
to John's bar after the hunting trip is eventually followed by
John's sensitive piano solo, toward the end of which the soundtrack blends the audible silence in the bar with the sounds
of a helicopter.   Cimino than has the film shift visually to
a shot of a Vietnamese field bursting into flame.

3. Later, of course we realize that the soldier's presence
has an additional fateful significance since Michael--the person most strongly affected by the man's response--essentially
becomes this soldier, right down to special services uniform,
Sergeant's rank, tilted beret, and withdrawn, virtually non-
communicative manner.
     However, as is clear from his refusal to shoot the
deer on his second hunting trip, Michael is superior to the
Green Beret in that he not only recognizes war's pointlessness but is seen actively (not just verbally) rejecting it by
turning away from killing.   Later, though, his homophilic

obsession with death--perhaps absent during the second hunting trip because Nicky, his death-oriented lover, is not with
him--returns in the Russian roulette game when he and Nicky
are reunited. Truly, together they are a deadly pair.

4. In an anticipation of his reaction to Michael's later "this
is this" statement (cf. Note 11), Stanley responds to Michael's
reading of the sun dogs manifestation by saying, "You're full
of shit ... you know, Mike, there's times when nobody but
a doctor can understand you." Characteristically, Stanley
must denigrate what he can neither appreciate nor understand.

5. Although Axel and John like the mountain scenery, they
differ from Michael and Nicky in that they only passively admire it instead of actively seeking, through direct physical
effort, to confront the landscape's stark beauty. Spiritually,
though, all of the friends can appreciate the sublimity and
tenderness of John's piano nocturne in a scene that acknowledges music's binding powers and thereby anticipates the effect of the "God Bless America" song at the film's end.

6. In a later scene, Cimino insures that the viewer will
draw such a connection between Steven and the deer. In
his trailer, after making love to Linda, Michael looks out of
the window at the Clairton nighttime. Cimino then cuts to a
shot of a mounted deer head, probably Michael's trophy from
the film's first hunt. The director then begins a reprise of
the initial zoom in on the dying deer's eye, framing the trophy
head tighter and tighter, after which Michael is seen going
out to make a phone call to Steven (who is in the Veterans
Administration hospital), as though the glimpse of the trophy
(and the dying deer) had been shot from Michael's point of
view (both zoom-ins would thus be read as analogues of Michael's increasing visual fixation on the animal). Apparently,
in the present sequence Michael has been reminded--through
an implicit linkage--of his deer/dear (cf. p. 173) wounded
friend. In essence, before hunting for Nicky in Vietnam, Michael hunts for Steven in the United States, scouting out the
latter's location by prying Steven's address out of the distraught Angela.

7. Michael's emphasis on the importance of the decisive
"one shot" is especially significant. Since this one shot--be
it the successful shot in hunting or the discharge of the bullet
in Russian roulette--signals death, Michael's assertion that
"that's what it's all about" indicates that for him death (and
the knowledge that an awareness of it brings) is the most im-

portant thing in life. If only judging by the way that, by the
film's end, Nicky's death unites all of the friends, male and
female, we must agree that in the universe of The Deer Hunter
this is certainly true.

8.   Significantly, on the second hunting trip, both Axel (with
John in tow) and Stanley fire two shots at a deer. They cannot hope to live up to Michael's stringent requirement.

9.   Note that Michael's "victims" are always male: either
buck deer or men.   Although in his pre-hunting exchange with
Nicky, Michael makes it clear that the one-shot requirement
is a characteristically male-oriented obsession with potency
(Nicky: "One shot?" Michael: "Two is pussy. "), one is tempted
to conclude from Michael's always killing male animals that
in some sense his hunting--either for deer or for Nicky--
also involves a subsconscious desire to confront, and finally
kill, an abhorred extension of his own fixation on death-
oriented homophilia (cf. Note 12, paragraph 3. Michael's
"hunt" for Steven, though, is clearly an affirmation of life;
cf. Note 6).
         For a confirmation of Nicky's self-destructiveness,
note his borderline anorexic attitude in the following exchange.
Axel: "How come I never see you eating?" Nicky: "I like
to starve myself ... keeps the fear up. " Axel: "It ain't
natural. "

10.   However, the constant use of the epithet "asshole" (e. g. ,
after mentioning liking the trees, Nicky says, "I sound like
some asshole, right?") also indicates how, at least in an implicit sense, all of these men are anally fixated.   Such a
realization explains why they are constantly accusing each
other of being "full of shit. "   Cf. Note 18 below.

11.   Interestingly, alone among the friends, Stanley seems
to recognize the true homophilic nature of Michael and Nicky's
relationship.   On the hunting trip, angry at Michael's denying
him the loan of his boots, Stanley retaliates verbally.   "I
fixed you up a million times.   I fixed him up a million times.
I don't know how many times I must have fixed him up with
girls.   And nothing ever happened--zero. "   Then, referring
to a statement Michael made earlier, Stanley says, "Your
trouble, Mike, nobody ever knows what the fuck you're talking about.   'This is this. ' I mean is that some faggot-sounding
bullshit or is that some faggot-sounding ... ?"   Actually,
Michael was responding to Stanley's lack of preparation for
the trip and thereby, since this is a hunting expedition, for

death, and had gestured with his single bullet, which symbolizes the lesson that one-shot games (hunting as essayed
by Michael; Russian roulette, whose wisdom he will soon
learn) teach, a lesson that Stanley fails to understand until
later, when Michael shoves Stanley's gun against his friend's
temple (cf. p. 175). In any case, given the fact that the single
bullet foreshadows the Russian roulette game between two male
lovers (Michael and Nicky), Stanley's comment about the remark's "faggot" overtones is amazingly perceptive and pre-
scient.

After Stanley's initial statement Nicky, looking some-
what embarrassed (perhaps in alarm over the accuracy of
what he knows is coming), says, "Shut up, Stan, will ya?
You're out of line." Stanley continues, though. Addressing
Michael, he says, "You know what I think? There's times
I swear I think you're a fucking faggot."

These remarks of Stanley's, taken in tandem with
Nicky's backhanded proposal to Linda (cf. p. 166) and Michael's curious sexual relationship with her (cf. p. 180),
dramatize quite clearly the homophilic bias that these men
demonstrate. Ultimately, whether Michael and Nicky are
actually lovers is thus less important than what is asserted
through them (as indeed through all of The Deer Hunter's
principal male characters): the primacy in the film of homophilic over heterosexual love. It is thus quite ironic that
at the wedding reception, Stanley initiates socially acceptable
(though nonetheless strongly homophilic) behavior by cutting
in on Michael and Linda (whose dance together is being watched
by Nicky with only a trace of jealousy) and choosing to dance
with Michael. Given Stanley's problems with women (cf. p.
216 and 179), Stanley's slight build (which invites comparison
with the only other svelte one of the friends, Nicky), and
Stanley's avoidance techniques and symbolically "little" gun
(cf. p. 179), it is possible that in some important sense,
Stanley's accusations derive from his jealously desiring Michael's affection without being able to solicit it effectively in
ways that the group of friends would find acceptable.

12. Michael and Nicky (like Thunderbolt and Lightfoot) can
thus only (in Lightfoot's words) "make it," then, when one
of the male partners is about to die; death is the ultimate
sexual consummation for the homophilic male.

There is also the suggestion in this scene that Nicky
would like Michael dead as well, a point Michael seems to
recognize when, placing the gun against his temple, he asks,
"Is this what you want?" (cf. p. 175).

Of significance as well is Michael's comment after he

convinces his and Nicky's North Vietnamese captors that the
two Americans should be able to play a Russian roulette game
with three bullets in the gun. "Now we got ourselves a game--
you and me," Michael says, suggesting through his statement
not only that he is eager for this confrontation (which may
lead to the escape of Michael, Nicky, and Steven) to begin,
but also that he indirectly enjoys the fact that this deadly encounter is with Nicky; this game is something he wants.   In
this latter sense, we may read Michael's killing of the deer
on the first hunting trip as his displaced murder of Nicky
(cf. Note 9).

13.   Some viewers might be tempted to read the game of
Russian roulette in the film as a metaphor for the political
suicide engaged in by overly self-confident countries which
become involved in guerilla-style wars for which they are
obviously not suited (cf. Scorsese's The Big Shave, which
figuratively dwells on this point).   This analysis is disavowed
by Cimino (Jean Vallely, "Michael Cimino's Battle to Make
a Great Movie," Esquire, January 2, 1979, p. 92).   Cimino
says of this reading, "That's too easy."   Such an interpreta-
tion fails to make coherent critical sense when applied to the
film as a whole, since The Deer Hunter not only has characters from relatively powerless countries (e. g., Vietnam)
engaging in the game, but further shows a representative
American (Michael) emerging from the first game triumphant.
        However, the final Russian roulette game between Mi-
chael and Nicky does assume political significance.   The news-
cast that Cimino inserts after the game's conclusion shows
a U. S. Army helicopter spilling (another fall; cf. Note 27)
off the side of an aircraft carrier while a commentator says,
"This seems to be the last chapter in U. S. involvement in
Vietnam," thus suggesting that political suicide in Vietnam
and the literal suicide of Nicky (whose death orientation is
similar to that of the nation as a political whole) are roughly
comparable.

14.   The game first appears in the film, though, through
the actions of an American, Michael, whose unusual hunting
practices anticipate it (cf. p. 173).

15.   Indeed, the North Vietnamese are symbolically criticized
in the opening Vietnam sequence.   As the North Vietnamese
soldier moves towards the pit where the women and children
are hiding, he passes a crib of grunting pigs.   Later, after
Michael has burned the soldier to death with a flame thrower
(the sexual symbol here employed invites comparison with the

flame-belching, phallic cannon in Thunderbolt and Lightfoot;
Cf. Note 2, Chapter 9), the pigs--which are already feeding
on what seem to be the remains of another soldier--begin squeal-
ing. The suggestion here is that this North Vietnamese soldier will, like his predecessor, be ripped apart and eaten by
the same pigs with which he was earlier compared.

We should also note that The Deer Hunter's metaphori-
cal passage from the opening shots of the mill fires to the
calm resignation of the end scene suggests that a movement
from damnation to redemption has been effected, as though
the film's intervening harsh events have somehow morally
and spiritually "improved" the characters.

16. However, when faced with a situation within which compromise seems impossible (as in the final Russian roulette
game with Nicky), Michael will once again invoke death.

17. As we might expect, though, none of The Deer Hunter's
characters truly perceive any of the film's deadly, negative
signs (the "sun dogs" are seen, but they are a positive omen).
The ominous Green Beret's significance; the spilled wine (the
bandleader notes, "If you don't spill a drop it's good luck for
the rest of your life."); Steven's losing his footing at the reception (when he returns home from the war, he has lost his
legs); the fatal allure of the Russian roulette game (which
virtually assures its repetition); the superficially innocent
bingo numbers called out at Steven's VA hospital (the "16
... sweet sixteen" ironically plays off the purity of Angela
and Steven's first sexual encounter--as Steven notes after the
reception, they have yet to make love; while the number "18,"
is, as the bingo caller notes, allusive to the age of majority,
which we should not only recognize as the age at which, in
the caller's words, a boy becomes "a man," but also as the
time when a male becomes subject to the draft; the two situations are therefore equated: maturity here equals one's
candidacy for fighting in a war)--the significance of all of
these messages goes unnoticed by the characters for whom
these "signs" have important consequences. However, it is
precisely this blindness to inevitability that gives The Deer
Hunter much of its awesomely touching, tragic beauty.

18. Michael acknowledges Nicky's importance to him when
they are preparing for the first hunting trip. Talking about
Nicky and the other people going along on the journey, Michael says, "I tell you, Nick, you're the only guy I go hunting with, you know? I like a guy with quick movement and
speed. I ain't gonna hunt with no assholes." When Nicky

responds by asking, "Who's an asshole?," Michael replies,
"They're all assholes.   I mean I love 'em, they're great
guys but, you know, they're all assholes.   Without you I hunt
alone."   As is characteristic for Nicky (as for all of the
friends), he cannot accept a tribute, and attempts to fend it
off with a jest.   "Well you're a fucking nut," he says, going
on accurately to assess Michael's obsessive penchant for dis-
cipline by jokingly calling him a "control freak."

19.   Actually, two other players who sit in the camera-left
position during a Russian roulette game have their guns go
off, but without significant (at least in the context of the film's
fiction) consequences.   During captivity, a South Vietnamese
prisoner fatally shoots himself, but he is obviously a relatively
unimportant character in the film.   Steven, also sitting in
the camera left chair, points the gun at his head and fires it,
but he only wounds himself slightly.   The only character in
The Deer Hunter who qualifies as a true conduit of death's
force is Michael.   Indeed, given the peculiarities of the hope-
less, dead-end relationship between Michael and Nicky, and
Michael's being compelled by circumstances to treat the second game between him and his friend as a prelude to Nicky's
coming home (but to what?   Even if both men were to return
alive, it would only be a return to a continuation of their ultimately unrealizable love), we can assume that Nicky, implicitly encouraged by Michael, shoots himself in order to
be delivered from Michael, who is acting here as an overly
importunate suitor.   Michael thus truly becomes the character
in the film who acts as the fateful focal point for everyone
he contacts.
        The physical placement of the players in the Russian
roulette games should also be noted if these sequences are
to be "read" correctly.   The camera left side in the first
game is clearly "the death side"; both shootings occur there.
Reflecting the change in the game's location (ostensibly from
North to South Vietnam), the second game makes the camera
right side the location where two men (a Vietnamese and
Nicky) shoot themselves.   However, one should note that
this "right side of death" view is balanced by the already-
alluded-to, placement-oriented symbols involving the referee's
dark patch and Michael's location, both of which favor camera
left.   Since the patch's dark lens draws attention to Michael,
and since Michael can in an important respect be seen as
attempting to kill off his homophilia through Nicky's death
(a desire aided by Nicky's already-noted subliminal predilec-
tions for death), we can here also regard death, in the person of Michael, manipulating Nicky across the table from him

in order to accomplish its fatalistic ends.   Indeed, Michael's
obsession with displays affirming his masculinity (driving
recklessly, hunting alone, using a high-powered rifle, killing
a deer with one shot) suggests an over-compensatory behavior
pattern that might very well result from an inability to accept
his homophilic affection for Nicky (this seems to be what Andrew Sarris suggests about all of the film's male characters
in general, and Michael in particular, through his ambigu-
ously-worded phrase, "homosexual terror"; cf. Village Voice,
December 18, 1978, p. 67; whether Sarris means fear of
homosexuals by heterosexuals or the feeling of fear experienced
by homosexuals is unclear).

Eventually, though, as pointed out elsewhere, Michael
confronts his true feelings for Nicky in the second, decisive
Russian roulette game, in which each man realizes (Michael
through saying, as he puts the gun to his head, "Is this what
you want?" although "it," death, is what he really wants for
Nicky; Nicky when, before he shoots himself, he says, "one
shot," thus suggesting by the appropriation of his friend's
phrase that he is the deer whom Michael is here shooting)
that only through death can their love achieve some form of
fulfillment.

Michael's role as the film's embodiment of fate is
recognized by Nicky during their captivity.   Michael tells
Nicky that they will have to "forget about" Steven if they are
to survive, to which Nicky responds, "Who do you think you
are, God?" This role of the man in power during fateful
games is affirmed when the North Vietnamese "referee" of
the game between Steven and Michael holds up for show a
single bullet before loading it into the gun, the precise gesture Michael exhibits when making the "This is this" speech
to Stanley (cf. Note 11).

Additionally, Michael himself unwittingly acknowledges
his fateful aspect; after being struck by the North Vietnamese
Russian roulette "referee," Michael tells the man, "You're
gonna die." Soon afterwards, Michael shoots the man to
death.

20.   Stanley's disgruntled status is reaffirmed during the
film's freeze-frame end credit sequence.   Each of the main
characters is shown in a pleasurable attitude, whereas Stanley is seen squinting into the distance with a pained expression on his face.

21.   There is always some obstacle between Michael and
Nicky (here, that obstacle is obviously Linda).   At the reception, Michael and Nicky's portraits (which are hung with Mi-

chael's on the right, Nicky's on the left, and which show Michael facing left and Nicky facing right) give us the two characters facing each other in positions that reverse those they assume in their two shared Russian roulette games.   Such a reversal occurs because these games ironically connote life, whereas the reception--both as a war-time send-off and an event full of fateful signs--connotes death.   Interestingly, the Russian roulette game positions are identically prefigured in the positions Michael and Nicky assume in the barroom tableau after John's piano solo.   While we would traditionally expect this fraternal bonding scene to suggest life, given the fact that it also functions as a prelude to the film's war sequences, such a deadly tone (communicated solely through the two friends' positions) is quite appropriate.   (In all currently available 16mm prints of The Deer Hunter, the feeling of doom thus created is complemented by the scene's last three frames.   Through a fortuitous example of inter-negative color mistiming, these frames shift to a greenish tinge that anticipates the green color of the field fronting a Vietnamese village.   Seconds after we first see them, the village and part of the field burst into flame as a result of a helicopter bombing attack.)

Notably, at the reception Steven's portrait is placed between Michael's and Nicky's, suggestively indicating that while any of the other friends are present, Michael and Nicky cannot reach a totally satisfactory consummation of their relationship.   (Significantly, Nicky looks at Linda's portrait when he is at the V. A. hospital, in whose courtyard he has just observed some men loading aluminum coffins into a transport.   As opposed to the unconscious deadly connotations Nicky associated with Michael, Linda's evocations obviously represent for him ideas of life.   Indeed, he misses her so much that he tells a Saigon prostitute to pretend that Linda is her name.)

22.   In an important scene, memory is twice invoked for Nicky.   After rejecting the Saigon prostitute (partially because her child is in the room, thus reminding Nicky of procreation: a life-associated process from which he obviously withdraws), Nicky looks down into the courtyard of her building and sees a jumbled collection of carved animals.   "Elephants," he says, identifying an animal notable for its supposed great memory.   Then, going into the street, Nicky hears one, and then another, gun shot, both of which apparently come from the Russian roulette game he is about to witness, and once again he is reminded of something--in this case, of the trauma

to which the North Vietnamese subjected him. Characteristically for Nicky (who has both vital and morbid tendencies), the two memories are complementary. The first connotes life; the second (for him at least), death.

23. This unsuccessful attempt at contact is followed by another when Nicky thinks he sees Michael on the street. Unfortunately, it is only someone who looks like Michael.

24. Steven's wife, Angela, is seen lying in her bedroom, but more out of inertia than out of a sense of belonging; without Steven, her house does not qualify as a home.

25. At the V. A. hospital, Steven again says that he wants "to go home," but he then changes his mind. Additionally, during the final Russian roulette game, Michael asks Nicky to "come home, just come home," going on to invoke a positive memory for his friend: "Remember the trees?"

26. Michael does directly give voice to his love for Nicky before the latter shoots himself (he twice says, "I love you"), but this statement is clearly an expression Michael is compelled to make out of desperation.

27. Actually, Steven and Stanley also slip at the reception, although Michael's fall is reprised as being the most symbolically significant. Since it results from a loss of power over his legs, Steven's fall anticipates his later amputation. Stanley's fall is, characteristically, a result of an argument he gets into (in this case, with Nicky) over his date's behavior (his date falls too, although as a result of Stanley's knocking her down). As usual, Stanley's relationships with women are far from satisfactory.

Other falls include Stanley's falling down in the bar towards the film's beginning; the fall of the two wine drops onto Angela's dress; Michael's fall off his car after the wedding and again after the reception, following which he begins running down the street, stripping off his clothes. Axel pursues him and falls. Nicky falls immediately after he and Michael escape from captivity; Steven and Michael fall from the airborne rescue helicopter (as a result, Steven's legs are seriously damaged).

Indeed, the entire tone of The Deer Hunter is fall-like, not only in terms of a fall from grace, but in a seasonal sense connoting loss, as well. The film's key opening (the wedding) and closing (the funeral) sequences are both set in the Winter, thereby assuming the full suggestivity of wintry extinction.

Ironically, the wedding reception leads to death (Nicky's) or near-death (Steven's), while Nicky's funeral results in a stronger, life-loving solidarity among the friends. In this sense, through the characters' actions, at least part of the church's death connotation in the film is transmuted into something positive.

28.   The viewer should note that in the film's extremely touching final gesture (the toast "To Nick," an amended version of Stanley's earlier-offered toast to two missing friends: "To Nick and Steve"), what is doubtless being remembered is not Nicky's death obsession but his more tender aspects, which the friends take pleasure in recalling.

The contrast with Heaven's Gate in this respect should be apparent. The friends in The Deer Hunter ultimately use memory as a means of reconciling them to past events and, one presumes, preparing them for the future. Heaven's Gate's Jim Averill, though, is trapped (albeit voluntarily) within his memories, and consequently is virtually unable to act.

Chapter Eleven

THE BEAUTY OF THINGS THAT FADE

It is quite difficult to find justification for the critical outrage that greeted the release of Cimino's third feature, Heaven's Gate, since the film is so clearly a restatement in more glorious and graceful terms of the themes and attitudes present in the director's first two films. However, in scope (the broad vistas of the Wyoming towns, the shots of the open prairie) and in the close attention paid to the recreation of historical and social detail, the film easily surpasses both the stark simplicity of Thunderbolt and Lightfoot and the impressive expansiveness of The Deer Hunter. In a number of significant ways, Heaven's Gate is a film that appropriates the best qualities of each earlier film and melds them in a more subtle and intelligent manner than Cimino has ever before demonstrated.

Like Thunderbolt and Lightfoot (which had only two central characters) and The Deer Hunter (again, a central pair: Michael and Nicky), Heaven's Gate concentrates on a limited number of personalities: in this case, Jim Averill (Kris Kristofferson), Ella Watson (Isabelle Huppert), Billy Irvine (John Hurt), and Nate Champion (Christopher Walken). The number of crucial main characters is doubled from previous efforts, a move in keeping with Heaven's Gate's panoramic action, yet as the film progresses it becomes clear that there is actually only one central character in its story: Jim Averill, who symbolizes the strengths and weaknesses of the growing American nation.

As did Thunderbolt and Lightfoot and The Deer Hunter, Heaven's Gate has a very simple story to tell. The film is concerned with depicting and investigating the nature of commitment. It accomplishes this purpose by following Jim Averill through a thirty-three-year period, from the innocence of

his college days to his maturity as a Johnson Country marshal during the range wars, and concludes with a coda that
finds Jim on the cusp of old age, having passed from innocence to experience to regret.

In its present wide-release, 147-minute version (edited
down from 219 minutes),[1] Heaven's Gate has a shorter running time than The Deer Hunter (183 minutes), but because
its action is somewhat less involved than its predecessor's,
Heaven's Gate seems longer, more stately.[2] In conjunction
with its leisurely pacing, and the fact that the story involves
only one major event (the open range confrontation between
the peasants and the land and cattle owners' Stockgrowers
Association), the film manages to evoke an atmosphere of
gracefulness that complements its concern with the role that
communally celebrated events play in a community's life.

From the film's very beginning, we are treated to a
number of ceremonies.   The setting is Harvard College, 1870.
After the opening titles, cinematographer Vilmos Zsigmond's
camera pans down to an empty street.   There is no noise
on the soundtrack; then, the silence is broken by the sound
of someone running and Jim Averill enters from frame left.
Averill goes off at frame right, rounds a corner, passes a
horse-drawn carriage moving in the opposite direction, and
catches up with a group of marching students who are walking behind a formally-attired band.   In the group is Jim's
friend, Billy Irvine, who effusively greets his late (but welcome) companion.

A number of themes are established by this opening
sequence.   The placidity and openness of the Cambridge street
setting is shattered by the sounds of the band and the cheering
students behind it, a violation of natural conditions (which
would tend towards stasis and silence) that prefigures both
the unnatural violations against the peasants' need to survive
and the figurative rape of the open country by the railroad[3]
(an invention which represents an inevitable progress that
nonetheless presages destruction as well as improvements).
Ironically, it is the railroad that brings load after load of
refugees into the Wyoming territory;[4] in taking up residence
there, these refugees prompt the stockgrowers to respond
with the kind of violence that actually hastens the country's
economic growth and the further polarization of rich and poor
that, unfortunately, necessarily attends it.

Jim is late for the parade (a woman in the carriage

he passes comments, "Late again, James?"),[5] a situation
suggesting figuratively that he is slow to join movements;
we see this to be so in his sluggish resistance throughout
the majority of the film to the Stockgrowers Association,
whose death-list plot--hatched in a rich man's club from
which Jim has been blackballed--he opposes.   His opposition,
however, is too little and too late; by the film's end, he has
capitulated to wealth's power and is seen in defeat, a man
who (if only reluctantly) bends to the winds of change, but
not in time to save those whom he loved.

Jim, Billy, and the students marching behind the band,
though, are also men who have consciously chosen to walk
in step to this drumbeat processional.   Although their lively
marching seems like an exercise of free choice, they are,
like anyone else caught up in a mass movement (e. g. , the
stockgrowers), a crowd, individual men marching to their
own drummers but a crowd acting as a crowd nonetheless.
The rather frightening implications of group activity, in which
a large number of people fall sway to a mass psychology that
seems to have an independent life of its own, are a chilling
foreshadowing of the forces that lead the stockgrowers, the
peasants, and the students (in the persons of Jim and Billy)
to the film's final slaughter.

Yet unlike the factions in the Johnson County range
wars, the marching group behind the band is celebrating a
positive and joyous event (they are headed for the Harvard
meeting hall where their commencement is to take place) that
supposedly marks some form of progress (out of academia,
into the real world) of which they can all be proud.   There
is indeed great joy and fun-making among the students: in
their delight at being graduated, in the pleasure they derive
from watching (and later dancing with) the pretty coeds who
observe them from the commencement hall balcony, in the
comedy engendered by Billy's clowning during the ceremony.

However, this is not a celebration untouched by serious considerations.   The speech of the Reverend Doctor
(Joseph Cotten), although it addresses the issue of commencement (which involves the hope that any new beginning represents, before compromise and possible defeat have set in),
is filled with references to the students' responsibility to the
uncultured, their supposed mission in bringing learning to
those on the frontier.   As we see in the film, these tired
liberal sentiments (clichés even in 1870) have no relation at
all to the real conditions on the prairie.   Yet the students

disregard the artificiality of the speech; in fact, they applaud
the oration. [6] Its call to action to educated men appeals to
their vanity, a vanity that in the person of Jim Averill is
soon to be put to a grievous and tragic trial.

The waltz scene that follows is the second musical
sequence that occurs in the film, already indicating how
strongly Heaven's Gate is concerned with the way that orchestrated movements work to achieve group cohesion.   The
students and their dates all share common goals; all seem
to derive from the same class.   The men, having earlier
marched to the militaristic strains of "The Battle Hymn of
the Republic" (a song whose fighting spirit is reinvoked in
the student fight and peasant massacre sequences), allow
themselves in the company of women to be swayed by a sim-
pler, gentler, less violent rhythm.   Strauss's "Blue Danube"
is played and the waltzing couples dance around a tree in the
middle of the Harvard yard, a tree whose relative permanence
and stability contrasts with the inherent changes that threaten
the lives of this upper class group.

It should be noted that throughout Heaven's Gate, Cimino employs the circle as the film's central symbol.   We
see it in the circular patterns created by the dancers here;
in the circles created by the dancers in the Heaven's Gate
meeting hall; in the circular patterns that the students assume in the upcoming student fight sequence.   Other 360°
movements appear in the shape of the peasants' assault against
the stockgrowers and their thugs; in the circles that the cavalry describe when they defend the stockgrowers; in the circles twice limned by the carriage that Jim buys for Ella's
birthday; and in the wheels of the mechanisms that play such
a key part in the film: the carriages, the railroad, even
the peasants' wagons, [7] roller skates, and those of the wooden
barricades that the peasants construct during their siege.
Given the film's overriding tone of ineluctability, we may
take all of Heaven's Gate's circles to be representations of
the wheel of fate (an impenetrable, closed circle) which, un-
heedful of man's vain actions, always steers events in the
direction of inevitability, an inevitability that none of the
film's characters--neither Jim, Billy, Nate, Ella, nor the
peasants--can successfully oppose. [8]   One must pay careful
attention in Heaven's Gate to both the appearance of these
circles and the directions of the movements that give rise
to them, since within this figurative schema may be found
the core of the film's meaning. [9]

The waltz's stateliness (which recalls the measured steps of the marching band members) pleases us with its form and grace.   Yet for all of its beauty (the scene is wondrously photographed with graceful, arcing camera movements), the waltz sequence has an antagonistic effect.   There is something premeditated and artificial in the way that the dancers move to the music.   Cimino shoots part of the sequence in long shot, allowing us to appreciate fully the dance's precision and geometry, yet at the same time (as in the film's opening shots, with Jim rushing off to join the parade) there are disquieting aspects to the scene as well.

Earlier, the direction of Jim's rush to join the parade was opposed by a carriage going the other way.   Now, another pair of opposed movements is created.   The outer ring of the dancing couples moves clockwise (the individual dancers in the ring move clockwise as well) but the inner ring moves counter-clockwise, thereby creating a disturbing image of discontinuity that presages some future rupture of the sense of order (suggested by the rhythmic dance) that is here created.

Additionally, midway through the dance a carriage enters the picture and is driven clockwise around the outer circle of dancers.   Although it moves along with half of the dancers, the carriage also opposes at least half of the shot's predominant direction (present in the inner ring's dancers), connoting some sort of contradiction (also suggested by the students' opposing movements) among the students--most likely an indecisiveness concerning their goals and purposes, which we shall shortly see reflected in the activities of the students' two representatives throughout the film: Jim and Billy. [10]

The waltz scene's carriage links up with two of the film's later significant images: that of Ella's carriage (a birthday gift to her from Jim), in which she is seen riding only during sequences involving either recklessness (the ride into town past the peasants) or violence (her later ride along a road where a thug shoots at her immediately comes to mind; indeed, the first ride's excessiveness anticipates the second's).   Additionally, the film's two early carriages (the one in the first scene, the one during the waltz) prefigure the carriage-like iron horse of the railroad, which in Heaven's Gate not only continues to bring more peasants into Johnson County (thus exacerbating the conflicts between rich and poor) but also delivers into town the shipment of thugs who carry out most of the murders against the poor people.   Indeed,

A symbol of perfection becomes a symbol of fateful entrapment: the dancing students in one of <u>Heaven's Gate</u>'s many
figurative circles.   Note the discordant carriage at frame bottom.

the scene in which Canton hires extra thugs takes place in
a railroad yard; Canton walks along the tracks, talking, while
sounds of engines are heard in the background. [11]   In essence,
then, the students' moving against the carriage and, most
significantly, Jim's moving in a direction opposite to that of
the film's first carriage, symbolize a resistance against the
elements of inevitable mechanization, progress (toward wealth)
and change (in favor of the rich)--tendencies symbolized by
the railroad, with which Canton and his men are equated--
that is as admirable as it is futile. [12]

     After the dance sequence, two more events occur that
presage tragedy for Jim and Ella. First, a group of students[13]
forms a protective ring around the tree in the yard's center
to guard a pink bouquet tied to the tree.   Jim and his com-
patriots penetrate the students' wagon-trainlike circular defense; in the midst of the ensuing brawl, Jim succeeds in
grasping and retaining this symbol of the group's honor.   The

suggestion here, then, is that the prize to be gained by pene-
trating a rival's camp is some sort of integrity. However,
as is evident from this melée in the Harvard yard and its
reappearance in the armed confrontation between the peasants
and the stockgrowers, such a symbolic victory (the bouquet
itself is not important; and even if the peasants did win, conditions on the range would still remain the same) is achieved
at a terrible price, since the yard fight results in numerous
injuries.

Characteristically, Billy, whose indecisiveness in the
film only marginally exceeds Jim's, reacts ambiguously. He
appears distressed (in apparent, pointless rejection of the
just-completed altercation; he will, somewhat similarly, reject the stockgrowers' violence although he does nothing to
prevent it either),14 but nonetheless joins in the rousing cheer
in support of "our dear old country." Somewhat less reflec-
tive at this point than his friend, Jim affirms his total support of the fight in his smiling and proud expression.

As in all of the film's scenes involving circular movement, determination of the direction of travel is vitally important if the meanings of a sequence are to be properly read.
Preparing for the attack by their lower classmen, the students
form two circles; the outer ring moves counter-clockwise,
the inner moves clockwise. This is just the opposite of the
dancing students, appropriately suggesting that the activity
here depicted--in contrast to the student's harmonious danc-
ing--connotes discord, a quality soon to be made manifest in
the upcoming student battle. 15 Within Heaven's Gate's precise symbolic system, these movements represent either an
acceptance of inevitability (toward wealth and power, a tendency represented by the natural, clockwise movements) or a
futile resistance to fate (as with the counter-clockwise dancing
during the waltz sequence, the symbology of which is here
repeated in the outer ring's direction). That the outer ring
(connoting external actions during times of conflict) suggests
a futile resistance to fate, while the inner ring (connoting
what, during times of stress, one knows deep down to be true)
suggests a reluctant acceptance of it, indicates that while the
outward actions of the students (whose naiveté is throughout
the film represented by Jim) may run counter to inevitability,
their inner selves know that such opposition is useless. True,
we may see Jim attempting to help the peasants in their fight;
we may even see Nate (whose wavering attitude towards the
stockgrowers is indicated during a sequence in which he first
rides against the direction described by a large group of new

immigrants, then along with them) begin to sympathize with
the poor, but none of their actions has any effect on what
must be.[16] Only the deplorable but successful landowner and
entrepreneur Frank Canton (Sam Waterston), and rich men
like him, act in concert with fate.

Appropriately, this precise circular pattern is duplicated in the movements of the attacking peasants during the
film's final siege sequence. Like the students (with whom
they are often implicitly compared), the peasants may vainly
resist, but they cannot hope to successfully oppose the inevitable. That the cavalry at the end of Heaven's Gate's re-
creates this two-circled defense (to protect the rich), and
that throughout the student assault sequence the marching
band returns to provide a musical accompaniment (first the
appropriate "Battle Hymn of the Republic,"[17] then a version
of "The Blue Danube" whose orchestration here converts the
music's beauty into a harsh-sounding cacophony of brass),
only adds further disquieting reactions to the disturbing feelings already created here.

Finally, Cimino closes the graduation sequence with
a shot of Jim's date and her friends looking down at the triumphant singing men. The women are framed in a window;
surrounding them are numerous lit candles, which point forward to the shots of the fireburning of the cabin in which
Nate--the lover and potential husband of Jim's later romantic
interest, Ella--is similarly surrounded by fire. This picture of Jim's date, who is crowded into the small window
opening along with other women, also anticipates Ella's assumption of the role of madame in her heavily populated
prairie house, within which she is boarded along with a number of her prostitutes.

Although the film at this point jumps ahead twenty
years, we find in our next glimpse of Jim Averill that his
situation is basically the same as before. As is evident
from his commentary voice-over,[18] Jim still clings to the
kind of liberal sentiments voiced by the Reverend Doctor; he
evidences a sympathy for the poor ("I saw hundreds leave
for the West with nothing but precious dignity and the clothes
on their backs") and demonstrates a curious vanity about his
mission towards these people ("I thought I could be of important service"). Nevertheless, one can derive from the way
the shot of Jim is set up that despite his efforts, nothing is
going to be changed. For one thing, while the train Jim rides
moves forward, Jim is seated with his back to the engine.

Cattle to the slaughter: the peasants in their Emigrant Car, part of the West-bound train that Jim Averill rides into Wyoming.

Thus, he does not look ahead to what is to come but backwards to what has been, figuratively indicating a clinging, regressive attitude that is in keeping with the insularity of his patronizing ideals.[19]

Additionally, the train that Jim takes (which also carries a group of peasants into the Johnson County town of Casper, Wyoming) moves towards camera left in a traditional representation of Westward travel, such travel connoting the country's expansionist, manifest-destiny thrust towards growth and prosperity. Since the peasants ride along with this tendency, they may be said to contribute to this progress, even if they will eventually serve only as cheap hired labor, rather than as the landowners they would like to be.[20] Jim's riding backwards, though, suggests that Jim is attempting to resist the inevitable movement towards national progress, which brings with it a greater concentration of wealth and power in the hands of the moneyed and propertied few. His look back towards the East of his youth presages not only his final appearance in the film (in which he is once again

in the East, in Newport, thus closing the deadly circle of his
journeys), but also points up his inherent melancholy attitude,
present in his treasuring of something that no longer exists:
the beautiful, innocent past that he can never hope to recover. [21]

Even the film's most vehement detractors must admit
that the milieu Heaven's Gate evokes is beautiful beyond words.
The recreation of the towns and buildings of Casper and Sweetwater seems letter-perfect. [22] Most importantly, by shooting
through dust-clouded atmospheres which soften and tone the
image to a pastel vagueness whose color seems a perfect
corollary of the kind of images that we summon forth from
memory, Vilmos Zsigmond gives us in every shot stunning
chromos whose tenderness perfectly evokes the bittersweet
sensations the film's story means to create.

There are, however, great scenes of happiness in the
film as well. The waltz sequence has its exhilarating aspects. The community dance roller-skating scene at J. B. 's
(Jeff Bridges) Heaven's Gate meeting hall[23] (whose slogan
promises "a moral and exhilarating experience") is quite joyous. Like the students earlier in the film, the peasants (on
roller skates waltz about, laughing and shouting. Yet, also
as in the students' scene, the viewer is given visual clues
to the tragic nature of the event. For one thing, the peasants
skate counter-clockwise around the room and counter-clockwise
around each other. In moving against the usual direction of
clocks, the dancers seem to be asserting their primacy over
"natural" forces. In light of the film's events (which leave
most of the peasants dead after their confrontation with the
Stockgrowers Association thugs), such audacity seems misplaced. Indeed, the peasants are shown to be incapable of
opposing the forces of fiscal and historical inevitability. [24]
The wheels on which they skate, like the wheels of the film's
carriages (the actual carriages and the trains) are fateful,
figurative embodiments of progress, [25] propelling everyone,
rich and poor alike, in the direction of the big-moneyed concerns towards which the country is heading. [26]

Significantly, Ella and Jim are among the peasants
and like them are caught up in the political tide (indicated in
the Wyoming sequences by clockwise movements) that will
soon either destroy or defeat all who, in one way or another,
oppose the stockgrowers, be they rich (like Jim) or merely
rich-aspiring (like Ella, Nate, and J. B.). [27] It is thus entirely fitting that since they act in opposition to the desires
of the rich (Ella accepts stolen cattle from peasants and, over

The peasant counterpart to the student dance: a roller-skating waltz in the Heaven's Gate meeting hall. At center, Isabelle Huppert and Kris Kristofferson, with Jeff Bridges to Huppert's right.

Nate's protests, entertains stockgrowers' employees as well; Jim initially tries to avoid the wholesale slaughter that the stockgrowers propose), Ella and Jim should describe in the film so many movements that run counter to what we realize is the deplorably natural (clockwise) movement of the country towards greater consolidation of wealth and power among the few. Thus, when Jim leads out on display Ella's birthday present of a horse and carriage, he walks around her counter-clockwise. In the ride past the peasants, who are having their picture taken, Ella drives her horse and carriage past the gathered crowd twice; in doing so, she traverses a circle in a counter-clockwise direction. Even after the peasants' roller-skate dance is over, Ella and Jim remain in the hall and perform a final, bittersweet pas de deux, moving counter-clockwise around the hall while dancing in a symbolic fashion around each other (first clockwise, as though attempting to bend with fate, then counter-clockwise as though resisting it). This is a reprise of the contradictory movements already de-

scribed by the students (although it inverts Jim and his student
partner's main, clockwise direction, an appropriate change in
that Ella is just the opposite of Jim's student date, who is
upper class and idle whereas Ella is lower class and works,
albeit as a prostitute. Both women, though, ultimately seem
to "sell" themselves by the film's end). Ella and Jim's dance
also anticipates the circles of attack (the peasants in their
assault against the Stockgrowers Association men) and defense
(the cavalry) created during the final battle sequence.

In Heaven's Gate there is not, as one might expect,
justice in the abstract sense of the word, only the enforce-
ment of the law's practicalities, particularly as these relate
to protecting the interests of the propertied men for whom
the law, and the country, exist. Canton tells the protesting
Nate at one point, "You were hired to enforce the law; we
are the law." Indeed, the peasants recognize the link between the government and essentially lawless (and illegal) repression when the mayor states, "They [the stockgrowers]
have the law on their side; the National Guard can't help us,"28
the implication being that the National Guard (supposed up-
holders of law and order) either act in compliance with, or
are powerless in the face of, fiscal force.

As Canton so tellingly points out, "This is no longer
a poor man's country." And the men in this private club
agree with his statement that "unenforced law is an invitation
to anarchy."29 What is obviously meant by the term "law"
here is law as it benefits the upper class, not a law that
would protect the peasants' rights to own land as well; if the
peasants act counter to this law, then, in Canton's words,
they must be "thieves and anarchists."

As Canton aptly states, "If we fail, the flag of the
United States fails," an assertion that anticipates the flag's
appearance, along with the cavalry (both are symbols of economic exploitation and repression), at the film's end. Clearly,
the America that Heaven's Gate gives us is not the land that
welcomes the homeless and dispossessed; it is an old and
dirty country biased in favor of the rich, a country whose
materialistic future is already mapped out. In this respect
the film complements Thunderbolt and Lightfoot's grim pessimism but is the opposite of The Deer Hunter, whose finale
suggests that the idealistic qualities inherent in America's
people may somehow revitalize the war-weary, dispirited nation. Aside from the renegade marshall, Jim Averill, the
forces of law in Heaven's Gate are on the side of the stock-

The meeting hall is also a place of discord.   The exhortation
by Mr. Eggleston (Brad Dourif), from the film's decisive
peasant gathering.   J. B. (Jeff Bridges), looking on, is significantly dressed (see note 27, paragraph 5).

growers, who with a calm faith in the power of their wealth
can blithely draw up a death list with the names of 125 men
on it (Jim is also slated to be murdered, although no attempt
is made on his life)[30] and have these men killed without the need
for what Jim and Billy refer to as "the necessary warrants."
Instead, from the cattlemen like Canton (whose lineage of
wealth and power is affirmed when he tells Nate, "My grand-
father was Secretary of War to Harrison; his brother was
the governor of the state of New York; my brother-in-law is
the Secretary of State") to the army major (also a member
of the association) who during the short version's massacre
drops his pants when there is a lull in the battle (at which
point Jim comments, " "That man is a friend of the president"),
the men of wealth and power are seen to be pigheaded (but

influential) villains.   Yet the governor and the president support the stockgrowers' actions: as Canton says to Nate when
Nate asks to see a warrant for a man's execution, "To you
I represent the full authority of the government of the United
States and the president"; and referring to the incoming thugs
the major says, "The president himself asked for these men
to go." We are left with no doubt that the president would
approve of the United States Cavalry's saving the rich and
their paid assassins from destruction.   Of course, we should
not be too surprised, since the cavalry has traditionally sided
with the oppressor (the white men) against the dispossessed
(e.g., the Indians).

After the cavalry arrives, Jim makes one last, pitiful
attempt to turn the slaughter to the peasants' account.   The
Army captain who had earlier accused Jim of only slumming
among the poor states, "These men [the remaining association
members and their hired killers] are under arrest by military
authority."[31]   Jim counters by saying to Canton, "Frank, you
know these men are under the jurisdiction of civil authorities."
Canton, though, has the decisive word, once again employing
political power (bought with money and wielded by the wealthy
men with which politics is riddled) to crush the peasants' opposition.   "I have here a telegram from the governor.   'Only
immediate drastic action on the part of authorities over and
above county officials can reduce the state of almost anarchy
in Johnson County' " (an ironic assertion when one realizes
that it is the stockgrowers' actions that have led to the present situation).

The captain adds the final ironic touch to these important exchanges: "Jim, you can let me take them out of
here peacefully or you can get shot for insurrection," he
says.   When Jim replies that "rescuing them is what you're
doing," the captain correctly identifies the horribly faceless
power that is the true deliverer of these men.   "It's not me
that's doing it to you; it's the rules."   Once again, the rich
man's law wins out.

Even members of the peasantry are corrupted by money.
The mayor of Sweetwater, himself a peasant, yields through
weakness and materialism to the temptation to appropriate
"the law" as a justification for the stockgrowers' planned actions, stating at the decisive meeting in the Heaven's Gate
hall, "We all know it's against the law to take branded cattle
from the open range."   The mayor is even prepared to sacrifice some of the peasants if he and those like him can be

spared. As he tells Jim in the film's short version (the
speech appears in the long version in only slightly different
form), "We want you to turn in the people on the list. We
are merchants, storekeepers, respectable citizens, not like
the others. " The mayor is mistaken, though; only wealth
and the proper social class guarantee one a privileged position; thus, all of Ella's, Nate's, J. B. 's and various peasants'
money-gathering is rather pointless.

Nor is the mayor alone in his cowardice. Immediately
after his statement at the meeting hall, another peasant chimes
in with, "The law is the law,"[32] ignoring the fact, as Heaven's
Gate so tellingly demonstrates, that the same law that the rich
use to their advantage is also employed to keep the peasants
poor and landless.

In Heaven's Gate, money does not aid one in deciding
what to do; it virtually determines choice. Among the film's
rich characters, money is seen to have either morally corrupted those individuals--like Canton--who are capable of acting, or to have crippled those characters --e. g. , Jim and
Billy--who despite their wealth retain a degree of moral recti-
tude but are in terms of action predominantly impotent. [33]
Jim's inability to save either the peasants or Ella demonstrates how a life of luxury has rendered him useless.   As
for Billy, right up to the point of his death he goes along
with the stockgrowers because, as he earlier tells Jim, in
response to being asked, "What'll you do" (about the death
list scheme), "I'm a victim of our class. "[34]

Although Billy applauds when Jim strikes Canton, and
supports Nate's later rebelliousness in Canton's tent, he either
sits still in the former instance and reclines in the latter,
instead of actively participating.   In essence, as is appropriate for a class orator (Billy's role at the graduation), Billy,
like that other orator, the Reverend Doctor, is all talk.   He
believes only in the abstract; when Jim says that the stockgrowers "can't get away with" their death list plans, Billy
replies, "In principle everything can be done--in principle. "
Yet Jim is identical to his friend in this respect.   Thus,
when J. B. asks Jim (in the long version) "How can people
declare war on a whole county?" (the short version has J. B.
ask, "How can the association declare war on the whole
county?"), Jim responds, "I guess on principle anything can
be done. " (This response does not appear in the short version, although considering Jim's overall evasion of action,
this would certainly be a characteristic reaction for him.)

The problem is, though, that the stockgrowers' activities are not taking place in an abstract realm, but in an eminently real one. Despite what Jim and Billy seem at times to believe, what is happening in Wyoming has actual, material consequences. The two men's metaphysics are just an excuse for their own shortcomings.

Ultimately, both versions of Heaven's Gate demonstrate overwhelmingly that Jim and Billy ignore the demands of and need for a pragmatic morality, just as they ignore the symbolic way that the billiard balls in their association club pool game fall into their designated pockets as readily as the film's events are already beginning fatefully to fall into place.

Billy may observe about the ongoing slaughter of the peasants that "It's not like the Indians, you know; you can't just kill them all," but such a statement only reveals his essential naiveté. Although they appear to be winning the battle (a temporary victory even if gained, since in Heaven's Gate's view big-moneyed interests will always predominate), practically all of the peasants will be slain by the rich and their hired thugs. 35

Whether we like it or not, for virtually the entirety of Heaven's Gate, Nate qualifies as one of these paid assassins. In fact, it is obvious that Nate works for the stockgrowers because they pay well. Cimino makes quite clear Nate's compromise of his values in exchange for money. Repeatedly, Nate is involved with activities or references relating to paper and writing, whose forms (e.g. money as written promissory gestures; as Nate says when he finds a couple of peasant men at Ella's, "Did you pay cash money?")36 figure prominently in his life. Thus, paper references appear in Nate's copying onto paper an entry about Nathaniel (his namesake) Hawthorne (an author virtually obsessed with fate and despair); in the newspapers with which he papers the walls of his cabin (the paper here obviously standing in as a symbol not only of civilization--Cf. the Reverend Doctor's speech-- but of literacy as well, and this despite the fact that Heaven's Gate shows literate men, for example Canton, committing some of the film's most barbarous acts); in a related, suggestive fashion, in the form of the essentially worthless pieces of land deed papers that the peasants initially believe in as testaments to their rights of property, rights which Nate opposes in his advocacy of the stockgrowers' possession of the land; and in the final death note that he leaves for Ella. Appropriately, during the siege on Nate's house, which has been set aflame, Cimino zooms in on the burning wallpaper (the embodiment of his unexpressed promise to Ella to improve his abode), suggesting that all of Nate's paper-related efforts are now pointless in the face of the Hell-fire death that the stockgrowers visit upon him.

Only his death note is spared, because it is an expression of spiritual feelings (e. g., "I hope they did not hurt Ella ... goodbye Ella and Jim"), not material desire (writing to improve one's station; decorating to impress someone with the place where one lives; earning money as a sign of power).   The note is in Nate's pocket, and thereby figuratively and literally near his heart; since it is in these senses close to him, it does not burn and emerges intact, thus telling us through its endurance (and the endurance of the memory of Nate shared by Ella and Jim) that the spiritual is what is ultimately important in life, a lesson that applies not only to Nate but to Jim (who only gives gifts--the rifle to J. B., although the film's short version has Jim uncharacteristically telling J. B. to "pay me later" for the firearm; the horse and carriage to Ella--instead of himself) and Ella, who, despite her emotional openness, nonetheless hoards money and cattle.

True, Nate does eventually leave the stockgrowers' employ, shooting one of their hirelings and, in response to Canton's remark about the president's support of the stockgrowers' actions, stating "Fuck him, too" (eliciting a "Bravo, sir!" from Billy) but his protests occur too late to do any good.

Indeed, Heaven's Gate makes it clear that Nate would probably have remained with the stockgrowers were it not for Ella's rape by association thugs.   Thus, neither his betrayal of his ancestry nor Jim's telling him that Ella's name is on the death list (assuming, of course, that Nate doesn't already know this) radicalize him; only when corruption threatens to touch him personally[37] (as does the rape of his fiancée) does Nate change from being a classical figure of death (symbolized in the traditional image of a shadow--in this case, Nate's-- which is here cast on the tent of Michael Kovach, a peasant whom he murders at the film's beginning, and suggested when, after entering Ella's cabin and finding some peasants there, Nate hears one of the men remark on the deadly coolness he has brought with him: "It's getting cold in here")[38] working for the association to a killer who turns against them before he is destroyed. Nate's and Billy's protests are either too

late, as in Nate's case, or too weak (Billy merely drunkenly
approves of the invective Nate aims at the president) to change
the fated course of events.

The assault on Nate Champion (Christopher Walken).   Canton
(Sam Waterston) will soon deliver the coup de grace.

      The killings of many of the film's characters are,
appropriately, carried out by significant individuals.   The
compromising mayor, who is telling J. B. that his "fears"--
presumably about the just-arrived thugs--"are unfounded,"
is shot by one of the peasants' most inspired agitators: the
uncompromising Widow Kovach. [39]   Canton retaliates against
Nate's shooting one of his aides by delivering the final, fatal
shot to Nate outside of the latter's cabin, an action that ironically satisfies our sense of order and balance, since Canton
and Nate represent respectively the upper and working class
characters most directly involved with the Stockgrowers Association's activities.   In addition, Canton pays Jim back for
his effrontery in the club by helping to kill Jim's two remaining friends, J. B. and Ella; while Jim, the only moneyed-class
member actively on the peasants' side, kills the highest rank-
ing member seen on the stockgrowers' side: the Army major.

The cavalry meets the thug-laden train, whose symbolic smoke
will soon (figuratively) carry many characters away.   Note
the allusive <u>Deer Hunter</u> antlers on the front of the train.

      Appropriately, during the final melée it is Ella who
shoots Billy. [40]   Each is an essentially weak character; each
qualifies as Jim's lover (one heterosexual, one homophilic).
Billy merely drifts along with the prevailing tide (his fate is
beautifully prefigured in his disappearing in a cloud of steam
that emanates from that symbol of progress, the locomotive). [41]
Like Billy, who stays, but does not fight, with the stockgrowers although he applauds the efforts of people like Jim
and Nate to thwart them, [42] Ella naively believes that she can
retain her personal integrity while remaining involved with the
moneyed interests.   By staying with the stockgrowers despite
his sympathies, Billy has sold out.   Ella also yields to money's
corruption; she literally sells out by selling her flesh (and
that of her "girls") for either money or cattle--she doesn't
care which.   As Nate correctly tells her at one point, "You're
getting too greedy."[43]

      Yet, by servicing both peasants and stockgrowers' em-
ployees, Ella is involved.   Thus, on the eve of the thugs'
vengeance raids, Ella is raped by a member of a three-man
group of hired killers who have already shot to death her pros-

titutes. The agents of the rich men who are raping the land
rape the woman whose wealth derives in part from that land's
rape. [44] The rape scene's symbolism is dramatically underscored when, before the rape, one of the thugs puts the barrel of his association-purchased rifle up under Ella's dress;
the gun-for-penis substitution is a concrete expression of the
political aspects of the impending physical assault.

    Cimino provides a number of actual and suggested
aural keys to complement the rape scene's fateful portentous-
ness. The presence in the cabin of Morrison, the association
man glimpsed early in the film playing a harmonica in the Casper
general store, is signaled before Ella enters the house. We
hear his harmonica playing as Ella drives up. Moreover,
when Ella enters the parlor, Morrison, sitting on her piano
stool, twists to face her; the creak from the stool's bearings
is ominous, although it has itself been anticipated in the sound
made when Ella opened the cabin's rusted screen door.

    More signals follow. Morrison's associate pours beer
over his head in an aural (and visual) travesty of the bloodletting (running liquid) that must have occurred when Ella's
prostitutes (who are lying dead in an upstairs room) were
killed. The creak of the upstairs window when Jim opens it
to see the slaughtered women suggests that Morrison's (the
creaker) role as leader of vengeance (Ella is, after all,
being rudely paid back for her avarice)[45] will soon pass to
him. All the while, both heard (during the rape scene) and
unheard (during the cutaway to Jim), a clock--symbolizing
an inevitability already made concrete in Ella's rape--ticks
away, drawing us closer to Heaven's Gate's end. Finally,
after the rape (which is audibly punctuated by Ella's screams
and groans and followed by the loud reports from Jim's guns),
Nate--his presence aurally anticipated by the sound of his
jangling spurs--arrives, and the sequence is complete.

    Actually, the rape scene is only one of a number of
related events in the latter half of Heaven's Gate, which is
comprised of a series of deadly occurrences that grow out
of one another like fateful circles emanating from a morbid
center. Tracing these events, we find that, first, the station-
master, Cully (Richard Masur), is repeatedly shot. This
barrage of shots leads into the immediately following scene,
in which the trapper (Geoffrey Lewis) says (in a statement
which at first seems a shocking reflection of the murder we
have just witnessed), "I've never been hit by a bullet [al-
though] I've been shot at many times." Soon, however, at

the beginning of the assault on Nate's cabin, he will be both
shot at and hit--many, many times.   The humorous interaction between the trapper and Nick (Mickey Rourke), which
involves some play with a knife (the action is amusing, but
has an underlying sense of violence), follows.   Chronologically, the murder of Ella's prostitutes (which in Heaven's
Gate's trimmed version may very well be taking place while
we are viewing this comic relief scene) then occurs, as
though the "wolf" (a traditional symbol of violence) that the
trapper talked about catching has somehow assumed concrete
form in the association men who kill Ella's women. [46]   Fate-
fully-related events continue.   The rape occurs; all but one
(ironically, Morrison) of the association men are shot by
Jim. [47]   Nate enters Ella's cabin, then leaves to find Canton.
Entering Canton's camp, he discovers that a firing squad is
preparing to shoot a man;[48] Nate then shoots Canton's aide,
a rebellious act (complemented by ensuing rebellious words)
which in economic terms significantly contrasts with his murder of a peasant towards the film's beginning, signals his
defection from Canton's cause, and ensures his (and his
friends') soon-to-occur death at the hands of Canton's men.
Another shooting, of the mayor, leading up through the film's
final assault and last depicted deaths, those of J. B. and Ella,
then takes place. [49]   Truly, Jim's statement to Ella after the
rape unwittingly identifies the deadly daisy chain of events
that rules the last hour of Heaven's Gate.   "Today was just
the beginning," he says; we may infer that similar chains of
death, all linked to the clash between rich and poor, are
historically destined to occur. [50]

The film's condemnation of Billy's and Ella's equivoca-
tions seems to imply that despite history's foregone conclusions, one has to take sides.   We must therefore admire
Jim's eventual determination to help the peasants even though
we know that he is fighting a losing battle.   Still, Jim only
enters the fight reluctantly.   At the meeting hall, one of the
peasants who refuses to fight tells the others, "You're cutting
your own throats" (Cf. Note 32).   By implicit contrast, Jim's
aloofness is underscored when he is later seen carefully shaving himself.   As the meeting continues, Jim stays in the upstairs room of the hotel near the hall, eventually going so
far as to signal his present distance from the peasants' fury
by casually buttoning his vest while watching hordes of poor
men ride off to meet the association men in armed conflict.

Even if he wanted to, though, Jim would still be pre-
vented by his class and position from achieving more than a

vicarious sympathy with people from other classes. [51]   Unlike
Nate (whose touching wallpapering of his shack for Ella's sake
seems a sweet, tender gesture that stands in opposition to
the opulent carriage that Jim gives Ella), [52] Jim is not predominantly a man of feelings but of thought (in this sense,
he is a great deal like Canton).   Nate is a poor man lured
by money; he acts instinctively and only at the film's end
thinks, realizing too late, after the rape, that he is fighting
on the wrong side.   As Jim rather smugly tells him during
the rape's aftermath, "Maybe you understand better the kind
of people you're working for now."

   By contrast, Jim is a wealthy man, slumming among
the peasants.   As the captain tells him, "You're a rich man
with a good name; you only pretend to be poor."   Jim knows
that the association is wrong but fails to act soon enough to
make any difference.   An emotional cripple and, quite possibly, a class-conscious bigot (like Canton), Jim can only
offer Ella material goods, not affection.   Thus Ella's com-

Ella, Jim, and the materialistic gift.   Ella: "You buy me
things; he [Nate] asked me to marry him."

ment to him: "You buy me things; he [Nate] asked me to
marry him." Jim replies, "Maybe it was always in my
mind to," but as Ella points out, "It's not good enough."
What matters in Heaven's Gate are actions, not words. 53
Yet Ella herself is not above reproach in this respect; like
Jim, she masks her feelings with monetary considerations.
"I thought you were getting to like me," Nate says when she
asks him to pay for sex. "I do," Ella replies, "but I like
money."

Ultimately, money wins out; neither love, idealism,
devotion, friendship, nor tenderness successfully stands in
the way of its great, destroying onslaught. In a final dance-
like movement that yokes together directions suggesting both
natural progression (half of the soldiers riding clockwise,
which symbolizes the inevitable movement towards greater
financial consolidation and national growth) and futile resistance to inevitability (present in the other soldiers riding
counter-clockwise, their direction mockingly reflecting the
peasants' futile resistance to progress), 54 the cavalry rein-
vokes the protective ring, not in defense of an ideal, as the
ring was employed in the student fight sequence, but in defense of a tragic, pessimistic realism.

Safely surrounded, the stockgrowers and their thugs
are thus saved from defeat. All of the peasants' efforts have
been in vain. 55 There is a powerful vitality behind the Heav-
en's Gate-centered meetings and dances and a lively spirit
in the peasants' activities; their communal events (like the
students' graduation ceremony and dance) indicate a strong
social need for group affirmation through rituals. But the
rich, too, have their social rites: mythically-garbed men,
all dressed alike in ritual slaughter robes; refined meetings
in straitened surroundings, with the customary death-oriented,
homophilic exclusion of women and the attendant serving--
also traditionally without women present--of brandy and ci-
gars by corpse-like waiters. And though the rituals of the
moneyed class represent death (in the persons of the lifeless
Canton and the uniformed thugs) while those of the peasants
and graduating students in an important sense suggest life
(the joyous dancing), the rich nevertheless prevail.

The finale of the cut version of Heaven's Gate56 gives
us the image of Jim Averill, a man who is wealthy (the fine
trappings, the expensive clothes) but now old and alone, pacing in his great yacht's cabin. He seems idle, morose, a
bit absurd. He closes the door to the cabin, shutting himself

in with his memories.   Lost in reveries of the past ("The
gone good days" which Jim told Billy he remembers "clearer
and better" as he grows older),[57] Jim can only impotently
replay in his mind the predominantly melancholy events we
have seen in the film.   Probably most significant among these
memories is Ella's fatal shooting, which occurred while Jim
was attempting to help her leave Wyoming.   The sounds of
that event come back to Jim in echo-chamber-processed, hollow replays (Jim calls out, "Ella!" while Ella, fatally wounded, gasps) and its inevitability is wonderfully communicated
in the incessant drumming of the yacht's engine (one of whose
parts is doubtless creating the noise by significantly turning
in a fateful circle), which is heard on the soundtrack during
this final recollection.   All of the men whom Jim, in his
fashion, loved--Billy, Nate, J. B.--are also dead.[58]   The
cut version has Jim recall a remark Ella made to him ("I'm
grateful to you for everything and I love you...") but omits
the last two words (the remark in full was, "I'm grateful to
you for everything and I love you for it"), suggesting through
the omission that what Jim is suppressing is the fact of Ella's
loving him because of what he did for her (Ella again is being materialistic),[59] not for how she felt about him.   Tragically, even at this late date, Jim fails to realize that his
emotional reticence--evident throughout the film--signals an
emotional deadness as well.   Both versions of Heaven's Gate
end with Jim gazing into the Western sun of his fading life,
leaving us with a sad picture of a useless man--ideals destroyed, intact in body but shattered in spirit, a pitiful embodiment of a rich man's country without purpose or direction, drifting aimlessly on an indifferent sea.

NOTES

1.   Although the present chapter takes cognizance of the more
significant differences between Heaven's Gate's two versions,
there is obviously little critical point in detailing extensively
the particulars of the divergences, especially now that Cimino's original cut is available on videotape.   However, a number of basic observations about the two films should be made.
     The long version of Heaven's Gate, while it differs
from the 147-minute film in the placement of certain sequences and in the employment of what appear to be alternate
takes of the same scene, draws the majority of its additional
72 minutes of footage from material that initially belonged to
sequences still present in the film's short version.   The restoration of this footage does not in most cases essentially

change the meaning of these sequences so much as it extends
them.   Thus, we are given more examples of Billy's clowning during the commencement exercises; a commencement
hall shot of policemen, whose presence at the ceremony foreshadows the repressive role that the cavalry and government
officials will play in the film; longer dance sequences involving the students and, later, the peasants; more scenes of the
Johnson County peasants being abused by stockgrowers thugs;
a longer version of the peasant men's Sunday morning cockfight gathering at the Heaven's Gate meeting hall; and an extended tracking shot of the butler weaving his way through
the ornate passages of Canton's club.

Present also is the significant piece of dialogue given
to the Army captain, who comments on Ella's prosperity and
the peasants' patronization of her establishment; and a clearer
accent on divisiveness among people, be they peasants (e. g. ,
the two men seen fighting at J. B. 's over property rights;
and later--in both versions--another form of divisiveness occurs when a peasant youth calls Nate, himself an immigrant,
a "goddamn foreigner") or others.   A stockgrowers' employee
tells Nate, "Ella ain't your friend, ain't nobody's friend."
Later, Nate echoes this sentiment when he says to Ella, "Jim
ain't your friend, ain't nobody's friend; he'd quit anybody if
it suits him."

Moreover, there is a stunning aptness about the long
version's inserted intermission (Cimino has even provided
for intermission music on the soundtrack), which occurs right
after Billy, having bid the departing death squad an ironic
farewell, seems to disappear in a cloud of steam (Cf. Note
41).   This is indeed an apt place to halt the film's action
temporarily, since the symbolic image with which we are left
heralds the beginning of many fateful disappearances in the
film.

Less successful, though, are some of the image/music
juxtapositions employed in the long version.   In particular,
two scenes--one involving Nate at Ella's, one occurring after
Nate's death--have their impact considerably diminished by
the presence of the music.   The mandolin version of "The
Blue Danube" heard on the soundtrack when Nate, upstairs
at Ella's, walks in on the sleeping Jim, seems more intrusive
than complementary, and distracts us somewhat from the ominous sound of the clock ticking away in the background, which
foreshadows the death knell clock that ticks during the prelude to Ella's rape.   The silence attendant with the short version's scene involving Ella's grieving over Nate's body is
much more telling than any music could ever be.

True, the short version sequence does eventually em-

ploy sound effects and music, but only after the emotional
impact has had time to take full effect. First, one hears the
sound of gunshots (here coming from the raging battle, thus
reminding us of the polarized conflict which, once he becomes
involved in it on the side of the peasants, ensures Nate's
death). Then gradually, towards the end of the sequence, the
musical selection "Snowfall" is brought in, an appropriate
choice, since this piece is a slow version of the "Village
Dance," which accompanied Ella's ride in her carriage past
the townspeople. It should be noted that in both instances,
it is recklessness that is musically being alluded to: in
Nate's case, recklessness is present in the form of his daring to oppose Canton; in Ella's case, it appears in the cross-
reference to her wild driving towards and through the town.

Perhaps most intriguing is the realization that the long
and short versions differ in the relative order of many scenes.
Since both cuts of Heaven's Gate are now available, a consideration of this aspect of the films is unwarranted. However, it should be realized that given the powerful influence
which adjacent scenes have on each other, the two versions
in an important respect constitute two significantly different
films, an aspect that may be confirmed by viewing them se-
quentially. Paradoxically, the film's unfortunate enforced -
editing has resulted in the availability of two great third films
by Cimino, instead of merely one.

2.   However, Heaven's Gate's 219-minute version passes just
as pleasurably as The Deer Hunter, which is 36 minutes
shorter.

3.   As we shall see, this figurative rape later assumes a
concrete form, at which time it has a somewhat different
meaning (cf. pp. 211-212).

4.   In fact, in both versions of the film the peasants ride
in their own unique conveyance; they either ride on top of a
cattle car or in a specially labeled "Emigrant Car," thus
suggesting their animal-like status in Heaven's Gate (Cf. Note
7).

5.   This piece of dialogue does not occur in the film's long
version.

6.   Indeed, as we learn from the short version's soon-to-
be-heard voice-over narration, Jim believes in what the Reverend Doctor is saying. However, as is made clear in Heav-
en's Gate's long version (which includes Billy Irvine's mock-

ing reply to the oration), Jim's friend clearly is not taken in
by such naive and presumptuous pontifications.   Thus, Billy
first belittles the relative oratorical weakness of the Reverend
Doctor's address, stating, "We must speak according to our
ability"; mocks the former speaker's age ("giving the dry
bones a long tongue"); and ends his peroration with a comic
rhyming verse which mockingly presents class privilege and
inequality as perfectly acceptable.   "We disclaim all intention
of making a change, in what we esteem on the whole well arranged. "   The students appreciate Billy's speech, but whether
they truly understand his satiric intent is not at all clear.

Also of note: the Reverend Doctor's address resurfaces later in Nate's comment to Ella about his shack's re-
decoration (Ella: "Wallpaper?" Nate: "Yeah, well, it civilizes
the wilderness.")   This only half-comic trivialization of the
Reverend Doctor's injunction to bring culture to the country's
rural areas ("the education of a nation") seems to affirm that
in Cimino's view, the good Reverend's address is nothing
more than sanctimonious, smug nonsense.

7.   Like cattle (both kinds of "animal" are led to slaughter
in the film; both kinds of beast are seen as merely animals
for use by the rich), the peasants in the film's long version
are often viewed pulling wagons, either because they are too
poor to purchase animals, because their animals have died
or--a more insidious reason--because their cattle or oxen
have been used as payment for time spent at Ella's.

8.   When in both versions of the film, Jim tries, without
success, to persuade Ella to leave Johnson County, he is
leaning against the prominently-figured wheel of the carriage
he has given her while, almost undetected in the background,
a dung beetle (traditional symbol of death) crawls up part of
the equipage.   This sequence, which occurs near a body of
water, invites comparison with similar scenes near water in
Thunderbolt and Lightfoot in which, as in the present Heaven's
Gate scene, the notion of moral and spiritual replenishment,
symbolized by the water, not only fails to occur but is replaced
by a decidedly morbid spirit.

The Deer Hunter, though, complicates this schema.
While it is true that the deliverance from North Vietnamese
captivity occurs near water, the film also invokes water as
a symbol of morbidity (in the form of the river of death across
which Michael passes on what turns out to be his deadly journey towards Nicky).   That the same body of water (the water
bordering the shack in which the first Russian roulette games
take place) should give forth men who are both reborn (Steven)

and condemned to death (the losers in the game) only further
demonstrates the complexity of water's imagery in The Deer
Hunter, a complexity matched in Heaven's Gate's shot of the
replenished Ella vibrantly emerging from her swim, only to
then refuse to leave Johnson County, thereby assuring her
doom.

9.   The reader will note that I am not drawing attention to
the direction in which the film's literal wheels turn.   Inter-
pretation in this respect is impossible because these directions vary depending upon from which side of the wheel one
views them (e. g. , a counter-clockwise-skating peasant's roller skate wheels appear to move either clockwise or counter-
clockwise according to whether the skater is perceived from
his right or left side; maintaining absolute consistency of
wheel movement in this respect would have created serious
problems in film continuity).   Ultimately, determination of
the specific figurative significance of these wheels must yield
to a concentration on the direction in which the conveyance
to which they are attached actually moves.   In the case of
the peasants' attack vehicles, though, determination of significance of movement is impossible because the vehicles
move in on the stockgrowers and their hirelings from all four
sides.   What can be said about these vehicles is that together
they describe a circle of fate that closes in on the rich and
their thugs.

10.   To add to the underlying sense of anxiety created during
the dance, Cimino makes certain that members of the marching band, along with their dates, are seen in all of the sequence's shots.   The picture of these frock-coated, top-hatted
men, all similarly dressed, links up with the images we are
later given of the stockgrowers' hired thugs, who all dress
alike (in virtually identical long coats and hats).   Thus, the
band members' dark, formal garb--which is already somewhat funereal in tone--has its morbid connotations complemented by its later invocation, thereby infusing into this sequence a note of both death (the clothing, its color, the band's
earlier stately march) and doom (what appears in retrospect
to be the clothing's almost inevitable reappearance).

11.   After making his speech, Canton--much like a train--
recedes back along the tracks.   In Heaven's Gate the peasants
only ride along on trains; the rich and their hirelings use
trains to achieve their ends.

     The symbolic equation here of Canton with a train is
rich in associations.   Since trains in Heaven's Gate symbolize

progress (manifest destiny and economic growth) and fate--
forces involved with America's move towards fiscal consolidation at the expense of the poor--it is quite apt that Canton,
the only major figure in the film who acts in concert with inevitability, should be identified with such a powerful symbol.
In an important sense, then, despite Heaven's Gate's condemnation of the peasants' loss of rights, Canton is the only important character who not only acts, but acts in harmony with
what must be.   Ironically, he thus emerges as the film's only
heroic figure.

Heaven's Gate gives us a range of characters who oc-
cupy various interesting positions on the continuum from rich
to poor, inactive to active.   Canton is rich; he acts on behalf of the rich.   Jim is rich, sympathizes with the poor,
and occasionally acts, albeit ineffectively.   Billy is rich,
sympathizes with the poor, but is incapable of acting.

There are also peasant characters who function as
roughly comparable counterparts to these individuals.   Agitators like the Widow Kovach are poor and act on behalf of the
poor.   Peasants like the mayor are relatively poor, sympathize with the peasants, but withdraw from action; they are
thus ineffectual.   Nate is poor, sympathizes with the peasants, and acts, albeit too late.   Ella occupies a median position in this paradigm; initially poor, she is working hard
to gain money; at first distant from the peasant/stockgrowers
conflict, she eventually takes an active role in it.

12.   Jim himself rides into the Wyoming town of Casper on
a train, but in a special way that alters the manner in which
his journey is to be read (see pages 200-202).

13.   Apparently, the defending students are members of the
class of 1871, who in a ritualistic activity wish to prevent
the present year's graduates from carrying away a symbolic
laurel of the school.   Alternately, the bouquet may be read
as a symbol of essential innocence, a state midway between
ignorance (tabula rasa white) and experience (symbolized by
a passionate red) which the pink-colored flowers represent
and which the graduating students vainly hope to maintain.

14.   Billy does, however, prevent--at least for a time--one
murder in the film (cf. Note 40).

15.   In fact, all of the film's battle-oriented sequences--
those involving either the defending students, the attacking
peasants, or the defending cavalry--describe the same pattern
of outer ring counter-clockwise, inner ring clockwise move-

ments, suggesting both conflict (within themselves) and similarity (among all of the examples). Cf. pp. 196, 198-200, 215,
Note 16.

16.   These meanings, virtually intact, carry over to the other
manifestations of these contrary patterns, which occur during
the peasant-assault and cavalry-defense sequences. Before
these sequences, Heaven's Gate has already prepared us for
a degree of indecisiveness in the actions of both the peasants
(e. g., the debate at the meeting hall) and the cavalry (e. g.,
the captain's possible sympathy with the peasants), thereby
justifying the symbolic reoccurrence of the opposed movements
described by these two groups. Although the earlier-identified
idealism of the students (pp. 199-200) may, in Heaven's Gate's
depressing latter half, long since have vanished, contradictory
impulses still remain. The peasants/cavalry counter-clockwise outer rings here symbolize the merest passing show of
reluctance to accept fate. Indeed, by these points in the film,
idealism (figuratively present earlier in the waltzing students'
outward ring's clockwise movement) has literally and symbolically moved inward, where it can only survive by being
cloaked by an outward display of pessimism. That the peasants in their dance sequence all move counter-clockwise indicates quite strongly that, unlike the students, they somehow already know that they are doomed, a fact constantly
brought home to them in the form of the numerous injustices
they suffer at the hands of the stockgrowers and their hirelings.

17.   When Jim disembarks in Casper, Wyoming twenty years
later, the "Battle Hymn" returns, albeit in a wistful form (it
is played on a guitar), suggesting that the militaristic tendencies it connotes are, at least for a brief period, in some
degree of abeyance; indeed, the theme replaces the just-heard
"Song of 70," which naturally recalls the innocence of Jim's
undergraduate days. The "Battle Hymn" then segues into a
version of the film's end-title theme, "Ella's Waltz," thus
musically anticipating Heaven's Gate's grim, melancholy resolution (itself additionally suggested through the finality-connot-
ing number "86" that appears on one of the railroad cars
past which Jim is seen walking).
       Students of the film are strongly encouraged to pur-
chase and review Heaven's Gate's soundtrack, available as
Liberty disc LOO 1073.

18.   This voice-over technique is not employed in the film's
long version; instead, the post-Harvard sequence merely opens
with the title (also used in the short version), "Wyoming,
Twenty Years Later." Interestingly, in a rare self-reflexive

homage, in both versions Cimino has the front of the train
that carries Jim into Wyoming adorned with a pair of deer
antlers that bear a striking resemblance to those used for
The Deer Hunter's advertising campaign.

    Jim narrates the shot of himself on the train in the
past tense ("I thought ... I could be ... "). The melancholy
distancing from the present created by the past tense, coupled
with Jim's observation, "so my life worked out differently,"
contributes an additional note of inevitability to what we watch,
as though history's outcome has already been written (a point
of view that complements the notion that the peasants' efforts
are basically futile). Since we see things in this short version of
Heaven's Gate from Jim's point of view, we are destined like
him to become outcasts too, watching past events from the
melancholy vantage point of the present, longing for what
might have been (the peasants' victory; a happy resolution to
Ella and Jim's relationship) but all the while knowing that
such things are not to be. This powerful additional effect
of fatefulness is unfortunately sacrificed in the film's long version, which tells its story in strict chronological fashion.
Cf. Note 56 below, and Note 15 in Chapter 12, for more
discussion of this aspect of the two films.

19. The film's long version makes quite plain Jim's basic
inability to confront the Wyoming situation adequately by showing him drinking from his flask on the train and then, when
the train arrives, depicting him crawling drunkenly on the
floor, looking for his boots. Later, in both versions of the
film, Jim will repeat the same activities--getting drunk and
searching for his boots--when the mayor and his party come
to see him, thereby once again displaying an avoidance technique and ineptness that suggest how basically unsuited and
unwilling he is to face the harsh realities of Wyoming politics. (For more on this aspect of Jim's personality, see
especially pp. 207-208 and Notes 24, 26, 57, and 58).

20. Cf. Notes 4, 7, and 51, which allude to the peasants'
inhuman status in Heaven's Gate.

21. Judging by his films' themes, Cimino himself must be
deemed a pronounced melancholic, a man virtually obsessed
with the past. All three of his films feature the loss of a
loved one as their resolution, leaving the characters who
have sustained the loss (Thunderbolt, the group in The Deer
Hunter, and Jim Averill) in emotionally depressed states.
Cimino's attitude is perhaps best summed up in the already-
mentioned phrase used in a pre-production flyer for Heaven's

Gate: "What one loves about life are the things that fade."
Complemented by the beautiful, evocative music in (most notably) The Deer Hunter (e. g. , the "Sarabande" and "Cavatina")
and Heaven's Gate (especially the selections "Slow Water" and
"The Long Road"), the films evoke a powerfully effective sentimentality, from which emerges a wondrously crafted, but
painful, beauty.

      However, the film's attitude towards the past is, at
best, ambivalent. While it condemns Jim's failure to act
(itself partially a function of his inability to live in the present), Heaven's Gate simultaneously romanticizes a past that
is clearly presented as unrecoverable (except, of course,
through a medium of representational art, like the film). Perhaps there is the suggestion here that we can only truly appreciate what is beautiful and meaningful ("what one loves about
life") after it has disappeared ("the things that fade"); such
an approach would rescue Jim from total condemnation and
would be in keeping with Cimino's romantic/melancholy dis-
position as evidenced through all three of his films.

22.   The viewer of the film may be a bit confused about the
distinction between the two towns. Casper is the opulent,
well-developed city where the stockgrowers' club is located;
Sweetwater (which, unlike Casper, is located in Johnson
County) is the town in which the peasants reside, and where
the counterpart of the rich men's club, the Heaven's Gate
meeting hall, is placed.

23.   Interestingly, Cimino chose a name for his film and for
the peasants' meeting hall which expresses the futility of the
poor ever successfully addressing the imbalance of wealth in
the United States. In Shotokan karate,
                there is a training technique known as "Gates of
                Heaven, " once called Kamikaze training. Defender
                and attacker stand at very close range, and when
                the attacker throws his reverse punch (a punch
                thrown with the hand on the opposite side from the
                attacker's forward leg) with full power to the de-
                fender's head, the defender may only respond in
                one way--moving straight in, as fast as he can.
                (The technical secret to this is that a reverse punch,
                properly executed, holds the attacker's shoulders
                square to the opponent, leaving an open triangle of
                space between his punching fist, his opposite shoul-
                der, and his punching shoulder. That space is the
                only safe territory for the defender--who has to get
                there at just the right time or be devastated. (Jim

Nail, "The Inner Mysteries: Hidden Potential in
    Martial Art," Black Belt, May, 1983, p. 44).
If one substitutes the terms "stockgrowers' thugs" for "at-
tacker" and "peasants" for "defender," one can see how apt
a description is here provided of Heaven's Gate's final assault
sequence. Unfortunately, as the article on Shotokan technique
points out, "until an advanced stage of training, this is not
a particularly useful technique to try ... but it is ideal for
forcing the defender to face himself, overcome his fears and
anxieties, and act."

The viewer should note that J.B. also appears to be
the owner of the saloon where the film's cockfight takes place.
Although the saloon is not identified by name in Heaven's Gate,
an article on Heaven's Gate's production which appeared in
American Cinematographer (November, 1980, p. 1113) identifies this establishment as the "Two Oceans Saloon."

24. When he later goes to visit Jim, the peasant mayor of
Sweetwater comments on the historical futility of resisting
the power of the rich. "In the end they will get it [the land]
anyway; if it takes 100 years they will get it," he says.

Curiously, the latter half of this speech is not present
in the film's short version, yet Jim's responding counsel to
the mayor and his associates is: "They're [the stockgrowers'
thugs] 50 men, Charlie; together you're 200." This implicit
advice to act seems inappropriate coming from a man who
is not only himself incapable of effective action, but who also
must realize, as does the mayor, that in the long run the
peasants simply can't win. Moreover, the remark renders
problematic Jim's subsequent behavior, in which he at first
blithely reacts to the peasants' mobilization and Nate's murder (Cf. Note 37), only quite late deciding, somewhat against
the odds, to act by joining the fight against the stockgrowers.

Jim's behavior throughout Heaven's Gate alternates
between two extremes. First he resists the stockgrowers,
stopping the fight outside of the general store, opposing Canton and his associates at their club, battling with Nate about
the death list, which has Ella's name on it. Then, after
Ella decides to marry Nate, Jim withdraws from the political conflict, almost as though having lost his peasant lover
he has lost interest in the peasants' struggle as well. He
thereby reveals himself as a man profoundly confused about
what is truly important to him. After his rival is killed,
Jim's wavering idealism once again surfaces, and he joins
the peasants' revolt, only eventually, at the film's end, to
retreat once again into despair and inactivity. Precisely how
much of Jim's indecisiveness is intended by Cimino to char-

acterize a morally weak character, and how much of it represents a confusion of fictional conceptualization on the part of the film's author, is impossible to determine.

However, Heaven's Gate's action may be partially rescued from the latter view by regarding it in the following manner: throughout the film, Jim (and, by extension, the audience as well) is placed in a double bind. If Jim does not act against the rich, he will be regarded both by himself and by us as a moral coward. Yet to act contrary to what seems destined to occur (fiscal consolidation), although a debatably noble activity, is also somewhat foolhardy. Ultimately, Heaven's Gate seems to be constructed in such a way that we tend to respect those characters whose actions run counter to inevitability, who in essence exercise a leap of faith; in this sense, the core of the film assumes an implicit existential tone.

25. Cf. Note 11.

26. A further similarity between the students and the peasants exists in the fact that each group "graduates" in the film, the students (in the persons of Jim and Billy) from an engaging innocence to a deplorable resignation, the peasants from hope for their future to despair over their present regrettable powerlessness in the face of the power of the rich. Interestingly, though, Heaven's Gate is constructed in such a way that this movement from ignorance to knowledge is (as in all of Cimino's films) at once both unfortunate and necessary: unfortunate in that one cannot realize the attainment of one's ideals in life, necessary in that if anything is ever to be achieved, one must have a clear understanding of the realities of the situations with which one comes in contact. As Heaven's Gate's end makes clear, though, Jim has learned nothing from his experiences. His bitter resignation at the film's finale involves a retreat from necessary action into a melancholy, but childish, withdrawal from the world.

27. Ella's obsession with money is clear from more than just her repeated statement that patrons at her house--including Nate but excluding Jim (from whom, nevertheless, she receives gifts)--must pay with either "cash or cattle" (she astutely drops the reference to cattle when the association men who, it turns out, are going to rape her are present). Nate recognizes her avarice when he somewhat diplomatically tells her, "The situation out back [where she keeps her cattle] is looking very prosperous." Similarly, the viewer is made aware of her materialism when, after she hears about Jim's birthday present to her, Ella immediately asks, "It's very

expensive, no?" We are thus not surprised when, in the film's
long version, Ella--speaking about how beholden she is to
Jim--uses a fiscal term to give voice to her feelings, talking
about her "debt" to Jim for his protection and her gratefulness
for "every<u>thing</u>' (emphasis added).   However, it must be
admitted that Jim actually somewhat encourages Ella's attitude by giving her the opulent present.   Additionally, in the
long version, Jim, referring to the carriage, warns Ella to
be careful with it, stating, "You have any idea what one of
these costs?   Watch out. "

Ella is also overtly concerned with keeping her book-
keeping in order, even to the point in the film's long version
of wanting to take her account books with her when she is
planning to leave Wyoming.   She has a rude counterpart in
the association man who during the peasants/stockgrowers
battle keeps track of peasant deaths in a ledger.

Ella's fiscal bent even extends to her morals, a condition evident from her ability to somehow equate emotional
fidelity with freedom from monetary considerations.   Thus,
she tells Jim at one point, "I never cheated on you.   I always made Nate pay. "   (For more on the cruel poignancy of
Ella's materialism, see the discussion of the short version's
end, pp. 215-216).

Nate's concern with money (cf. pp. 208-209 for an extensive discussion of this characteristic) is evident as well, both
in his hiring himself out to the stockgrowers--an act motivated solely by the desire for personal gain (he tells Jim,
"What? How the hell do I know?   Get rich like you")--and
in his fascination with Ella's entering (in Nate's word) "figures" into her books.

Jim's friend J. B. is similarly obsessed with capital.
Like Nate, who is also apparently of peasant background, J. B.
makes money by taking advantage of the peasants.   He first
affects sympathy with the poor ("These people don't have a
pot to piss in," he says), but then reveals his typical, ego-
istic, entrepreneurial bent.   "But people always get thirsty
after a funeral and I'm not about to sit and watch the grass
grow when there's money to be made," he tells Jim.   Later,
during the land deeds meeting, J. B. (wearing a full-length
coat much like the one that his rich friend, Jim Averill, carried with him into Casper; thus the identification between the
two characters' materialism is strongly affirmed) characteristically emphasizes material progress and self-interest over
group solidarity, telling the peasants, "We all want to hold
together--to push ourselves ahead, to protect what we have,"
as though unity was important predominantly for the sake of
individual advancement.

28.   In the film's long version, J. B. refers to the peasants'
abandonment by a traditional bulwark against insurrection when
he says to Jim, "The captain told me the National Guard can't
do anything but I'm sure you already know that." Curiously,
the film's short version loops out this statement, replacing
it with J. B. saying, "Sure feels like Monday; it was a hell
of a Sunday, though, wasn't it?"

29.   During this sequence, following a shot of Billy, Cimino
cuts to Billy's memory of two coeds taking a leisurely walk.
The contrast between this apparent reminiscence of student
life--with all of its attendant idealism--and the harsh discussion that is depicted in the film's present tense is obvious,
although the memory is also quite selective, in that Billy
remembers the lyricism of his college days but leaves out
the violent student images (e. g. , the fight and its aftermath)
to which we have been exposed.

30.   It is only the film's short version which suggests that
Jim is to be eliminated. As Canton there puts it, "We will
first go to Johnson County; we will dispose of the Marshal,
James G. Averill." This line is not present in the uncut
film, which has Canton say, "We will depose the incompetent
civil authority there," thus effectively skirting the issue of
whether or not deposition refers to murder or mere removal
from office. However, the former meaning does seem to be
suggested by the remark's proximity to Canton's soon-to-be-
heard statement, "We have placed 125 names on a death list."

31.   The captain even goes so far as to make a further mock-
ery of the battle. Addressing no one in particular (how many
peasants, after all, are still alive?), he says, "You can all
go home now," as though they have all been on some pleasant afternoon outing.

32.   Ironically, this latter statement is a precise duplicate
of the one earlier made by the mayor to Jim in the film's
uncut version. It is appropriate that the conciliatory peasant
who presently makes this statement is the one who later in
the meeting tells the peasants that they are "cutting [their]
own throats" since, like the mayor, he obviously has a vested
interest in maintaining the unjust economic status quo. It
is, therefore, an accurate assessment of all characters in
the film who somehow repudiate their class that they have
directly betrayed their people. (Could this judgment possibly
include Jim as well? Canton certainly thinks so. After Jim
warns Canton and his club members to "stay out of my county, "

Canton replies, "You offset every effort we make to protect
our own property and that of members of your own class."
Jim's response that "You're not in my class, Canton; you'd
have to die first and be born again" fails to address the eco-
nomically-determined meaning of "class" that Canton here invokes.) Thus, the man who in the short version's meeting
hall scene gives the moving speech about the rich leaving the
peasants "nothing" (cf. Note 39) calls the mayor a "traitor"
after the mayor offers his already-mentioned comment (which
overlooks the mitigating circumstances of the peasants' desti-
tution) about it being "against the law to take branded cattle
from the open range."   This exchange is obviously a replay
of the one between Nate and the "married man" peasant whom
Nate catches about to shoot a steer.   When the peasant had
said to Nate, "My family starving," Nate had pointed out that
that didn't give him "the right to steal."   In response, the
young man had observed, "You look like one of us; you work
for them?" thus in effect calling Nate a traitor to his people
(just like the mayor).   Indeed, the sequence affirms Nate's
alienated status when it ends with the young man referring to
Nate as a "goddamn foreigner."
    Nate's response, like the mayor's, is quite predictable,
since both men, through their monetary selfishness, have implicitly (and, in Nate's case, literally) allied themselves with
the stockgrowers.   In essence, this situation points up the
deplorability of possessing money or goods in a capitalistic
society since possession, almost by definition, compels one
to assume a conservative, egotistic stand with respect to one's
rights of property.   In essence, as Cimino implies throughout
Heaven's Gate, money dictates one's politics.
    Somewhat surprisingly, after Ella's rape, Jim--in ap-
parent reference to stockgrowers' attempts to legally prevent
the peasants from stealing cattle (and, possibly, squatting on
land as well?)--says to Nate, "You people were in the right
legally, but they [the rapists] just threw that away," a statement whose first half recalls Jim's remark to Canton and his
club members that "Legally you bastards have a right to protect your own property."   However, Jim then went on to tell
the rich men, "But unless you have a signed legal warrant
for every name on that death list, stay out of my county."
Yet when three peasants in the long version tell Jim that Nate
shot Michael Kovach, Jim does nothing about it, neither attempting to determine if the meat Kovach was trimming when
shot was rightfully his, nor questioning Nate--who enters the
room just as the peasants are leaving--about the incident.
Once again, we are faced with a virtually maddening inconsistency in Jim's behavior.

33.   Money thus becomes one of the forms through which de-
terminism--an overriding characteristic in all of Cimino's
films--acts in Heaven's Gate.   One can see that money similarly fuels much of the fateful action in Thunderbolt and Lightfoot and The Deer Hunter as well.   Thus, the earlier film's
armored car company job, which ultimately leads to such
melancholy and, in most cases, deadly consequences for all
four main characters, is motivated predominantly by a desire for wealth; while in the later film, the excessive amounts
of money that Michael uses to bribe the Frenchman and the
organizers of the South Vietnam Russian roulette game make
possible his deadly, dead-end game with Nicky.

34.   Typically, Billy chooses to do nothing, seeking refuge
in victimization rather than action.   Nevertheless, despite
Jim's expected reaction, Billy is correct.   Jim--and anyone
else in the film who has a vested interest in the status quo--
cannot by definition escape from the moral and philosophic
dictates of his economically-limned position.   All of Heaven's
Gate's characters--from Jim to Billy to Nate to Ella to the
property-owning or business-operating peasants--are so affected by money that regardless of their class, their owner-
ship of "goods" converts them into people who are virtually
compelled by the nature of the capitalist system to forsake
their friends and associates and, if necessary, eventually to
compromise their integrity in the name of a form of self-
protection that in the film is usually capitalistically defined.

35.   This view of the inevitable dominance of the rich over
the poor is embodied in the unfair fight outside the Casper
general store.   In this early confrontation between stockgrowers' representatives and peasants, a peasant is brutally
beaten by one of three association men, who continues hitting
his victim long after the man has lapsed into submission.
Jim significantly tells the association man, "That's enough,
friend; you've won," although his statement has no effect.
Characteristically, Jim only interferes physically in the fight
when the man hits Jim, after which Jim knocks him down.
Like Nate (after Ella's rape), Jim must somehow be personally affected by events in order to even begin to react to
them.

36.   Nate is also at this point making sure that the form that
the peasants' payment for sex has taken is not stolen association cattle.   Cf. Notes 43 and 44.

37.   Appropriately, this critique of Nate's behavior also ap-

plies to the two other members of the film's fateful menage
à trois, Jim (cf. Note 3) and Ella.   Although Jim is emotionally reserved, it seems likely that his main reason for joining the peasant battle is Ella's rape; however, he only allows
this to affect him after Nate is dead (as though before that
point, becoming outraged enough to act would have been pointless since Nate was present to "defend" Ella's honor).   With
this consideration in mind, Jim's pontifical speech to Nate
after the rape (cf. Note 32) is merely a Reverend Doctor-like
example of empty, grandstand rhetoric.   In fact, Jim is characteristically cold about Nate's death, telling Ella, "He knew
what was coming and he made his own decision; so did you."
This is a harsh but--it must be admitted--accurate assessment, since both Nate and Ella seemed quite aware of the
consequences of opposing the association.

    As for Ella, the film's long version makes it clear
that she, too, only becomes motivated to join the peasants
after Nate's death.   She enters the Heaven's Gate meeting
hall to inform the gathered assembly that "They're [the thugs]
here," an act doubtless prompted more by grief and frustration than a desire to warn the peasants about the county's invasion.   The film's short version does not show her attend-
ing the meeting at all.

38.   As in The Deer Hunter, Cimino uses Walken predominantly to connote death.   In the earlier film, Nicky's obsession with death was suggested through his refusal to eat (in
evidence during the first hunting trip) and his fixation with
Russian roulette.   In Heaven's Gate, in addition to his character's hired killer activities, Walken's deadly connotation is
heightened not only by his usually emotionless expressions
but also by his makeup, which accentuates his eyes in such
a way as to make him appear almost ghoulish.   Given his
deadly aspect, it is thus fitting that Nate's death is the event
that finally impels Jim and Ella to join the peasants' battle,
with disastrous consequences for them both.

39.   The shooting occurs at the end of the debate about how
the peasants should respond to the arrival of the stockgrowers'
thugs in Wyoming.   This debate takes different forms in Heav-
en's Gate's two versions with respect to speakers, action,
etc., although there is some duplication of footage as well.
Of particular note, though, is the long version's overt emphasis on discord among the peasants, a factor present in the
short version but not given as much prominence there.
    However, two very effective pieces of dialogue are
present only in the film's cut version: the sequence in which

a man, in despair, tears up his land deed claim, picks up
some dirt from the meeting hall floor, and tosses it into the
air, emphasizing his assertion that the rich "leave us nothing,
nothing." Again only in the short version, there is the Widow
Kovach's effective statement about the rich ("Nothing is bother-
ing them so much as when they see a cabin on the open range").
The absence of this speech in the film's long version not only
virtually eliminates Mrs. Kovach's role as a peasant agita-
tor, but renders somewhat meaningless her gesture--still included in the long version--of rising from her seat after one
of Mr. Eggleston's (Brad Dourif) stirring statements and urging the peasants on to ever greater outrage and solidarity.
Both versions of the scene, though, contain the final, stirring
bit of dialogue in which a peasant boldly shouts, "We're going
to shoot all of the sons of bitches and even the army won't
stop us."

40.   This shooting is highly ironic, since Billy had earlier,
in the long version's battle, intentionally tripped a rifleman who
had Ella in his sights.

41.   The cloud-as-fate image is stunningly employed in the
immediately following sequence, in which the railroad station-
master, Cully, is murdered by an association hireling.   As
Cully attempts to mount his horse to escape from the thug
(whose long coat billows cloud-like in the breeze), a dark
cloud fortuitously passes before the sun, creating a black
shadow on the ground that moves forward and encloses him.
Before that, the wind, that traditional symbol of change, blows
off his hat.
        This serendipitous cloud image is so potently sugges-
tive that Cimino reprises it for two successive shots.   As
Cully rides away, he encounters an army of mounted association men, who rise up over the edge of a hill like a dark,
avenging cloud; it is one of these men who shoots him.   Similarly when, in a later scene, the Trapper innocently heads
out to take a bath, he is, like Cully, first confronted by a
single association member, then by a phalanx of men (Canton, the major, and Billy among them) who loom up over the
edge of a rise in a comparable "dark cloud of vengeance"
manner.

42.   Billy's later support of protests against either faits ac-
complis or the inevitable is prefigured in his actions after
the student melée when he somewhat ambiguously shakes his
head from side to side in rejection of the fight, which is already unalterably finished.

43. Ella's avarice is widely recognized in the film. As
one of the stockgrowers' hirelings correctly points out to
Nate, "We break our backs out here [protecting the stockgrowers' interests] and Ella breaks her back on these hunky
mudfuckers." The comparison being made between the men
working for the stockgrowers and Ella is obvious; in one way
or another, they have all prostituted themselves in exchange
for money.

44. This may seem a rather crude way of describing the
scene, but this view is encouraged by the film. Thus, when
Ella, realizing the impending physical threat from the association men, says, "You pay in advance here--cash," one of
Morrison's men modifies her statement, adding the words,
"or cattle." When Morrison then says, "You have enough of
the association's cattle out back to pay for all of us without
coming up for air ... the whole month of April," we realize
that Cimino intends us to view the rape as, in essence, Ella's
"due," as the payment of a bill owed by Ella to the association in exchange for her appropriation of their property. Cf.
Note 45 for more on this theme.

45. A number of the peasants in the film's uncut version
appropriate the notion of Ella's greediness as a cause for
the stockgrowers' reprisals. After Ella's name is read from
the death list, some peasants shout, "Whore, it's all her
fault! Give her to them! Give them the whore!" thus correctly recognizing Ella's role in exacerbating tensions between rich and poor while at the same time mistakenly believing that one sacrifice will at this point appease the Stockgrowers Association. The notion of vegeance is ironically
being complemented at this point, since in the long version
it is during this meeting that the murder of Ella's prostitutes--
the first act of mass retribution perpetrated by association
thugs--is taking place.
        However, it should be clear that Ella would never have
become so prosperous--and therefore such a visible symbol
of defiance of the stockgrowers' property rights--had not the
peasants, among others, patronized and supported her establishment. As the army captain correctly observes to Jim at
one point, "I guess some of these new citizens would rather
get laid than feed their families."

46. Indeed, if we take Heaven's Gate's true wolf to be the
force behind these men (the rich), we can see how apposite
is the trapper's only literally amusing advice on how to catch
a wolf properly: "Grab hold his tongue" and don't let go.

Towards the film's end, when the peasants, despite heavy
losses, have the rich at bay, they only "let go" when they
are compelled to do so by the cavalry.   Unfortunately, as
the trapper points out, when you let go (as you inevitably
must), the wolf "kills you."   The trapper ends his story by
recommending that one "hang on until help comes," ironic
advice considering that although the poor do "hang on" in the
battle sequence, when "help comes" it is in the form of the
cavalry, who rescue the enemies of the poor from destruction.

47.   Morrison's fate is never made known to the viewer.

48.   In both versions of the film, the following exchange between Canton and Nate then takes place--Canton: "Let's not
have any last minute sentimentalism about the killing of a
few thieves and anarchists."   Nate: "You ever kill a man
yourself, Canton?" The film's short version drops the issue
at this point, leaving us with the impression of Canton as an
essential coward, a man who either hires others to commit
murder or who (as when he shoots Nate, J. B. , and Ella)
does his killing from a distance.   In Heaven's Gate's full-
length version, though, Canton proceeds to go outside and
shoot through the head the man destined for the firing squad.
Even admitting the gesture's histrionic tone, one must grant
Canton the ability to act decisively, a quality that could ar-
guably render him less of a total moral weakling than he might
at first appear.   Cf. Note 57 for a contrast to Canton's behavior here.   Nate's defection from Canton's cause is wonderfully symbolized by his appropriation of the dead man's scarf
immediately before his departure from what is itself a symbol: Canton's camp.

49.   The uncut Heaven's Gate interposes more events between
Cully's death (which is much more graphically portrayed in
the long version) and the mayor's shooting, including a scene
between Jim and Ella in which Ella is reluctant to leave the
county, sequences involving Jim's return to J.B.'s and his
getting drunk, the mayor's visit to Jim's room, the trapper's
death, and the shooting of Nate and his friend Nick.   All of
these events, though, may be viewed as contributing to the
film's interlocking series of fateful occurrences.

50.   Given the structural and symbolic unity that underlies
Heaven's Gate, it could also be said that the string of cau-
sality and fatality operates throughout the entire film, from
its very first to its last scenes.   From the disturbed placidity

of the Harvard street at its beginning, which is mirrored in the only literally calm sea on which Jim's yacht floats at the film's end, Heaven's Gate may be read as an interlocked series of fateful events, all of which lead one inexorably to its terrible, and violent, conclusion. The film contains such a multiplicity of foreshadowings precisely because its true subject matter is the inescapability of one's fate.

The following list of initial events from the first half of Heaven's Gate (before the more obvious series of interlocking events takes over) indicates how vitally linked with later corollary occurrences virtually all of the film's events are.

INITIAL EVENT	COROLLARY EVENT
(Opening shot of empty street)	(End shot of virtually blank ocean)
Jim running (he is late)	(implied; end of film) Jim too late, everything is over
Marching band	(implied) Peasants file into Heaven's Gate meeting hall
Entrance into commencement hall	(implied) Entrance into Heaven's Gate hall
Reverend Doctor's speech exhorting students to bring culture to the provinces	Speeches made by peasants exhorting them to fight
Student dance sequence	Peasant dance sequence
Student fight	Peasants vs. stockgrowers fight
Students singing after fight	Peasants singing between battles
Jim traveling Westward	(simultaneous) Peasants (on foot) traveling Westward
Man playing harmonica in general store	Harmonica playing heard outside Ella's cabin
Jim fights stockgrowers' thug outside general store	Jim joins peasant fight against stockgrowers

(implied) Stockgrowers make up death list	Jim reads death list to peasants
Jim visits Canton's club	Peasant leisure activities (cockfight)
Nate shoots peasant	Nate shoots Canton aide; Canton shoots Nate
Nate tells Ella she's "getting too greedy"	Ella raped
Ella rides into town in new carriage	Ella rides along road in carriage, gets shot at

51.   Early on in the film's long version, a female peasant
recognizes the patronizing and ineffective nature of Jim's
half-hearted concern for the poor's welfare.   After Jim tells
the woman that he will redress the murder of her husband,
who has apparently been killed by stockgrowers' employees
(Jim says, "I'll settle this; I promise you that"), the woman
in essence tells Jim to mind his own business.   "We'll work
our land, thank you," she says.   Cimino underscores the un-
bridgeable gap between these two representative class members by then showing us the woman pulling her wagon while
Jim rides off in his carriage.

52.   One should not overlook the fact, made more prominent
in the film's long version, that like Jim and Billy (Cf. pp. 207-
208), Jim and Nate--the respectively rich and poor suitors
for Ella's love--not only have known each other previous to
their Wyoming meetings, but are also psychologically linked.
Thus, when Nate enters Ella's, he is already aware of Jim's
presence, which in the long version he not only deduces from
the existence of Ella's opulent carriage (Nate: "Saw a new
rig out in the barn ... Jim back, is he?") but also in a
purely intuitive way.   Nate: "He's here now, is he?"   Ella:
"Upstairs."   Nate: " ... I felt him" (the short version appropriates this notion by having Nate ask, "Jim back, is he?").
This special cognizance has its counterpart in Jim's suspicion
--which, I believe, many viewers share--that Nate (who is,
as the long version makes clear, the stockgrowers' foreman)
is lying when he says he didn't know that Ella's name was on
the death list.

53.   Although there seems to be genuine affection between
them, Jim's attitude does suggest that to some degree he attempts to purchase Ella's love with money.

54. The configuration of the cavalry's riding precisely duplicates the movements described by the peasants during their
initial horseback assault. This similarity should occasion no
surprise, though, since many of the cavalry are, traditionally, culled from the ranks of the working classes. Indeed,
there may even be a hint of sympathy with the peasants'
plight inherent in the captain's turning over the death list
to Jim (assuming, of course, that the gesture--which nevertheless results only in the peasants' mobilization--is nothing
more than a favor done for a wealthy man). In any case,
like the stockgrowers' thugs whom they rescue, the cavalry
in Heaven's Gate can, predominantly, be seen as dupes, men
who have compromised their values in exchange for money.

It should also be noted that at dawn, before the second
peasant/stockgrowers fight sequence, Jim scouts the battle-
field by characteristically (given his admirable but nonetheless futile commitment to the peasants' cause) riding counter-
clockwise around the stockgrowers' defenses.

Significantly, when the stockgrowers' thugs (who are
doubtless all from the working class) earlier rode into Wyoming in their special railroad car, they, too, demonstrated
dual tendencies. The men were seated so that half of them
faced forward (in the direction of travel) and half faced the
rear. The physical placement of the rear-facing men ironically duplicates Jim's attitude on his train ride into Casper.

55. The pointlessness of the entire conflict is strikingly
communicated in the film's long version, in which, after the
battle scene, Cimino has the camera roam among the conflict's human and material wreckage, which is eventually
covered by blowing dust, while on the soundtrack only the
wind is heard. Then gradually, "The Blue Danube"--played
on guitar--blends in, reminding us that the result of this
battle, the film's last waltz (a circle-of-fate-dominated conflict), was foretold in the film's student waltz sequence, which
presaged two battles (students versus students; peasants versus stockgrowers), both fought over ultimately useless prizes:
in the former conflict, the bouquet at Harvard; in the latter,
the at-best-temporary possession of property by the poor in
Johnson County.

56. The end of the film's uncut version is as follows: we
find Jim pacing the deck of his yacht; the setting sun is behind him. He goes below deck, where the engine's drumming
sound can now be heard. The "beautiful girl" (she is so
identified in the film's credits) with whom Jim had danced
at Harvard, and whose photo he had carried with him, is

asleep on a divan.   A servant enters (Cf. the corpse-like butler at Canton's club) and then leaves.   The woman stirs, saying rather lazily, "I'd like a cigarette."   (Is there the suggestion here that she is drugged?)   Jim gives her a cigarette
and has to lean far over to light it for her.   The woman,
looking at the sullen Averill, shakes her head, exhibiting a
cruel mixture of pity and disdain.   The college theme, "Song
of 70"--which reminds us of the past and its irrecoverable
innocence--emerges at this point.

Jim rises, goes to the cabin door (neither version of
the film shows us Jim escaping from the cabin's figurative
enclosure), and stands there.   The setting sun, again reminding us of the end of Jim's youthful idealism, once again lights
his face.   Jim glances to frame right to look at the fading
glow, the image freezes, and the film fades out.

It's clear that the same notions of entrapment, regret,
and despair permeate both endings, although the cut version's
end, with its more telling evocation of memory (Ella's and
J. B. 's deaths are recollected by Jim, rather than depicted in
the present tense), outdistances the same quality's evocation
in the film's long version, where it surfaces mainly through
the music and by virtue of suggestion.   For more commentary
on the film's two endings, see Chapter 12, Note 15.

57.   Given his reluctance to help the peasants until events
have gone too far and his not telling Ella he loves her (two
characteristic behaviors), it can be said that Jim has always
been too late for everything (cf. his tardiness at the film's
beginning; although he does avenge Ella's rape, he is not present to prevent it or the murder of Ella's prostitutes).   Now
that Ella, Nate, Billy, and J. B. are dead and Jim is trapped
in his useless middle age, it is too late for him as well.

Jim and Billy may be viewed as men virtually paralyzed
by their obsession with what has been, not what is and will
be.   Each routinely gets drunk either to avoid involvement in
situations or to escape facing up to unpleasant facts.   Billy
seems to be always inebriated; Jim is drunk during his train
ride into Casper (cf. Note 19).   In fact, after stopping the
fight outside the Casper general store, Jim stoops down
to carefully retrieve the bottle of brandy he has just
purchased.   Jim drinks again when he reaches J. B. 's, and
passes out from drinking after Ella chooses Nate over him.
Jim and Billy are also apparently drunk in the aftermath of
the student fight, a conflict whose terrible aspects they both
fail to totally perceive.   Cf. p. 231.

Each man also has an escapist fixation on images of
purity that are firmly locked in the past.   Thus, Billy's mem-

ory vision during the club sequence (Cf. Note 29)--which re-
moves him for a while from the ugly realities of the death
list discussion--is matched by Jim's ever-present photo of
himself and the beautiful girl with whom he waltzed at the
commencement dance. (At one point in the film's long version, while drinking and looking at the photo, Jim tells J.B.,
"I hate getting old," thus incorrectly blaming the passage of
time--instead of his own moral indecisiveness--for his present depressing situation.) In an important sense, Jim and
Billy are truly, in Billy's rationalizing (albeit somewhat valid)
words, "victim[s] of [their] class," which through wealth and
ease has rendered them virtually incapable of acting.

58.   Intriguingly, Canton and Jim, both of whom are rich,
are the only two major survivors of Heaven's Gate's battles.
Given Jim's manifold weaknesses, we may take the doctri-
naire triumph in the film to be totally Canton's.

59.   Alternatively, it is possible that Ella qualifies her expression of love in defensive response to Jim's traditionally
guarded emotional attitude; however, given her clearly expressed love for money throughout Heaven's Gate, it is more
likely that the reading for this line that I have provided in
the text is the correct one. The reader is referred to Note
27 for more discussion of this aspect of Ella's personality.

Chapter Twelve

THE SABOTAGING OF HEAVEN'S GATE

The facts surrounding the production, initial screening, withdrawal, re-editing (from 219 to 147 minutes)[1] and final distribution of Heaven's Gate deserve to be fully detailed, not only because of the film's astoundingly poor box-office performance (the re-edited version averaged $1605 per screen for the week of April 29, 1981)[2] and the factors that contributed to making Heaven's Gate one of the most expensive (especially in terms of the discrepancy between a film's production costs and grosses) films ever made[3] but, more importantly, because of the curious nature of the reaction that the film elicited.

In many ways, Heaven's Gate was not significantly more costly than a number of other contemporary films which initially failed to recoup their expenses. Both Warren Beatty's Reds and John Milius's Conan The Barbarian cost over 20 million dollars to produce. In the case of these films, the latter especially, it is difficult to understand where the money went; indeed, neither film has the scope or intensity of Heaven's Gate. Dino de Laurentiis' production of Flash Gordon cost 25 million dollars; Steven Spielberg's 1941 required $27 million. The 30 million dollars allocated to John Landis's The Blues Brothers[4] would appear to have been spent on purchasing cars that could be destroyed in the film's supposedly amusing final chase. The topper is Robert Wise's Star Trek-- The Motion Picture. This film required 45 million dollars to produce, yet its sets and special effects are far inferior to those of its sequel, Star Trek II--The Wrath of Khan, which was brought in under budget for less than a third of its predecessor's cost.[5] Happily for the producers, although the first Star Trek film lost money, it was saved by the marketing of toys, books, and other spin-off items, which rescued the project from financial ruin.[6] Unfortunately, as we shall later

see, the promotion of Heaven's Gate was so poor that the
film was never given a chance to recoup its costs.

There is not space here to construct an adequately
comprehensive critical methodology for an objective assessment of all of the above films in order to compare them with
Heaven's Gate. However, we can note a number of salient
features about a few films that were virtual "box office poison"
which may have been brought to bear against Heaven's Gate.

There would seem to be an unusual psychological reaction to the work of directors who receive the Academy Award
for Best Direction and then do not demonstrate adequate de-
ference either to the Academy itself or to the critical community. William Friedkin won the Academy Award for 1971's
The French Connection, Cimino for 1978's The Deer Hunter,
Woody Allen for 1979's Annie Hall. In each case, subsequent
films by these directors were generally greeted with astoundingly negative critical response. Although Friedkin's The
Exorcist (with its virtually guaranteed audience) was a financial success, the film garnered mixed reviews. Friedkin's
Sorcerer, The Brink's Job, and Cruising received mostly
negative reviews. [7] Allen's Manhattan not only received mixed
reviews[8] but was passed over for the year's Best Film Oscar nomination. This was probably a result of Allen's not
coming to the previous year's ceremony to accept his awards
for Annie Hall. As Roy Scheider put it in a September 1980
Playboy interview, Allen's failure to attend the ceremony
"was saying 'fuck you' to the industry that had given him the
job."[9] Allen's following film, Stardust Memories, was either
strongly damned or equivocally touted. [10]

To add practical insult to critical injury, Heaven's
Gate and Cruising were quickly withdrawn from exhibition by
their distribution company. After a disastrous November
18, 1980 advance screening and November 19 theatrical opening, Heaven's Gate was pulled on November 20. The film's
planned November 21 Los Angeles premiere was cancelled
at the last minute. (In fact, while United Artists' West Coast
office was busily trying to inform the more than 2000 people
who planned to attend the Los Angeles premiere of the cancellation, Michael Cimino, Kris Kristofferson, Isabelle Huppert, and Jeff Bridges were in Toronto watching the film at
a showing that, given time constraints, the studio had been
unable to cancel.)[11] Cruising virtually disappeared entirely,
only to resurface in 1982, two years after its initial release. [12]
The poor critical response to both versions of Heaven's Gate

was, as we shall see, unfounded and excessive. As for Cruising, while it was ostensibly withdrawn because of its approach to homosexuality, a close study of the film suggests that it was Friedkin's daring to deal with the sado-masochistic undercurrents in the homosexual subculture, rather than his realization of the plot, that caused the film harm.

Now, while it is quite within the realm of possibility that Stardust Memories, Heaven's Gate, and Cruising were all of poor quality, it is just as likely, given the confluence of factors surrounding these productions, that some additional variable contributed to the negative reception that greeted these films.

I believe it is fair to say that the critical drubbing that Allen, Cimino, and Friedkin experienced occurred not so much as a response to the quality of the films they produced but rather as a reaction to their confident realization of projects of which they were in full artistic control. To some people, such self-confidence might smack of arrogance; I strongly suspect that in these directors' cases it did, and that an appreciable amount of the hostility towards (to take the most notable examples) Stardust Memories, Heaven's Gate, and Cruising may be attributed to reviewers' alienation from the work of three men who despite the accolades of the Academy (which almost always seems to give its awards to safe-- i. e. , widely acclaimed--projects) proceeded to tackle daring and potentially problematic themes anyway: self-reflexivity in Stardust Memories, the drive towards socialism as a reaction to capitalism and manifest destiny in Heaven's Gate, homosexuality and violence in Cruising.

What, precisely, was the critical reaction to Heaven's Gate? First we need briefly to chronicle what happened following the film's initial screening. After the negative reception to its advance showings, Heaven's Gate was re-edited by Michael Cimino. However, it is not clear whether the film's shortened version actually reflects its director's real intentions. Following the film's first screenings, Cimino claimed that "the missing step of public previews clouded my perception of the film" and that he was "unable to benefit from audience reaction."[13]

What makes suspect the essential plausibility of Cimino's capitulation to re-editing is his documented reaction to the threatened editing of The Deer Hunter. Cimino had been pressured by Universal Studios, The Deer Hunter's releasing

company, to severely trim his earlier film, which was originally assembled in rough-cut form at a length of three and
a half hours. Universal wanted the film reduced to approximately 140 minutes. Cimino protested. At one point in the
dispute EMI, the film's backer, reportedly removed Cimino
from the project. Eventually, after a successful sneak pre-
view of The Deer Hunter, both backer and distributor relented.
The Deer Hunter emerged with a final running time of 183
minutes, 43 minutes longer than Universal's "ideal" length
and only 23 minutes short of the film's rough-cut version. [14]
Had Cimino been given a chance to take the original version
of Heaven's Gate to the general public (Cf. Note 59), it is
quite possible that the film might never have been withdrawn
and re-edited. [15]

Writing about the full-length film, Stanley Kauffmann
said, "I'm not inclined to exculpate Cimino: Heaven's Gate,
as shown, is the work of a gifted man spaced out on ego." [16]
After seeing the re-edited version, Kauffmann still was not
pleased. "Kristofferson graduates in 1870 from Harvard ...
and goes through a lot of Commencement Day shenanigans
that, though sparser now, are still disproportionate to their
relevance. All that was needed was to establish that he came
from a good family, was well-educated, and met a girl. Five
minutes, tops." [17]

Clearly this is an unwarranted reaction to the film.
The graduation day events are not "shenanigans" if one recognizes their link with the peasants' meetings and the massacre at the film's end. And why, one wonders, should Kauffmann be displeased with the pacing of both versions' student
dance sequences (the major "Commencement Day" event), since
the wedding reception in The Deer Hunter--which was far less
stately and contained less fateful and figurative information--
was clearly appreciated by Kauffmann in his review of the
earlier film? [18]

Is it fair to state, as Kauffmann does, that Billy Irvine is "inexplicably a member" of the Stockgrowers Association? [19] Even the reduced version of Heaven's Gate makes
it quite clear that Billy is an equivocating character who is
merely along for the ride. As Billy explicitly tells Jim (in
a weak apology for his actions) when Jim asks him why he
remains with the stockgrowers, "I'm a victim of our class."
Is any further explanation (which we nonetheless receive; cf.
Chapter 11, pp. 207, 209-211, and Notes 29, 34, 41, and 55)
necessary?

Kauffmann also disliked the film's cinematography.
"The incessant sidewise filtering of sunlight through windows
and shutters, the consistently syrupy lighting convert the harsh-
ness and immediacy that this history ought to have into pret-
tiness."[20] Kauffmann goes on to imply that this is the only
kind of work of which cinematographer Vilmos Zsigmond seems
capable (Kauffmann refers to this kind of cinematography as
"gauzy and soft").[21] To ignore the evocative effect of Zsigmond's photography in Heaven's Gate is to batter the film un-
justly, while Kauffmann's latter claim is simply unfounded.
A glance at the work Zsigmond did on (for example) Deliverance, Scarecrow, Obsession, The Last Waltz, The Rose, and
the "realistic" parts of Close Encounters of the Third Kind
indicates how capable Zsigmond is of achieving crisp, detailed images whenever he feels that they are aesthetically
appropriate.   Contrary to Kauffmann's implied claim, Heav-
en's Gate's "look" is not due to a failing on the part of the
film's cinematographer but is the intentional result of that
cinematographer's painstaking efforts to create mood through
photographic technique. [22]

Andrew Sarris remarked on "the stupidity and inco-
herence" of (the 219-minute) Heaven's Gate, calling the film
"an undeniably ponderous spectacle."[23] Yet how much attention did Sarris actually pay to the film?   Admitting that he
has "a great deal of difficulty in reading [Cimino] as an ar-
tist" (a highly ambiguous assertion; is the difficulty in the
reading of Heaven's Gate or in the acceptance--reading--of
Cimino as a craftsman?) and that he "was almost deafened
by the Dolby sound"[24] (two admissions which, together, virtually suggest that Sarris was unable to monitor the film
either visually or auditorially), Sarris then goes on to make
some unusual claims.

He states that "most of the action in Heaven's Gate
is centered around the bloody conflict between ranchers and
settlers in Johnson County, Wyoming, in 1886."[25] Yet the
film makes it clear that the Wyoming events take place in
1890: in the words of a title, "Twenty Years Later" than
the 1870 of the film's Harvard sequences.   Sarris continues
by asserting that he

> never understood the point of the [commencement
> hall] proceedings. Joseph Cotten [as the Reverend
> Doctor] and John Hurt [as the graduating class or-
> ator] make speeches that sound like gibberish ... [26]
> [bracketed material added]

although Cotten and Hurt's orations not only clearly play off against each other but, in their comments about rank and privilege, have profound relevance to later events (e. g. , the antipathy between the stockgrowers and the peasants; Jim's difficulties with bridging the gap between himself and those in a different class).

Sarris refers to the film's "rollicking circles and ovals of camera movement"[27] but makes no attempt to relate these patterns to the film's themes, and ends his article by dubbing Heaven's Gate an "ambitious monstrosity. "[28]

Although he states early on in his review that "nothing ... could induce me to sit through any recut variation of this tortured work,"[29] Sarris returned to a consideration of Heaven's Gate in 1981. Mistakenly referring to the film's budget as "$33. 5 million,"[30] Sarris manages to remain consistent with his earlier review's inaccuracy and negative attitude. Thus, he calls Ella "more exploited than examined,"[31] thereby asserting for Ella a quality (exploitation) that one would be hard pressed to find in the film, while at the same time passing over Heaven's Gate's presentation (which amounts to an examination) of Ella's obsessive materialism (cf. Note 37, Chapter 11).

In the only other factually verifiable statement in the entire review, Sarris maintains that "by cutting the boisterous mob scenes, Cimino enables [Brad] Dourif's Mr. Eggleston to achieve a modicum of eloquence as he exhorts the persecuted peasants to fight against the hired hordes of the cattle association. "[32] Despite the plural word "scenes," Sarris is here obviously referring to the Heaven's Gate meeting hall sequence (the only scene in which Dourif's character urges on the peasants; what other mob scenes, as candidates for potential cutting, would have brought Eggleston's exhortations into greater relief?), and he is wrong. The meeting hall scene in Heaven's Gate's uncut version has a running time of 4 minutes 35 seconds, while the short version's scene (which contains some alternate footage) is 50 seconds longer at a running time of 5 minutes 25 seconds. Eggleston's speech is identical in length (approximately 47 seconds) and content in both versions; thus his speech would, if anything, seem less obscured in the film's cut version--just the opposite of what Sarris maintains. Despite his well-intentioned expression of admiration for the film's politics ("There are not many films nowadays with the gumption to take on the special interests with a collective faith rather than an anar-

chically individualistic self-absorption"),[33] Sarris's conclusions
appear to be as unjustified as those of his critical colleagues.

Like Kauffmann and Sarris, the New York Times'
Vincent Canby was singularly displeased with the 219-minute
version of Heaven's Gate. Canby did not like the film's cinematography, claimed that Heaven's Gate's narrative line "is
virtually non-existent" (a statement with which it is difficult
to deal, since the film's story is extraordinarily clear), and
ended his review by rhetorically asking, "You thought the
wedding feast that opened The Deer Hunter went on too long?
Wait till you see Heaven's Gate."[34]

This latter assertion is really quite perplexing, since
(again like Kauffmann) Canby seems to imply that he didn't
like this sequence in The Deer Hunter (a sequence which did
not, in any case, open the film, as Canby claims). However, a glance back at Canby's Deer Hunter review reveals
that while the article refers to the reception as "huge" and
"hysterical" (words which are not, in this case, necessarily
pejoratively used; Canby's contextual framework is quite vague),
it goes on to state that the reception "sets out in rich detail
what I take to be one of the movie's principal concerns--what
happens to Americans when their rituals have become only
quaint reminders of the past rather than life ordering rules
of the present...."[35] Since (like Kauffmann's) Canby's rhetoric in his Heaven's Gate review implicitly equates the two
ceremonies, he must, to avoid inconsistency, judge Heaven's
Gate's graduation dance as performing the same vital function
as its Deer Hunter counterpart. Nevertheless, Mr. Canby is
sufficiently inconsistent, both in his recollection of his past
evaluations and with regard to his present assertions, to deem
Heaven's Gate anything other than "something quite rare in
movies these days--an unqualified disaster."[36]

Let's sample a few more reactions to Heaven's Gate.
Referring to the full-length film, Newsweek's David Ansen
claimed that Cimino had not created any characters in Heav-
en's Gate--only postures and clichés.[37] He thus ignores the
manner in which we become emotionally involved with Jim,
Ella, and Nate (it is true that Cimino intentionally keeps us
at a distance from these characters, but only in order to
avoid unnecessary sentimentalization). Ansen goes on to assert that "Heaven's Gate confirms my suspicion that Cimino's
true obsession (and weakness) is for the spectacle of mascu-
line self pity."[38] Admittedly, Cimino is interested in mascu-
line characters' loneliness, but do the men in Heaven's Gate

(or Cimino's other films for that matter) seem self-pitying, or are they simply silent sufferers?

Reviewers writing about the film's trimmed version were similarly upset. Richard Corliss observed that "narrative coherence is to Cimino as a snake is to an elephant: he doesn't ignore it so much as he tramples all over it."[39] Again, I must assume that Corliss, like many critics, simply wasn't watching the film. Heaven's Gate's story is extremely simple; even in the truncated version of Heaven's Gate the unified plot is presented quite directly. I can only hypothesize that just as critics sometimes remember bits of action or dialogue in a film that they only imagined were there (a relatively common occurrence that doubtless happens to any movie-goer at least once), so too is it possible to miss significant portions of a film that are there. This would seem to be the situation operating in Corliss' case.

Jack Kroll observed that the dance sequence in the Heaven's Gate meeting hall amounted to nothing more than "sheer vertiginous silliness."[40] Even allowing for taste, how can one avoid the conclusion that Kroll is simply going out of his way to attack the film? This dance sequence is well edited and to the point; even its music (Doug Kershaw's "Mamou Two-Step") is appealing (as a sampling of the film's soundtrack recording will indicate). In a similar vein, Stanley Kauffmann felt that the beautiful waltz between Ella and Jim in the near-deserted meeting hall "aches for excision."[41] Maybe Kroll and Kauffmann simply don't like to watch dancing.

Of all the reviewers of Heaven's Gate, Pauline Kael is the most thorough. In speculating on why the film's original cut was so poorly received (Kael didn't like it, either), Kael hits on a salient point.

> It could be that the press had been waiting to ambush Cimino. His public remarks over the last couple of years since The Deer Hunter had invited it, and so had the cost of Heaven's Gate.... There's no observation (in the film), no hint of anything resembling direct knowledge--or even intuition--of what people are about. It's the work of a poseur who got caught out.[42]

While we may dispute Kael's assertions about the film's value, there's no denying the likely validity of her hypothesis about the film's reception.

United Artists' Domestic Sales Chief Jerry Esbin noted
that "It looks like somebody had told people all over America, don't go see the picture."[43]   This is a mild assessment.
Reviewers did more than just advise people not to see Heav-
en's Gate; they used their columns as platforms from which
to roast Cimino publicly, turning him into a scapegoat/repre-
sentative for everything that is supposedly wrong with contemporary American filmmaking.   In a review whose unjustifiable ferocity rivals that of Vincent Canby's article (a ferocity that inadvertently seems to support Kael's hypothesis
about a vendetta against Cimino), Jeffrey Wells, writing in
Films in Review, stated,

> As a narrative drama, Heaven's Gate is so over-
> whelmingly bad, so determinedly insulting to the
> intelligence that one has to summon the will to crit-
> icize it, as it is clearly not worth the effort....
>   The overall blame [for the film's failure] belongs
> to Cimino, and since there was no end to the talk
> of his genius back in The Deer Hunter days, many
> of us who saw that film for the dreck that it was
> are heartily enjoying ourselves as his former ad-
> mirers eat their words.[44]

It is hardly necessary to comment at length on Wells'
unsupported assertions, sloppy logic (the conclusion at the
end of the quote's first paragraph is a classic non sequitur,
since Wells is deriving statements from premises whose validity he never demonstrates), and tactless critiques (e. g.,
"dreck").   Wells was not content, however, to let the issue
remain there.

> It [the 219-minute version of Heaven's Gate]
> should be preserved in cold storage as an eternal
> reminder of what can happen when a witless wonder
> is handed a blank check by studio executives too
> in awe of 'genius' to assert common sense.
>   The Heaven's Gate debacle is, by anyone's meas-
> ure, the last nail in the coffin of big-spending wun-
> derkinds like Cimino, Steven Spielberg, John Landis
> and others.[45]

Obviously, Wells' prognostications have proved to be
wrong.   Spielberg's latest effort, E. T., is the top-grossing
film of all time[46] while Landis is quite actively engaged in
directing motion pictures (his most recent films include An
American Werewolf in London and a segment of The Twilight
Zone).

Need anything be done about the power of directors? Spielberg doesn't think so. In one interview, he observed that filmmaking virtually requires an autonomous individual at the helm.

> All of us are sort of overreacting to what's taking place with Heaven's Gate. I really don't think any apocalyptic changes are going to occur against film-makers and for corporations in Hollywood. Movies aren't made in the boardroom. They're made standing 12,000 feet up on the top of Mount Shasta with a camera in your hand and 20 out-of-breath actors around. If a lot of executives can make it up to 12,000 feet, maybe they've earned the right to have a say. [47]

However, a director's responsible position invariably subjects him to exposure, which almost inevitably leads to praise or scorn. The re-edited version of Heaven's Gate did disastrously at the box office, killed by word of mouth (unchecked by the film's distributor), fostered by vengeful and, most regrettably, far from perspicacious reviewers. Only Pauline Kael tempered her criticism with forthright, unconcealed admiration. Writing that much of the film does not seem to follow the logic of accepted characterization, Kael nevertheless concluded her review by stating, "[Cimino] does have an eye, though; he may not be able to think straight but he's a movie director. "[48]

It wasn't only other reviewers who seemed to disagree with Kael's final assessment of Cimino's talent, though. United Artists, Heaven's Gate's distributor and backer, must share the blame for the film's deplorable (and unnecessary) commercial failure.

While UA's pre-release advertising campaign for Heaven's Gate was impressive (the sepia-toned "Coming for Christmas" advance one-sheet is truly gorgeous), at no time after the film opened did United Artists avail itself of media support for Heaven's Gate by selectively culling the random positive remarks that reviewers, even those who mostly disliked the film (e. g. , Kael), expressed, and then printing these reactions in their advertising.

Interestingly, United Artists also distributed Cruising, Stardust Memories, and Gordon Willis's Windows (the latter

a visually interesting companion piece to the Friedkin film),
and committed the same type of "running scared" errors with
these productions.   Another UA release, Francis Ford Coppola's Apocalypse Now, was--despite mixed reviews[49]--ad-
mittedly saved from financial ruin by successful marketing
strategies, a high-priced, reserved seats only initial engage-
ment, [50] and the sales of the film overseas; [51] however, the first
two approaches may very well have been engineered and orchestrated by Coppola himself,

    Ultimately, neither the critics (against whose aesthetic
objections a good advertising campaign can always achieve
positive results) nor the public (who never really had the opportunity to judge the film properly) can be faulted for Heav-
en's Gate's fiscal failure.   The blame must reside predominantly with United Artists.   In a discussion with Jean-Luc Godard, Pauline Kael made the following point regarding Heaven's
Gate.

> If the company [United Artists] had thought that the
> critics were wrong, they would have put millions in
> advertising and they might have recouped on the pic-
> ture.   A lot of terrible movies get by if the com-
> panies believe in them.   But [United Artists] didn't
> believe in [Heaven's Gate] and that is why they lis-
> tened to the press. [52]

    There is even more to the story about United Artists'
ineptitude with respect to Heaven's Gate's exhibition.   Less
than a week after the full-length version of Heaven's Gate
opened in New York City (November 19, 1980), United Artists
officials were already at work ignorantly undermining the film's
chances of future success.   A scant five days after the film's
premiere, the company released the following facts to Variety:
"An unspecified part of the cost of Heaven's Gate is being
written off by United Artists per UA's parent Transamerica
Corp, which admitted Nov. 24 that it considered the film to
be a loser ... a spokesman for TA ... conceded TA now
takes the position that the film has no chance of turning a
profit. "[53]

    Is it too far-fetched to assume that UA was somehow
playing out some perverse death wish here in willing the film
into overall failure?   Didn't they realize what kind of effect
such trumpeted statements about lack of confidence in their
own product would have not only on industry insiders (exhibitors, programmers) but on patrons outside the industry who
would be likely through reprintings of these astounding claims

to hear what a film company was saying about one of its own
films?

In its November 26 edition, Variety reported that Michael Cimino had reputedly called Hy Smith, United Artists'
Vice President for Worldwide Advertising-Publicity and Promotion and, according to Smith, stated that "He wants to
finish the film, and that he prematurely rushed the picture
to make a deadline and now wants as few people to see it as
possible."[54] This claim about Cimino's artistic indecisiveness, especially when considered alongside his staunch self-
assured defense of the integrity of The Deer Hunter's original
cut (which was also advance-screened, in order to qualify for
any possible Academy Award nominations) and the number and
severity of cuts to which Heaven's Gate was eventually subjected (is it likely that Cimino's aesthetic judgment was so
disordered that he delivered a version of his film which was
70 minutes longer than the way he really wanted it?), sounds
less like an admission of changed attitude by Cimino than a
simple, implied request for support from his film's releasing
company, who (unbeknownst to the director) was probably
already willing to treat the film as a flop.   It's likely that
Cimino read Vincent Canby's irresponsible review of Heaven's
Gate, which appeared hours before Cimino's call to Smith,
and, suspecting that he could expect little support from United
Artists, panicked and called Smith for some modicum of re-
assurance.   At this point, Smith probably told Cimino that
United Artists wanted the film radically cut, and the two
worked out the previously quoted, supposedly face-saving statement to justify the film's withdrawal from exhibition (a pre-
cipitous move that doubtless scared off a significant number
of future potential viewers)[55] and save United Artists (but
not, as we might expect, Michael Cimino) from embarrass-
ment.

Although she wasn't specifically referring to them,
Pauline Kael nevertheless does a fine job of aptly characterizing the psychology of United Artists' executives, individuals
who (as a number of industry insiders have told me), having
never been involved in actual film production, only know (and
this only slightly) how to sell things--although movies don't
seem to be among the items they can successfully market.

> If the people at the top of the movie company are
> not primarily interested in movies, but come either
> from agencies or law firms or the business com-
> munity itself, if they are from the Harvard Business

Four ill-fated films distributed by United Artists: above, Al
Pacino and Richard Cox in Cruising; below, Woody Allen and
Jessica Harper in Allen's Stardust Memories ...

... above, Talia Shire and Elizabeth Ashley in Windows; and below, Marlon Brando and Martin Sheen in Apocalypse Now.

School, as many of them are, and they are put in
to rationalize the business, and if they look strictly
in terms of how much money they can get out of
a project before it goes into production, that is to
say of how much they can be sure of from television,
from overseas television, from cable, from cassettes, they know they can get the most money from
pictures that have stars or have a big bestseller
property. Those pictures are the easiest to market, and so it is the marketing decisions that determine which pictures they will make. And often
if a picture comes along that they did not have much
confidence in and really couldn't sell in advance,
they don't do anything for it, so that a picture like
Melvin and Howard or, say, All Night Long or At-
lantic City doesn't get anything like the promotion
of those movies that they are sure of. As a matter of fact, they are embarrassed to be connected
with those movies because they assume those movies
are going to fail financially and so, inadvertently,
they make those pictures fail. 56

Add the title Heaven's Gate to those films listed above
and you can see how apposite, with one exception, Kael's
comments are. The exception? Given the extent of United
Artists' lack of professionalism in the Heaven's Gate affair,
I believe that applying the word "ineptitude" to the company's
activities is an unwarranted kindness. 57

Prelude to a Conclusion

Early in 1983, American Film noted that the full-length
version of Heaven's Gate had been resurrected for showing on
Los Angeles' Z Channel cable television network in December,
1982. "In January 1983, other cable television systems offered Heaven's Gate as a pay-per-view option for around four
dollars per showing. Between Z Channel and pay-per-view,
as many as 225,000 viewers may have gotten the first look
at the complete film since it was pulled from distribution in
1980."58

Most tragic, though, are two important pieces of information that are only implied in this article: first, that
the film was exhibited as something of a freak attraction (as
Jerry Harvey, programming director of the Z Channel, put
it, "[People] want to see the $42 million film by the man who

made The Deer Hunter");[59] and second, that the theatre-
quality, 70mm, six-channel Dolby stereo print that was used
for the television broadcasts was to be received in monophonic
sound on home screens tragically smaller than the ones on
which the film would have played in theatrical situations.

A Bitter, and Then Sweet, Coda

On June 18, 1983, the Associated Press reported that
the full-length version of Heaven's Gate (which only exists in
the 70mm format) was exhibited at the Library of Congress.[60]
The A. P. reporter was hardly objective in his chronicling of
the facts.   The story's lead notes that " 'Heaven's Gate,' the
biggest flop in motion picture history, is a box-office smash
at the Library of Congress," yet the cutesy second paragraph
points out that "admission is free at the library's tiny the-
ater."[61]   The same deplorable rhetorical technique is used
to observe that "many were turned away in their attempt to
see just how bad a $45 million failure could be."   A few par-
agraphs later, the story notes that "the library's film thea-
ter ... seats only 64 people...."[62]

Other milestones of quality journalism in this nation-
ally-syndicated article include a reference to the film as a
"3 hour 45 minute bomb" (the writer is obviously wrong about
the film's running time), an incorrect assertion that the film's
critical rejection was "universally shared,"[63] and a claim
that the people who showed up to see the film were only "cu-
riosity buffs."[64]

Fortunately, there is a relatively happy ending to the
Heaven's Gate sabotage story, although as is for some strange
reason characteristic, it took the Europeans to rescue one of
our films.   On August 11, 1983, Michael Cimino was featured
in the British Film Institute's Guardian Lecture and was in-
terviewed on stage at the National Film Theatre by Nigel Andrews,[65] an event that represents a beautiful tribute to Cimino's artistry.   From August 13 to 16, 1983, the NFT re-
vived the original, full-length version of Heaven's Gate, which
commentator John Gillett in the BFI's program notes referred
to as "a new and thrilling experience."[66]   Every one of the
nine NFT screenings was completely sold out.[67]

Hailed as "a masterpiece," "an outstanding film ...
moving and exciting from start to finish," and "one of the
great American films,"[68] the full-length version of Heaven's

Gate (in 70mm and Dolby stereo) theatrically reopened in Brit-
ain, at London's Plaza Theatre, [69] a scant two years after
it initially opened at the West End's Odeon Haymarket. [70]
Surely if the British can give Cimino's film this serious second chance at theatrical success, don't we owe him at least
as much?

NOTES

1. Actually, three versions of Heaven's Gate exist. Cimino's
original cut of the film for the 70mm, 6-track Dolby stereo
version ran about 217 minutes (some reports list the running
time as 219 minutes; the additional two minutes are doubtless
comprised of the intermission music inserted between the
film's first and second "acts"--Cf. Chapter 11, Note 1). When
re-edited for the film's 70mm 1981 re-release, Heaven's Gate
was 153 minutes long; this edition included "pre-title and post-
ending musical segments." ("Trimmed 'Gate' Still a Long
Way from Profitable Paradise," Variety, April 29, 1981, p.
6. This same article claims--on page 26--that Ella is "gun-
ned down" on the day she is to marry Jim). Apparently,
when the film was released in 35mm, these musical sections
were eliminated; these excisions would account for the 35mm
running time of 147 minutes. Since the 70mm re-edited version enjoyed limited play, it would seem wise (and, in the
process, would avoid unnecessary complications) to talk about
two versions of Heaven's Gate with the following running times:
219 and 147 minutes.

2. " 'Gate' Creaks Open to Disastrous Biz: UA Laying Low, "
Variety, April 29, 1981, p. 3. Figuring a three dollar admission charge and two shows per day, seven days a week,
means that only 535 people per theatre per week (or roughly
75 people per day) attended the film in the theatres that Variety surveyed.
    Further information on Heaven's Gate's grosses can
be gleaned from "Revised 'Heaven's Gate' Collapses at Box
Office," New York Times, April 28, 1981, p. C7. The Times
noted that:

> A computerized service that breaks down theatrical
> grosses in California showed that the movie had
> averaged only $2880 per print over the weekend in
> Southern California. Usually, 65 percent of the
> money that will be earned by a movie its first week
> comes the first weekend. At the Regency in San
> Francisco, where a mediocre opening week is above

$30,000, "Heaven's Gate" managed to gross only
$8827. At Loew's Astor Plaza in New York, it
grossed $10,105--less than half that of the the-
ater's expenses for a week ... [nationwide], by
yesterday the grosses were dropping rapidly.

3. Figures on Heaven's Gate's exact costs vary from 35 to
42 million dollars; some of this discrepancy can be accounted
for, though, since the higher figure (cited, for example, in
" 'Gate' Creaks Open to Disastrous Biz; UA Laying Low,"
Variety, April 29, 1981, p. 3) includes not only negative costs
but also an additional $8 million: $2 million for the film's
re-editing and $6 million for marketing ("Revised 'Heaven's
Gate' Collapses at Box Office," New York Times, April 28,
1981, p. C7). Nevertheless, even the film's negative costs
are open to dispute. The just-cited Times article lists the
film's cost as both 37 and 38 million dollars (I derive the
latter figure by subtracting the Times-claimed $2 million for
re-editing from what they refer to elsewhere in the article
as the film's 40 million dollar cost). Yet just five months
previously, the same newspaper reported that Heaven's Gate
represented a 36 million dollar investment in production and
promotion. ("A Loss Fund Set Up for 'Heaven's Gate'," New
York Times, November 25, 1980, p. D6). Variety variously
lists the film's cost. The story "UA Faces Economics of
210-Minute Film," (Variety, October 1, 1980, p. 7), asserts
that Heaven's Gate cost 35 million dollars. Astoundingly,
the November 26 issue of Variety lists two different cost
figures for the film; two stories ("UA, Directors' Paradise,
Under Loss Cloud; 'Heaven's Gate' Is Hellish Dilemma" and
" 'Gate' Pullout Has Exhibs Scrambling; Cimino to Scissor"
cite a cost of 35 million, while on the same page three,
"Transamerica Writes Off 'Gate' As Admitted Loss; No Specifics" lists the film's cost as 36 million. Sight and Sound
("Public Relations," Winter, 1981/1982, p. 29) said that the
film cost "almost forty million dollars," while American Film
("Cable Heaven for Cimino's Gate?" March, 1983, p. 28)
quoted an aggregate figure of 42 million.

4. Michael Dempsey, "After The Fall--Post-Cimino Hollywood," American Film, September, 1981, p. 53. For more
information on the production costs of Star Trek and The
Blues Brothers, see Variety, January 14, 1981, p. 3.

5. Cinefantastique, Volume 12, Nos. 5 and 6 (double issue),
p. 52. Star Trek II's actual budget: 12 million dollars.

6. Ibid. The sale of television and overseas film rights
similarly rescued Conan from financial disaster. Indeed,
the film's producer, Edward Pressman, reported that Conan
garnered over 60 million dollars in worldwide rentals ("'Plenty
on Pressman's Pic Slate: 'Conan' Sequel, Lo-Cost 'Rourkes,'"
Variety, March 23, 1983, p. 26). Thanks to United Artists,
though, Heaven's Gate was never afforded such an opportunity.

7. For Sorcerer, see Films in Review, October, 1977, pp.
500-501; Variety, June 29, 1977, p. 26; and New York Times,
July 10, Section III, p. 11. For The Brink's Job, see Motion Picture Product Digest, December 20, 1978, p. 60; Variety, December 13, 1978, p. 24; Playboy, April 1979, pp.
47-48. For Cruising, see Variety, February 13, 1980, p.
16; The New Yorker, February 18, 1980, pp. 126-128; and
New York Times, February 15, 1980, Section III, p. 6.

8. See, for example, National Review, June 22, 1979, pp.
818-820 and National Review, July 6, 1979, pp. 868-870;
New Republic, May 19, 1979, pp. 22-23; The New Yorker,
April 30, 1979, pp. 110-113; Variety, April 25, 1979, p. 18;
and Films in Review, June/July, 1979, pp. 371-372. Only
the last two reviews are definitely supportive of the film.

9. Playboy, June, 1980, p. 88.

10. See, for example, The New Yorker, October 27, 1980,
pp. 183-190; New Republic, October 11, 1980, p. 20; Films
in Review, December, 1980, p. 628; Time, September 29,
1980, p. 68; and Newsweek, Octobor 6, 1980, p. 71. All
of these reviews are either negative (The New Yorker; New
Republic; Films in Review) or mixed (Time), with the exception of Newsweek's.

11. The general story of Heaven's Gate's withdrawal may be
gleaned from Jean Vallely's "The Opening and Closing of
Heaven's Gate," Rolling Stone, February 5, 1981, pp. 33-36,
59. However, Vallely's article does not cite specific dates.
The reader is therefore referred to the following articles:
"Film 'Heaven's Gate' Taken off Market, New York Times
November 20, 1980, Section III, p. 24; "Behind the Fiasco
of "'Heaven's Gate,'" New York Times, November 21, 1980,
Section III, p. 8; "Hollywood Shaken by 'Heaven's Gate',"
New York Times, November 22, 1980, p. 12; and Vincent
Canby's "The System That Let 'Heaven's Gate' Run Wild,"
New York Times, November 30, 1980, Section II, p. 1.
        On this same topic, Variety's issue of January 21,

1981 (which contains the story, "Slimmed-Down 'Gate' Due
Spring; Bach Gushes; 'GWTW' Parallels?", p. 5) is interesting, but its chronology is incorrect. Steven Bach, UA Senior
Vice President for Worldwide Distribution, told Variety that
Heaven's Gate was pulled on November 25; Bach may mean
that some exhibitors continued to show the film for a few
days after the film was officially withdrawn. Also, see "Heav-
en's Gate Leaves Theatre Owners Fuming," Business Week,
December 8, 1980, pp. 29-30, for exhibitor reactions to the
film's cancellation. Many theatres, contractually locked into
playing Heaven's Gate, were faced with nothing to screen once
the film disappeared.

12. See "Gen'l Cinema Cancels, Restores 'Cruising' Dates;
Fears Gay Tactics," Variety, February 6, 1980, p. 4, for
an idea of the problems United Artists and Lorimar (respectively, the film's distributor and producing company) had with
Cruising; many theatres, legally committed to play the film,
tried to back out on their obligations. The film's grosses
were phenomenally low (on the order of $7-9 million on a
$6 million investment), which along with the uniformly nega-
tive critical response and United Artists' poor marketing practices hastened Cruising's death.

13. "How to Play Hollywood Hara-Kiri," Time, December
1, 1980, p. 104.

14. Jean Vallely, "Michael Cimino's Battle to Make a Great
Movie," Esquire, January 2, 1979, p. 93. The following
quote from Vallely's article is quite apposite to the Heaven's
Gate debacle.

> There was talk of cutting it [The Deer Hunter] to
> two hours, then two hours and ten minutes, then
> two hours and twenty minutes. 'If we had done
> that,' says Cimino, 'we would have lost important
> things. The first places people attack are those
> scenes that involve character development. A film
> lives, becomes alive, because of its shadows, its
> spaces, and that's what people wanted to cut.' (p.
> 93)

Was it these missing "shadows" and "spaces" that accounted
for at least some of the hostility to Heaven's Gate's trimmed
version?

15. A comparison of Heaven's Gate's two versions indicates
that the full-length 219-minute cut is superior to the film's
147-minute counterpart, in that the graduation ceremony, stu-

dent dance, and peasant roller skating sequences are more expansive and sumptuous; relationships among the characters are made more clear; speeches (such as Billy Irvine's address to the graduates) exist that extend our appreciation of dramatic scenes' purposes; and additional characterization sequences (such as those involving the peasants) are present to add dramatic resonance to the plot.

Of the two versions' different endings, though, I find that of the shortened film to be more successful, since it not only seems dramatically preferable to have Jim (an essentially selfish, unemotional man) alone and unmarried at the end, but also creates more poignance if the film's ultimate Wyoming events are portrayed through the reminiscences (more glances back to the past, so typical of Averill) of this past-fixated, tragically memory-laden man.

For additional discussion of Heaven's Gate's alternate endings, see Chapter 11, Notes 18 and 56.

16.   New Republic, December 13, 1980, p. 26.

17.   New Republic, May 16, 1981, p. 24.

18.   New Republic, December 23 and 30, 1978 (double issue), pp. 22-23.   Although Kauffmann did not like The Deer Hunter, one can see through his almost uniformly negative assertions to some thinly-veiled admiration of the film's manner of representing communal events.   For example: "One key ritual, a Russian Orthodox wedding, is the core of the opening section.   Both the ceremony and the following celebration tell us a good deal about organization and hierarchy." (p. 22).

19.   New Republic, May 16, 1981, p. 24.

20.   Ibid.

21.   Ibid.

22.   For a notable appreciation of Zsigmond's work on Heaven's Gate, see American Cinematographer, November, 1980, which contains four articles on the film's shooting, along with numerous production photos.

23.   "Cimino: from Colossal to Titanic," Village Voice, November 26-December 2, 1980, p. 45.

24.   Ibid.

25. Ibid.

26. Ibid.

27. Ibid.

28. Ibid.

29. Ibid.

30. "We'll Save It in the Cutting Room!," Village Voice,
April 29-May 5, 1981, p. 47.

31. Ibid.

32. Ibid.

33. Ibid.

34. New York Times, November 19, 1980, Section 3, p. 29.

35. New York Times, December 15, 1978, Section 3, p. 5.

36. New York Times, November 19, 1980, Section 3, p. 29.

37. Newsweek, December 1, 1980, p. 88.

38. Ibid.

39. Time, May 4, 1981, p. 87.

40. Film Comment, January/February, 1981, p. 58.

41. New Republic, May 16, 1981, p. 24.

42. The New Yorker, December 22, 1980, p. 102.

43. Variety, May 6, 1981, p. 44.

44. Films in Review, January, 1981, p. 56.

45. Ibid, p. 55.

46. For a general idea of E. T. 's phenomenal box office power,
see "E. T. , Rocky III Took 25% of Summer's Box Biz; Fewer
Pix Carved Bigger Pie in 82," Variety, September 15, 1982,
pp. 3 and 34. Referred to in the story as "the fastest earner

in the business," E.T., "after just 66 days of release," had already earned its distributor, Universal Pictures, "approximately $140,000,000 in rentals." After 88 days in release, the film's gross was $240,160,446. (Sidebar story, p. 6). See also " 'E.T.' Chasing 'Star Wars' Record; New B.O. Highs, As Other Pix Lag," Variety, July 7, 1982, p. 3.

47. " 'Heaven' Turns into Hell," Newsweek, December 1, 1980, p. 88. For comments on Spielberg's brand of filmmaking, see the introductory pages to Part Two of this book.
    For an alternate opinion about studio producers, see Stanley Kauffmann's review of Heaven's Gate's original cut (New Republic, December 13, 1980, pp. 26-27). Kauffmann feels that the entire Heaven's Gate project never should have been approved.

48. The New Yorker, December 22, 1980, p. 102.

49. Ambivalent reviews appeared in: New York Times, August 15, 1979, Section III, p. 15; Films in Review, October 1979, pp. 495-496. Variety's review of May 16, 1979 (p. 21), though, was generally favorable.

50. See, for example, Box Office, August 6, 1979, p. 2; and New York Times, August 3, 1979, Section III, p. 6 (an article that reported advance sales for Apocalypse Now of $76,480 as of August 3 for a scheduled opening date of August 15).

51. As of December 26, 1979 (after only a little more than four months of exhibition), Apocalypse Now's worldwide box office gross was almost 59 million dollars, a strong return on a 31 million dollar (negative cost) investment. Coppola estimated the film's break-even point as between 75 and 80 million dollars (" 'Apocalypse' Near Break-Even," Variety, December 26, 1979, pp. 1 and 62).

52. Jean-Luc Godard and Pauline Kael, "The Economics of Film Criticism: A Debate," Camera Obscura, 8, 9, 10 (Fall 1982), p. 170. Cf. "Public relations," Sight and Sound, Winter 1981/1982, p. 29 for a similar assertion.

53. "Transamerica Writes Off 'Gate' As Admitted Loss; No Specifics," Variety, November 26, 1980, p. 3. Even after UA was sold to MGM (a sale commonly believed to have been precipitated by the Heaven's Gate crisis, but actually the result of years of motion picture fiscal mismanagement and

marketing bungling by the company on scores of movies. For details of the sale, see "Transamerica Sells United Artists; Metro Pays $250-Million in Cash, Balance on 12% Promissory Note," Variety, May 27, 1981, p. 3), MGM/UA spokesmen continued to downgrade their own product. MGM/UA's President for Ancillary Rights, Peter Kuyper, continued the company's fine tradition of maligning the film, thereby demonstrating that UA's ignorance of good business tactics flows on unabated. Although Kuyper thought that exhibiting the film's full-length version on cable television "was the best idea I'd heard," he also stated

> I don't think at this point it [presumably, Heaven's Gate's full-length version] has a big future in the-atrical distribution. Let's not forget this is the biggest failure ever made. We shouldn't get caught up in the euphoria that this is a great picture that somehow fell through the cracks. ("Born Again," The Movies, September, 1983, p. 12).

54. " 'Gate' Pullout Has Exhibs Scrambling; Cimino to Scissor," Variety, November 26, 1980, p. 3.

55. Although he ignores UA's other shortcomings, Andrew Sarris makes this same point in his review of Heaven's Gate's short version.

> It strikes me that United Artists sealed the fate of Heaven's Gate when its moguls panicked so soon after the original screening. It was the studio's pulling of the film even more than the negative reviews that insured for Heaven's Gate and Michael Cimino a secure place in the folklore of spectacular failure. ("We'll Save It in the Cutting Room," Village Voice, April 29-May 5, 1981, p. 47).

56. Godard and Kael, op. cit., pp. 164-165.

Writing in the Village Voice ("Rules of the Game," December 3, 1980, p. 77), Stuart Byron credited supposed re-editing done by Francis Coppola on Apocalypse Now and John Landis on The Blues Brothers with aiding these films' eventual box-office performance, and went on to suggest that it was UA executives' temerity in not suggesting earlier that Cimino trim his film which virtually ensured Heaven's Gate's negative reception.

Like Kael, Byron also derides the business-major mentality of UA's executives, who (like 1980 UA president Andy Albeck) he claims are "detail m[e]n who had little creative or even decision-making experience." Byron's point of

view is confused, though; are men like Albeck capable of dis-
pensing sage advice (e. g. , that certain films be re-edited)
or not?   And if not, then what are we to make of Byron's
hypothetical scenario, which involves UA's urging Cimino
(just as Universal had reputedly done with Landis) to cut his
film before it was exhibited?

57.   UA's "ineptitude" does not pertain solely to domestic
productions.   No less a figure than François Truffaut told
Variety ("Truffaut Wants Rights Back to Pix, Sez UA Handling
Lethargic," Variety, August 17, 1983, pp. 5 and 44) that UA
had done a horrendous job of promoting his UA-distributed
and co-produced films.

> Director Francois Truffaut, whose new film, "Vive-
> ment Dimanche," has just opened in France, says
> he's started legal proceedings against United Artists
> in order to recover all commercial rights to the
> seven of his pictures coproduced by the American
> major.
>   The director's chief complaint is that the films
> in question--"Stolen Kisses," "Mississippi Mermaid,"
> "The Wild Child," "The Story Of Adele H. ," "Small
> Change," "The Man Who Loved Women" and "The
> Green Room"--have virtually disappeared from the-
> atre screens, and that UA is doing nothing to put
> them back into circulation.
>   "UA contracted to have world distribution rights
> on all these films (with the exception of English-
> speaking territories for four titles) and to have them
> on a long-term basis; from 20 to 30 years, " Truf-
> faut told Variety.   "But they're no longer doing any-
> thing to maximize their commercial potential."
>   As an example of alleged UA inertia, Truffaut
> cited the current blockbuster success of Jean Beck-
> er's local thriller, "One Deadly Summer, " which
> has confirmed actress Isabelle Adjani as one of the
> industry's hottest star properties.
>   "Four million French filmgoers have seen it since
> it opened in May, " he noted.   "You'd think it would
> have been the right moment to rerelease 'The Story
> of Adele H,' in which Adjani established an inter-
> national reputation.   But UA has done nothing.   As
> coproducer of my pictures, I am asking for all my
> rights back...."
>   Truffaut said that he enjoyed a valuable collabor-
> ation with UA during their 10-year association, but
> noted that UA had badly declined in the past 20 years.

"I had very good relationships with the old UA crowd,
like Eric Pleskow and Ernst Goldschmidt, but especially when they left to form Orion Pictures, things
really went to seed there."

58.   "Cable Heaven for Cimino's Gate?," American Film,
March, 1983, p. 28.

59.   Ibid. Nevertheless, Heaven's Gate's uncut version was
appreciated by Z Channel's viewers. Over 45,000 subscribers
opted to watch the film; according to Z Channel's Jerry Harvey, "75 per cent of those people liked it more than they disliked it." ("Born Again," The Movies, September, 1983, p.
12).

60.   Associated Press dispatch, June 18, 1983.

61.   Ibid.

62.   Ibid.

63.   See, for example, "Public Relations," Sight and Sound,
Winter 1981/1982, p. 29, which mentions the extremely
favorable reviews the film received from British critics like
Philip French, Neil Sinyard, and Nigel Andrews.

64.   In the text paragraph, all quotes from the news article
refer to the aforementioned Associated Press dispatch.

65.   Publication of the National Film Theatre, BFI, August,
1983, p. 3.

66.   Ibid, pp. 2-3.

67.   "Uncut 'Gate' Gets Comm'l UK Launch," Variety, September 14, 1982, p. 35. The Variety article also reported
that business on the videotape version of Heaven's Gate was
"steady," and that Warner Home Video (the tape's British
distributor) expected "the [film's] theatrical launch to boost
sales still further." Current indications are that the tape is
also doing quite well here in the United States (see, for example, the videotape and videodisc column in The Big Reel,
February, 1984, p. 71).

68.   Advertisement for Heaven's Gate in Time Out, September 8-14, 1983, p. 46. Jack Gordon, President of International Distribution at MGM/UA, had this to say about the pos-

sibility that <u>Heaven's Gate</u>'s London reception might signal a come-back for the film: "There is no full-blown revival of any type" (<u>The Movies</u>, op. cit.). Thus, MGM/UA maintains its negative attitude toward the film.

69.   Time Out, <u>op. cit.</u>

70.   James Ivory, "What's the name of this movie?," <u>Sight and Sound</u>, Winter 1981/1982, p. 24.

BIOGRAPHICAL NOTES

Martin Scorsese

Martin Scorsese was born in Flushing, New York on November 17, 1942. When he was eight years old, his parents moved back to Manhattan's Little Italy, where he lived until he was 24. Scorsese's retiring nature, partially a result of his being asthmatic, was early on complemented by his education as a Roman Catholic. Scorsese studied for the priesthood, but he was expelled from his seminary. Subsequently, he enrolled at New York University, where he was attracted to the school's film program. As a student, Scorsese wrote and directed such films as What's a Nice Girl Like You Doing in a Place Like This? (1963), It's Not Just You, Murray (1964), and The Big Shave (1967-68). He holds a B. S. in Film Communications and an M. A. from New York University; he returned to N. Y. U. as an Instructor of Film in 1970.

Scorsese's first feature film, Who's That Knocking at My Door? (1969), was an invitational entry in the Chicago Film Festival. After completing his second feature film, Boxcar Bertha (1972), Scorsese took the advice of John Cassavetes to quit wasting his talents. The result was Mean Streets (1973). His next film, Alice Doesn't Live Here Anymore (1974), garnered a Best Actress Oscar for Ellen Burstyn. In 1976, Taxi Driver secured Scorsese's reputation as an important force in American filmmaking. Since then, Scorsese has directed four films, including the Oscar-winning (for Best Actor) Raging Bull (1980).

Although he has in the past joked about directing a religious movie, Scorsese eventually plans to film an adaptation of Nikos Kazantzakis' The Last Temptation of Christ.

Michael Cimino

Michael Cimino is extremely reluctant to reveal details about his personal life. Some sources list his birthdate as 1943, although it is generally believed that he was born in 1940. He grew up in New York City and Old Westbury, Long Island, attended private schools, and majored in Fine Arts at Yale University. In 1962, while still at Yale, Cimino enlisted in the U.S. Army Reserve.

In 1963, Cimino graduated from Yale with an M.F.A. He subsequently studied ballet and acting, and later worked for a New York-based company that produced industrial and documentary films, where, he claims, he learned how to operate a Movieola.

In 1971, Cimino moved to Los Angeles in order to work in motion pictures. He collaborated with Deric Washburn and Steve Bochco on the script for Douglas Trumbull's Silent Running (1971) and with John Milius on Magnum Force, (1973), which was directed by Ted Post.

With the help of Magnum Force's star, Clint Eastwood, Cimino was given the directorial job for Thunderbolt and Lightfoot (1974), which was scripted by Cimino and starred Eastwood. Then, in 1976, with the approval of the British entertainment conglomerate EMI, Cimino and Deric Washburn began work on the script for The Deer Hunter; the film premiered in December 1978, and went on to win Oscars for Best Director, Best Picture, Best Supporting Actor, Best Editing, and Best Sound.

In 1980 Heaven's Gate premiered, occasioning (like Mr. Cimino's previous film) a storm of controversy. Mr. Cimino is currently involved in the pre-production activities for two films: the Carl Foreman-scripted The Yellow Jersey, starring Dustin Hoffman; and Year of the Dragon, starring Mickey Rourke.

FILMOGRAPHY--MARTIN SCORSESE

WHO'S THAT KNOCKING AT MY DOOR? (1969)

Direction: Martin Scorsese
Script: Martin Scorsese (with additional dialogue by Betzi Manoogian)
Cinematography (black-and-white): Michael Wadleigh, Richard Coll, Max Fisher
Editing: Thelma Schoonmaker
Sound: John Binder, Jim Datri
Art Direction: Victor Magnotta
Production manager: Barbara Battle
Assistant Director: Mardik Martin
Produced by Joseph Weil, Haig Manoogian, and Betzi Manoogian (Trimrod) for Joseph Brenner Associates.
Running tume: 90 minutes.
Alternate titles: J.R.; Bring on the Dancing Girls; I Call First.

  Cast: Harvey Keitel (J.R.), Zina Bethune (the girl), Lennard Kuras (Joey), Michael Scala (Sally Gaga), Anne Collette (young girl in dream), Harry Northrup (Harry, the rapist), Robert Uricola (young man at party with gun), Bill Minkin (Iggy/radio announcer), Wendy Russell (Gaga's girlfriend), Phil Carlson (the guide on the mountain), Susan Wood (Susan), Marissa Joffrey (Rosie), Catherine Scorsese (J.R.'s mother), Tsuai Yu-Lan, Saskia Holleman, Ann Marieka (dream girls), Victor Magnotta and Paul de Bionde (boys in street fight), Martin Scorsese (gangster), Thomas Aiello.

  Synopsis: The activities of three friends--J.R., Joey, and Sally Gaga--are followed over the course of a number of days. All three seem to prefer each other's company to that of women, although the film is interspersed with J.R.'s recollections of his relationship with a young woman, known only as "the girl." Eventually, after much anxiety over his relationship's break-up, J.R. returns to tell the girl that he forgives her for not being a virgin. He is summarily thrown

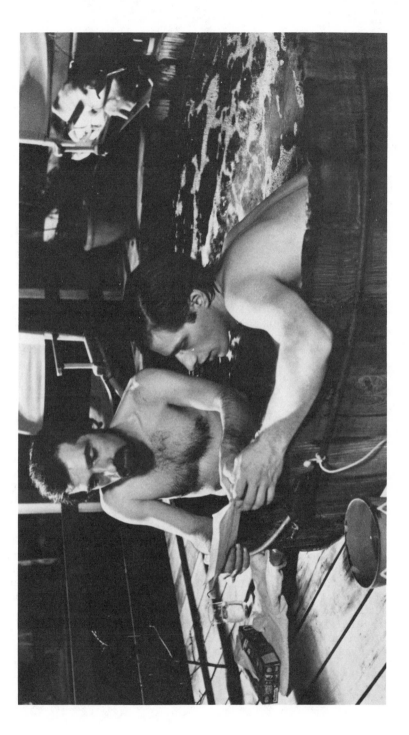

out of her apartment and goes back to his lonely life with
his male companions.

BOXCAR BERTHA (1972)

Direction: Martin Scorsese
Script: Joyce H. Corrington and John William Corrington,
from the book Sister of the Road by Boxcar Bertha Thompson
as told to Ben L. Reitman.
Cinematography (color): John Stephens
Editing: Buzz Feitshans
Music: Gib Guilbeau, Thad Maxwell
Sound: Don F. Johnson
Visual Consultant: David Nichols
Associate Producer: Julie Corman
Produced by Roger Corman; released by American Interna-
tional Pictures.
Running time: 88 minutes.
    Cast: Barbara Hershey (Bertha), David Carradine
(Bill Shelley), Barry Primus (Rake Brown), Bernie Casey
(Von Morton), John Carradine (H. Buckram Sartoris), David
R. Osterhout and Victor Argo (the McIvers), Grahame Pratt
(Emeric Pressburger), Chicken Holleman (Michael Powell),
Marianne Dole (Mrs. Mailer), Harry Northrup (Harvey Hall),
Joe Reynolds (Joe), Martin Scorsese and Gayne Rescher (cli-
ents in brothel).
    Synopsis: After the death of her crop-dusting father,
Bertha Thompson and her companion, Von, link up with Bill
Shelley, a labor activist agitating for fair treatment of the
country's disadvantaged poor, who are being victimized by
The Great Depression. In league with Bill, Von, and Rake
(a luckless gambler), Bertha begins to rob the most obvious
target of oppression: The Reader Railroad. After a number
of daring hold-ups, Rake is killed; Bill and Von are sent to
prison. Bill escapes, although he is eventually crucified by
thugs employed by the railroad's president, Sartoris. Von
avenges Bill's death, after which Bertha strikes out on her
own.

MEAN STREETS (1973)

Direction: Martin Scorsese

Opposite: Martin Scorsese and Steven Prince on the "set" of
American Boy: A Profile of Steven Prince.

Script: Martin Scorsese, Mardik Martin
Cinematography (color): Kent Wakeford
Additional Photography: Norman Gerard
Editing: Sid Levin
Sound: Glen Glenn
Visual Consultant: David Nichols
Special Effects: Bill Bales
Produced by Jonathan T. Taplin for Taplin-Perry-Scorsese
Productions. Released by Warner Bros.
Running time: 110 minutes.
      Cast: Harvey Keitel (Charlie), Robert De Niro (Johnny
Boy), David Proval (Tony), Amy Robinson (Teresa), Richard
Romanus (Michael), Cesare Danova (Giovanni), George Mem-
moli (Joey Catucci), Victor Argo (Mario), Lenny Scaletta
(Jimmy), Murray Moston (Oscar), David Carradine (drunk),
Robert Carradine (assassin), Jeannie Bell (Diane), Lois Wal-
den (Jewish girl in bar), D' Mitch Davis (black cop), Dino
Seragusa (old man), Julie Andelman (girl Charlie dances with
at party), Peter Fain (George), Harry Northrup (soldier),
Robert Wilder (Benton), Jaime Alba (first young boy), Ken
Konstantin (second young boy), Nicki "Ack" Aquiulino (man on
docks), Catherine Scorsese (woman on landing), Ken Sinclair
(Sammy), B. Mitchell Reed (disc jockey), Martin Scorsese
(Michael's hired killer).
      Synopsis: An unflinching look at life in New York's
Little Italy. Charlie, the nephew of a local Mafioso, cannot
decide between his allegiances to his girlfriend, Teresa, and
her reckless cousin, Johnny Boy, and his desire to inherit
his uncle's influential position. After numerous incidents involving Charlie, Johnny, Teresa, and other local residents
(notably the loan shark, Michael, and the bar owner, Tony),
Charlie attempts to take Johnny out of the city in order to
escape Michael's anger over Johnny's failed loan payments.
Michael catches up with them, though, and has his hired
killer wound both Johnny and Charlie while Teresa, who is
traveling with them, suffers injuries after the car Charlie is
driving crashes.

ALICE DOESN'T LIVE HERE ANYMORE (1974)

Direction: Martin Scorsese
Script: Robert Getchell
Cinematography (color): Kent Wakeford
Editing: Marcia Lucas
Music: Richard Lasalle
Sound: Don Parker

THE LAST WALTZ (1978)

Direction: Martin Scorsese
Cinematography (color): Michael Chapman, Laszlo Kovacs, Vilmos Zsigmond, David Myers, Bobby Byrne, Michael Watkins, Hiro Narita.
Editing: Yeu-Bun Lee, Jan Roblee
Music Editors: Ken Wannenberg, Bob Raff
Concert Music production: John Simon
Concert Audio: Rob Fraboni
Concert producer: Bill Graham
Production design: Boris Leven
Treatment and creative consultant: Mardik Martin
Produced by Robbie Robertson. Executive producer: Jonathan Taplin. Associate producer: Steven Prince. Released by United Artists.
Running time: 117 minutes.
Interviewer: Martin Scorsese
Performers: Ronnie Hawkins, Dr. John, Neil Young, The Staples, Neil Diamond, Joni Mitchell, Paul Butterfield, Muddy Waters, Eric Clapton, Emmylou Harris, Van Morrison, Bob Dylan, Ringo Starr, Ron Wood.
The Band: Robbie Robertson, Rick Danko, Levon Helm, Garth Hudson, Richard Manuel.
Horn section: Jim Gordon, Tom Malone, Howard Johnson, Jerry Hay, Richard Cooper, Charlie Keagle.
Electric violin: Larry Packer.
Poetry read by Lawrence Ferlinghetti, Michael McClure, Sweet William Fritsch.
Synopsis: An interview/concert film detailing The Band's farewell performance.

RAGING BULL (1980)

Direction: Martin Scorsese
Screenplay: Paul Schrader, Mardik Martin from the book Raging Bull by Jake La Motta, with Joseph Carter and Peter Savage
Cinematography (black and white and color): Michael Chapman
Editing: Thelma Schoonmaker
Music: from pre-recorded classical and popular sources.
Sound: Les Lazarowitz, Michael Evje, Donald W. Mitchell, Bill Nicholson, David J. Kimball
Production design and visual consultant: Gene Rudolf

Production Design: Toby Carr Rafelson
Associate Producer: Sandra Weintraub
Produced by David Susskind and Audrey Maas. Released by Warner Bros.
Running Time: 112 minutes.
Cast: Ellen Burstyn (Alice Hyatt), Kris Kristofferson (David), Alfred Lutter (Tommy), Diane Ladd (Flo), Billy Green Bush (Donald), Vic Tayback (Mel), Jodie Foster (Audrey), Harvey Keitel (Ben), Lelia Goldoni (Bea), Lane Bradbury (Rita), Valeria Curtin (Vera), Harry Northrup (bartender), Murray Moston (Jacobs), Mia Bendixsen (Alice at age 8), Ola Moore (old woman), Dean Casper (Chicken), Henry M. Kendrick (shop assistant), Martin Brinton (Lenny), Mardik Martin (customer in club during Alice's audition), Martin Scorsese and Larry Cohen (patrons at the diner).
Synopsis: The death of her unresponsive husband prompts Alice Hyatt--with her son in tow--to try her luck on the road. After a job as a singer and a disastrous run-in with a violence-prone married man, Alice becomes a waitress at Mel's diner, where she meets David, a ranch owner. Alice and David's relationship develops to the point at which she wins some important concessions from him concerning her future plans.

TAXI DRIVER (1976)

Direction: Martin Scorsese
Script: Paul Schrader
Cinematography (color): Michael Chapman
Editing: Marcia Lucas, Tom Rolf, Melvin Shapiro
Music: Bernard Herrmann
Art Direction: Charles Rosen
Visual consultant: David Nichols
Special Make-up: Dick Smith
Special effects: Tony Parmelee
Produced by Michael and Julia Phillips; Associate Producer: Phillip Goldfarb; released by Columbia Pictures.
Running time: 112 minutes.
Cast: Robert De Niro (Travis Bickle), Jodie Foster (Iris), Cybill Shepherd (Betsy), Harvey Keitel (Sport), Steven Prince (Andy, the gun salesman), Albert Brooks (Tom), Peter Boyle (Wizard), Leonard Harris (Charles Palantine), Diahnne Abbott (woman at concession stand in porno theatre), Frank Adu (angry black man), Richard Higgs (secret service agent at Palantine rallies), Gino Ardito (policeman at rally), Garth Avery (Iris' companion), Copper Cunningham (prostitute in

cab), Harry Fischler (cab dispatcher), Harry Cohn (cabbie in Bellmore), Brenda Dickson (woman on soap opera), Nat Grant (stick-up man), Robert Maroff (mafioso), Beau Kayser (man on soap opera), Vic Magnotta (secret service photographer), Norman Matlock (Charlie T.), Murray Mostin (caretaker at Iris' apartment house), Harry Northrup (soldier), Bill Minkin (Tom's assistant), Gene Palma (street drummer), Peter Savage (the john), Robert Shields (Palantine aide), Robin Utt (campaign worker), Joe Spinell (personnel officer), Maria Turner (angry prostitute on street), Carey Poe (campaign worker), Ralph Singelton (television interviewer), Martin Scorsese (angry man with gun in Travis' cab).

Synopsis: Travis Bickle, an insomniac Vietnam veteran, becomes an all-night taxi driver, thereby directly confronting his hatred of blacks, prostitutes, and other street people, all of whom he considers degenerate. Following the failure of his relationship with a presidential contender's campaign worker, and his unsuccessful attempt to assassinate the candidate, he returns to the neighborhood of a young prostitute whom he has met, where he kills her pimp, her caretaker, and a local hoodlum. Travis inadvertently becomes a media hero, but this fails to quell his lust for vengeance.

NEW YORK, NEW YORK (1977)

Direction: Martin Scorsese
Script: Earl Mac Rauch, Mardik Martin; story by Earl Mac Rauch
Cinematography (color): Laszlo Kovacs
Editing: Tom Rolf, B. Lovitt
Supervising Film Editors: Irving Lerner, Marcia Lucas
Original music and songs: John Kander and Fred Ebb
Musical supervisor and conductor: Ralph Burns
Sound Editing: Michael Colgan, James Fritch
Saxophone solos: Georgie Auld
Choreography: Ron Field
Production Design: Boris Leven
Visual Consultant: David Nichols
Special effects: Richard Albain
Costumes: Theadora van Runkle
Produced by Irwin Winkler and Robert Chartoff. Associate Producer: Gene Kirkwood. Executive in charge of production: Hal W. Polaire. Released by United Artists.
Running Time: 163 minutes (uncut version); 155 minutes.
    Cast: Robert De Niro (Jimmy Doyle), Liza Minnelli (Francine Evans), Lionel Stander (Tony Harwell), Barry Pri-

mus (Paul Wilson), Mary Kay Place (Bernice), Georgie (Frankie Harte), George Memmoli (Nicky), Dick Miller Club owner), Murray Moston (Horace Morris), Lenny (Artie Kirks), Clarence Clemons (Cecil Powell), Kathi Ginnis (Ellen Flannery), Norman Palmer (desk clerk), David Winkler (Jimmy Doyle, Jr.), Dimitri Logothetis clerk), Frank Sivera (Eddie di Muzio), Diahnne Abbott lem club singer), Margo Winkler (argumentative woma Steven Prince (record producer), Don Calfa (Gilbert), Kuby (Justice of the Peace), Selma Archerd (wife of of the Peace), Bill Baldwin (announcer in Moonlit Ter Mary Lindsay (hatcheck girl in Meadows), Jon Cutler in Frankie Hart's band), Nicky Blair (cab driver), C Kasem (D. J.), Jay Salerno (bus driver), William To Dorsey), Sydney Guilaroff (hairdresser), Peter Savag Morris' assistant), Gene Castle (dancing sailor), Lo (Fowler), Shera Danese (Doyle's girl in Major Chor McMillan (D. J.), David Nichols (Arnold Trench), Ha rup (Alabama), Marty Zagon (manager of South Ben room), Timothy Blake (nurse), Betty Cole (chairwo Forest Covan (porter), Phil Gray (trombone player band), Roosevelt Smith (bouncer in Major Chord), Lucoff (cab driver), Bill Phillips Murry (waiter in club), Clint Arnold (trombone player in Palm Club) Alan Berk (drummer in Palm Club), Jack R. Clint tender in Palm Club), Wilfred R. Middlebrooks (ba in Palm Club), Jake Vernon Porter (trumpet playe Club), Nat Pierce (piano player in Palm Club), M cobosa (fighter in Moonlit Terrace), Susan Kay Hu Jenkins (girls at Moonlit Terrace), Mardik Martin at Moonlit Terrace), Leslie Summers (woman in Moonlit Terrace), Brock Michaels (man at table i Terrace), Washington Rucker, Booty Reed (music ing hall), David Armstrong, Robert Buckingham, rett, Nico Stevens (reporters), Peter Fain (greet Club), Angelo Lamonea (waiter in Up Club), Cha burro, Wallace McClesky (bouncers in Up Club), (dancer in Up Club), Robert Petersen (photograph Raymond (railroad conductor), Hank Robinson (Fr guard), Harold Ross (cab driver), Eddie Smith (room at Harlem club).

Synopsis: The story of Jimmy Doyle, ja player, and Francine Evans, his girlfriend, who lead singer with the band in which Jimmy plays. break-up of their marriage, both go on to fame spective fields, Francine through popular recordi musicals, Jimmy through innovative playing.

Art Direction: Alan Manser, Kirk Axtell (Los Angeles),
Sheldon Haber (New York)
Set decorations: Fred Weiler, Phil Abramson
Stunt coordination: Jim Nickerson
Boxing technical advisor: Al Silvani
Technical advisor: Frank Topham
Assistant directors: Alan Wertheim, Jerry Grandey
Produced by Irwin Winker and Robert Chartoff in association
with Peter Savage.
Associate producer: Hal W. Polaire. Released by United
Artists.
Running time: 119 minutes.
    Cast: Robert De Niro (Jake La Motta), Cathy Mor-
iarty (Vickie La Motta), Joe Pesci (Joey La Motta), Frank
Vincent (Salvy), Nicholas Colasanto (Tommy Como), Theresa
Saldana (Lenore), Mario Gallo (Mario), Frank Adonis (Patsy),
Joseph Bono (Guido), Frank Topham (Toppy), Lori Anne Flax
(Irma), Charles Scorsese (Charlie, man with Como), Don
Dunphy (Himself), Bill Hanrahan (Eddie Eagan), Rita Bennett
(Emma, Miss 48's), James V. Christy (Dr. Pinto), Bernie
Allen (Comedian), Michael Badalucco (Soda Fountain Clerk),
Thomas Beansy Lobasso (Beansy), Paul Forrest (Monsignor),
Peter Petrella (Johnny), Sal Serafino Thomassetti (Webster
Hall Bouncer), Geraldine Smith (Janet), Mardik Martin (Copa
Waiter), Maryjane Lauria (1st Girl), Linda Artuso (2nd Girl),
Peter Savage (Jackie Curtie), Daniel P. Conte (Detroit Pro-
moter), Joe Malanga (Bodyguard), Sabine Turco Jnr., Steve
Orlando and Silvio Garcia Jnr. (Bouncers at Copa), John Ar-
ceri (Maitre D'), Joseph A. Morale (1st Man at Table), James
Dimodica (2nd Man at Table), Robert Uricola (Man outside
Cab), Andrea Orlando (Woman in Cab), Allan Malamud (Re-
porter at Jake's House), D. J. Blair (State Attorney Bron-
son), Laura James (Mrs. Bronson), Richard McMurray (J. R.),
Mary Albee (Underage ID Girl), Liza Katz (Woman with ID
Girl), Candy Moore (Linda), Richard A. Berk (1st Musician),
Theodore Saunders (2nd Musician), Noah Young (3rd Musician),
Nick Trisko (Bartender Carlo), Lou Tiano (Ricky), Rob Evan
Collins (1st Arresting Deputy), Wally Berns (2nd Arresting
Deputy), Allan Joseph (Jeweller), Bob Aaron (1st Prison
Guard), Glenn Leigh Marshall (2nd Prison Guard), Martin
Scorsese (Barbizon Stagehand); Reeves Fight: Floyd Anderson
(Jimmy Reeves), Gene Lebell (Ring Announcer), Harold Valan
(Referee), Victor Magnotta (Fighting Soldier); 1st Robinson
Fight: Johnny Barnes ("Sugar" Ray Robinson), John Thomas
(Trainer), Kenny Davis (Referee), Paul Carmello (Ring An-
nouncer); 2nd Robinson Fight: Jimmy Lennon (Ring Announ-
cer), Bobby Rings (Referee); Janiro Fight: Kevin Mahon (Tony

Janiro), Martin Denkin (Referee), Shay Duffin (Ring Announ-
cer); Fox Fight: Eddie Mastafa Muhammad (Billy Fox), "Sweet"
Dick Whittington (Ring Announcer), Jack Lotz (Referee), Kevin
Breslin (Heckler); Cerdan Fight: Louis Raftis (Marcel Cer-
dan), Frank Shain (Ring Announcer), Coley Wallace (Joe Louis),
Fritzie Higgins (Woman with Vickie), George Latka (Referee),
Fred Dennis (1st Cornerman), Robert B. Loring (2nd Cornerman); Dauthuille Fight: Johnny Turner (Laurent Dauthuille),
Jimmy Lennon (Ring Announcer), Vern De Paul (Dauthuille's
Trainer), Chuck Hassett (Referee), Ken Richards (Reporter
at Phonebooth), Peter Fain (Dauthuille Cornerman); 3rd Robinson Fight: Count Billy Varga (Ring Announcer), Harvey
Parry (Referee), Ted Husing (TV Announcer).
    Synopsis: The career of Jake La Motta--the tough,
violent middleweight fighter--is chronicled. La Motta's conflicts in the ring with numerous fighters, and out of the ring
with his wife and his brother (both of whom he physically and
verbally abuses), is portrayed. Jake's arrest on a morals
charge and his supposed resultant redemption provide the
film's denouement.

THE KING OF COMEDY (1983)

Direction: Martin Scorsese
Script: Paul D. Zimmerman
Cinematography (color): Fred Schuler
Editing and production supervision: Thelma Schoonmaker
Supervising sound editor: Frank Warner
Songs performed by Ray Charles, The Pretenders, Rickie Lee
Jones, B. B. King, Talking Heads, Van Morrison, David San-
born, Ric Ocasek, Bob James, Robbie Robertson
Music Production: Robbie Robertson
Production design: Boris Leven
Set decoration: George De Titta Sr., Daniel Robert
Art direction: Edward Pisoni, Lawrence Miller
Produced by Arnon Milchan. Executive producer: Robert
Greenhut.
Released by Twentieth Century-Fox.
Running time: 101 minutes.
    Cast: Robert De Niro (Rupert Pupkin), Jerry Lewis
(Jerry Langford), Diahnne Abbott (Rita), Sandra Bernhard
(Masha), Ed Herlihy (Ed Herlihy), Lou Brown (bandleader),
Loretta Tupper, Peter Potulski, Vinnie Gonzales (stage door
fans), Whitey Ryan (stage door guard), Doc Lawless (chauf-
feur), Marta Heflin (young girl), Catherine Scorsese (Rupert's
mom), Cathy Scorsese (Dolores), Chuck Low (man in Chinese

restaurant), Margo Winkler (receptionist), Shelley Hack (Cathy Long), Mick Jones, Joe Strummer, Paul Simonon, Kosmo Vynil, Ellen Foley, Pearl Harbour, Gabu Salter, Jerry Baxter-Worman, Dom Letts (street scum), Fred de Cordova (Bert Thomas), Edgar J. Scherick (Wilson Crockett), Kim Chan (Jonno), Dr. Joyce Brothers, Victor Borge, Tony Randall (themselves), Jay Julien (Langford's lawyer), Harry Ufland (Langford's agent), Martin Scorsese (television director).

Synopsis: Rupert Pupkin, a third-rate comedian who aspires to greatness, and his side-kick, Masha, kidnap late-night talk show host Jerry Langford, whom they both idolize. With Langford bound and gagged, Rupert is able to appear on the Langford show as a featured performer, while Masha realizes her desire to have a romantic evening rendezvous with the kidnapped star. Although Rupert is caught and sent to prison, he emerges as a celebrity, with a best-selling book (soon to be turned into a movie) and a television show of his own.

Short Films by Scorsese

WHAT'S A NICE GIRL LIKE YOU DOING IN A PLACE LIKE THIS? (1963)

Direction: Martin Scorsese
Script: Martin Scorsese
Cinematography: James Newman
Editing: Robert Hunsicker
Music: Richard H. Cole; lyrics by Sandor Reich
Sound: Sandor Reich
Stills: Frank Truglio
Produced by the New York University Department of Television, Motion Pictures, and Radio as part of their Summer Motion Picture Workshop.
Faculty Advisors: Haig Manoogian, John Mahon
Running Time: 9 minutes.
Cast: Zeph Michaelis (Harry), Mimi Stark (wife), Sarah Braveman (analyst), Fred Sica (friend), Robert Uricola (singer).
Synopsis: A young man becomes so obsessed with a photograph that he eventually disappears into it.

IT'S NOT JUST YOU, MURRAY (1964)

Direction: Martin Scorsese

Script: Martin Scorsese, Mardik Martin
Cinematography: Richard Coll
Editing: Eli Bleich
Art Direction: Lancelot Braithwaite, Victor Magnotta
Produced by the New York University Department of Television, Motion Pictures, and Radio.
Running Time: 15 minutes.
    Cast: Ira Rubin (Murray), Andrea Martin (the wife), Sam DeFazio (Joe), Robert Uricola (the singer), Catherine Scorsese (the mother), Victor Magnotta, Richard Sweeton, Mardik Martin, John Bivona, Bernard Weisberger.
    Synopsis: A hucksterer meets his come-uppance in a most appropriate way.

THE BIG SHAVE   (1967-68)

Direction: Martin Scorsese
Script: Martin Scorsese
Cinematography: Arres Demertzis
Music: Bunny Berrigan
Blood: Eli Bleich
Bathroom: Ken Gaulin
Whiteness: Herman Melville
Sponsored by the Cinemathèque Royale de Belgique.
Running Time: 6 minutes.
    Cast: Peter Bernuth (young man)
    Synopsis: A man shaves himself so well that he literally cuts his throat.

ITALIAN AMERICAN   (1974)

Direction: Martin Scorsese
Treatment: Mardik Martin, Larry Cohen
Cinematography: Alex Hirschfeld
Editing: B. Lovitt; Associate Editor: Tom Walls; Assistant Editor: Randy Jon Morgan
Sound: Lee Osborne
Electrician and stills: Martin Andrews.
Still Photos: Courtesy of the Scorsese family.
Produced by Saul Rubin and Elaine Attias; Assistant Producer: Susan Rubin; Associate Producer: B. Lovitt. Funded by the National Endowment for the Humanities and the National Communication Foundation.
Running Time: 48 minutes.
    Cast: Catherine, Charles, and Martin Scorsese.

Note: The following recipe appears in <u>Italian Ameri-</u>
<u>can's</u> credits.

The sauce:

Singe an onion and a pinch of garlic in oil.

Throw in a piece of veal, a piece of beef, some pork
sausage and a lamb neck bone.

Add a basil leaf

When the meat is brown, take it out and put it on a
plate.

Put in a can of tomato paste and some water.

Pass a can of packed whole tomatos through a blender
and pour it in.

Let it boil.

Add salt, pepper, and a pinch of sugar.

Let it cook for awhile.

Throw the meat back in.

Cook for one hour.

Now make the meatballs.

Put a slice of bread without crust, 2 eggs and a drop
of milk into a bowl of ground veal and beef.

Add salt, pepper, some cheese, and a few spoons of
sauce.

Mix it with your hands.

Roll them up, throw them in.

Let it cook for another hour.

Synopsis: A diverting 48 minutes is spent with Scorsese's parents; Catherine Scorsese, who does most of the
talking, reminisces about her own parents and also demonstrates her technique for making tomato sauce.

AMERICAN BOY: A PROFILE OF STEVEN PRINCE   (1978)

Direction: Martin Scorsese
Treatment: Mardik Martin, Julia Cameron
Cinematography: Michael Chapman
Editing: Amy Jones, Bertram Lovitt
Sound: Darin Knight; song by Neil Young
Produced by Bertram Lovitt for New Empire Films/Scorsese
Films.   Executive producers: Ken and Jim Wheat.
Running Time: 55 minutes.

Cast: Steven Prince, Martin Scorsese, Mardik Martin, George Memmoli, Julia Cameron, Kathy McGinnis.

Synopsis: An interview/discussion with actor Steven
Prince.

THUNDERBOLT AND LIGHTFOOT   (1974)

Direction: Michael Cimino
Script: Michael Cimino
Cinematography (color): Frank Stanley
Editing: Ferris Webster
Music: Dee Barton; song by Paul Williams
Sound: Richard Portman, Bert Hallberg
Sound editing: Keith Stafford
Art direction: Tambi Larsen
Set decoration: James Berkey
Special effects: Sass Bedig
Stunt work and special effects supervision: Carey Loftin,
Buddy van Horn
Produced by Robert Daley; released by United Artists
Running time: 114 minutes.
      Cast: Clint Eastwood (Thunderbolt), Jeff Bridges
(Lightfoot), George Kennedy (Red Leary), Geoffrey Lewis
(Eddie Goody), Gary Busey (Curly), Jack Dodson (vault man-
ager), Gene Elman (tourist), Burton Gilliam (welder), Roy
Jenson (Dunlop), Claudia Lennear (secretary), Bill McKinney
(crazy driver), Vic Tayback (Mario), Dub Taylor (station at-
tendant), Gregory Walcott (used car salesman), Erica Hagen
(waitress), Alvin Childress (janitor), Virginia Baker, Stuart
Nisset (couple at station), June Fairchild (Gloria), Catherine
Bach (Melody), Irene K. Cooper (cashier), Karen Lamm
(woman on motorcycle), Luann Roberts (suburban housewife),
Lila Teigh (tourist), Cliff Emmich (the fat man), Ted Foulkes
(young boy), Leslie Oliver, Mark Montgomery (teenagers),
Tito Vandis (counterman).
      Synopsis: John Doherty, nicknamed Thunderbolt, has

Opposite: Clint Eastwood as Dirty Harry Callahan--down,
but hardly out, in a scene from the Cimino/John Milius-
scripted Magnum Force.

his assumed identity as a preacher exposed by a member of
his former gang, who comes to his church to kill him.   The
attempt is unsuccessful.   In flight, he meets up with a young
drifter, Lightfoot.   After another failed attempt on Doherty's
life (by two other former gang members: Red Leary and
Eddie Goody), the new foursome go on to rob the same armored car company that was previously attacked.   Although
the job is successful, the getaway is botched: Red and Goody
die.   The hiding place of the money from the first job is re-
discovered, although it is found only a short while before
Lightfoot succumbs to injuries inflicted on him by Red.   Once
again, Thunderbolt is alone.

THE DEER HUNTER   (1978)

Direction: Michael Cimino
Script: Deric Washburn, from a story by Cimino, Washburn,
Louis Garfinkle and Quinn K. Redeker
Cinematography (color):   Vilmos Zsigmond
Editing: Peter Zinner
Music: Stanley Myers; "Cavatina" and "Sarabande" performed
by John Williams
Sound (Dolby Stereo):   Darin Knight
Sound editing: Teri E. Dorman, James Feitch
Set decoration: Dick Goddard (U. S. A.), Alan Hicks (Thai-
land)
Production consultant: Joann Carelli
Assistant director: Charles Okun
Produced by Barry Spikings, Michael Deeley, Michael Cim-
ino, and Jon Peverall
Associate producers: Marion Rosenberg, Joann Carelli.
Released by Universal/EMI.
Running Time: 183 minutes
          Cast: Robert De Niro (Michael Vronsky), John Cazale
(Stan, "Stosh"), John Savage (Steven), Christopher Walken
(Nikanor Chevotarevich, known as Nick), Meryl Streep (Linda),
George Dzundza (John), Chuck Aspegren (Axel), Shirley Stoler
(Steven's Mother), Rutanya Alda (Angela), Pierre Segui (Ju-
lien), Mady Kaplan (Axel's Girl), Amy Wright (Bridesmaid),
Mary Ann Haenel (Stan's Girl), Richard Kuss (Linda's Father),
Joe Grifasi (Bandleader), Christopher Colombi, Jr. (Wedding
Man), Victoria Karnafel (Sad-looking Girl), Jack Scardino
(Cold Old Man), Joe Strand (Bingo Caller), Helen Tomko
(Helen), Paul D'Amato (Sergeant), Dennis Watlington (Cab
Driver), Charlene Darrow (Red-head), Jane-Colette Disko
(Girl Checker), Michael Wollett (Stock Boy), Robert Beard

and Joe Dzizmba (World War Veterans), Father Stephen Kopes-
tonsky (Priest), John F. Buchmelter III (Bar Patron), Frank
Devore (Barman), Tom Becker (Doctor), Lynn Kongkham
(Nurse), Nongnuj Timruang (Bar Girl), Po Pao Pee (Chinese
Refugee), Dale Burroughs (Embassy Guard), Parris Hicks
(Sergeant), Samui Muang-Intata (Chinese Bodyguard), Sapox
Colisium (Chinese Man), Vitoon Winwitoon (N. V. A. Officer),
Somsak Sengvilai (Viet Cong Referee), Charan Nusvanon (Chin-
ese Boss), Jiam Gongtongsmoot (Chinese Man at Door), Chai
Peyawan, Mana Hansa and Sombot Jumpanoi (South Vietnamese
Prisoners), Phip Manee (Woman in Village), Ding Santos,
Krieng Chaiyapuk, Ot Palapoo and Chok Chai Mahasoke (Viet
Cong Guards), Hillary Brown (Herself), Choir of St. Theo-
dosius Cathedral, Cleveland, Ohio.

    Synopsis: Six friends from a Pennsylvania steel town--
Michael, Nicky, Stanley, Linda, John, and Axel--attend the
wedding of a seventh friend, Steven. Soon after, three of the
men (Michael, Nicky, and Steven) leave for Vietnam. They
are eventually captured by the North Vietnamese, who force
them to participate in Russian roulette games. The three
escape, although Steven is badly injured. Nicky goes AWOL;
Steven, now a cripple, returns home to a V. A. hospital.
After a stateside liaison with Nicky's girlfriend, Linda, Michael goes back to Vietnam, where he finds Nicky playing
Russian roulette in the South. During a game in which Michael participates, Nicky shoots himself. After Nicky's funeral, the friends reunite in John's bar, where they successfully resign themselves to their fates.

HEAVEN'S GATE (1980)

Direction: Michael Cimino
Script: Michael Cimino
Cinematography (color): Vilmos Zsigmond
Editing: Tom Rolf, William Reynolds, Lisa Fruchtman,
Gerald Greenberg
Music: Adapted, arranged, and performed by David Mans-
field; "Mamou Two-Step" composed by Doug Kershaw; "The
Blue Danube" performed by The New York Philharmonic, con-
ducted by Leonard Bernstein
Supervising sound editor (Dolby Stereo): James J. Klinger
Sound editing: Richard W. Adams, Winston Ryder
Music supervision: Joann Carelli
Art direction: Tambi Larsen
Art directors: Spencer Deverill, Maurice Fowler
Set decoration: Jim Berkey, Josie MacAvin

Costume design: Allen Highfill
Stunt coordination: Buddy van Horn
Produced by Joann Carelli; executives in charge of post-
production: Denis O'Dell, Charles Okun
Executive in charge of post-production: William Reynolds.
Released by United Artists.
Running time: 219 minutes (originally), 147 minutes (edited
re-release length); reputedly now being edited to an approxi-
mately 90 minute version, to be retitled The Johnson County
Wars.

   Cast: Kris Kristofferson (Jim Averill), Christopher
Walken (Nate Champion), John Hurt (William C. "Billy" Irv-
ine), Sam Waterston (Frank Canton), Brad Dourif (Mr. Egg-
leston), Isabelle Huppert (Ella Watson), Joseph Cotten (The
Reverend Doctor), Jeff Bridges (John H. Bridges), Roseanna
Vela (Beautiful Girl), Ronnie Hawkins (Wolcott), Geoffrey
Lewis (Trapper), Nicholas Woodeson (Small Man), Stefan
Shcherby (Big Man), Waldemar Kalinowski (Photographer),
Terry Quinn (Captain Minardi), John Conley (Morrison), Mar-
garet Benczak (Mrs. Eggleston), James Knobeloch (Kopeston-
sky), Erika Petersen (Mrs. Kopestonsky), Paul Koslo (Mayor
Lezak), Robin Bartlett (Mrs. Lezak), Marat Yusim (Russian
Merchant), Aivars Smits (Kovach), Gordana Rashovich (Mrs.
Kovach), Neil Wilson (Kovach's son), Tom Noonan (Jake),
Jarlath Conroy (Mercenary in New Suit), Allen Keller (Dud-
ley), Richard Masur (Cully), Mary C. Wright (Nell), Caro-
line Kava (Stefka), Mady Kaplan (Kathia), Anna Levine (Little
Dot), Pat Hodges (Jessie), Mickey Rourke (Nick Ray), Kevin
McClarnon (Arapaho Brown), Kai Wulff, Norbert Weisser,
Rege Hastings (German Merchants), Steve Majstorovic (Czech
Merchant), Gabriel Walsh (Zindel's Clerk), Norton Buffalo
(Private), Jack Blessing (Emigrant Boy), Jerry Sullivan (Gov-
ernor of Wyoming), Jerry McGee, Cleve Dupin, Stephen Bru-
ton, Sean Hopper, David Mansfield (Heaven's Gate Band),
David Cass (Moustached Mercenary), Paul D'Amato (Bearded
Mercenary), Peter Osusky (Peter), Ivan Kormanik (Ivan),
Vasil Kormanik, Paul Junas (Slovak Emigrant Singers), Luba
Dmytryk, Oresta Kachala, Bohdanna Kachala, Irene Wisoff
(Ukranian Emigrant Singers), T-Bone Burnett (J. B.'s assis-
tant), Michael Christensen (Juggler), Anatoly Davydov (Fight-
ing Bulgarian Emigrant), Nina Gaidarova (Bulgarian Emi-
grant's Wife), Wally McCleskey (chicken fighter), Gary [Buzz]
Vezane (Canton's bodyguard), H. P. Evetts (Wolcott's body-
guard), Bruce Morgan (Miner--Mercenary), Bobby Faber
(Class Marshall--Harvard), Judi Trot (Irvine's girlfriend).
   Synopsis: The story of Jim Averill--the joy of his
Harvard University days, the tenderness and bitterness of

his life as a Marshal in Johnson County, Wyoming, where a bitter feud rages between rich cattlemen and peasants who desire to work the land.   The cattlemen draw up a death list containing the names of 125 peasants.   Despite Jim's efforts, most of the peasants are killed, along with Billy Irvine, Jim's best friend from college and Nate Champion, the fiancé of Jim's love interest: a local madam, Ella Watson.   Ella and Jim plan to leave the territory but Ella is shot to death by some of the cattlemen's hired thugs.   The film's coda finds Jim alone, musing over the way his life has turned out.

Scripts by Michael Cimino

<u>Silent Running</u> (1971).   Directed by Douglas Trumbull.   Script by Cimino, Deric Washburn, and Steve Bochco.

<u>Magnum Force</u> (1973).   Directed by Ted Post.   Script by Cimino and John Milius.

SOURCES

A detailed study like Martin Scorsese and Michael Cimino operates on the implied principle that the films under discussion are available for the viewing and reviewing necessary to bring out their essential structural and symbolic complexity. To that end, I offer here a guide to the availability of Scorsese and Cimino's work on both film and tape.

Note that especially in the case of Michael Cimino's films, all of which are photographed in the Panavision 2.35:1 anamorphic format, the frame's entirety is not represented on tape (the resultant video image has a 1.33:1 aspect ratio). Fortunately, the videocassettes of Thunderbolt and Lightfoot, The Deer Hunter and Heaven's Gate represent intelligent film-to-tape transfers, with virtually no distracting panning and scanning, and only a small amount of image squeezing in the tape of The Deer Hunter. Regrettably, the available 16mm anamorphic prints of these titles have lost over 13 per cent of their image area in the transfer to 16mm; this loss is evidenced by the scope frame's having been drastically trimmed at the top. This defect is carried over into The Deer Hunter's adapted scope version, which for some strange reason has been masked for the 1.85:1 format, thus yielding prints with a 21 per cent loss of picture information.

All of Martin Scorsese's films seem to have survived transfers to film and tape virtually intact.

LISTING KEY: Availability is listed for the following formats: 35mm, 16mm, and videocassette. Certain 16mm non-theatrical distributors also rent videocassette titles; these distributors are noted, although invariably, rental of these titles will be less expensive if cassettes are obtained through local video stores. Video-cassette label names are provided for the benefit of those individuals interested in purchasing films on tape. Such purchases should be made through licensed videocassette dealers.

288

In addition to rental, What's A Nice Girl Like You Doing In A Place Like This? and The Big Shave are available for purchase on 16mm and video through distributor GPS.

Full addresses for 35mm theatrical and 16mm non-theatrical film companies appear in the KEY TO ABBREVIA-TIONS; phone numbers for 16mm non-theatrical distributors are also provided in order to made rental and information requests easier.

Note that in the availability chart, "NA" means "Not Available at this time."

MARTIN SCORSESE

FEATURE FILMS	35mm	16mm	Video
Who's That Knocking At My Door?	NA	D	NA
Boxcar Bertha	O	NA	V
Mean Streets	WB	S	WHV;SVR
Alice Doesn't Live Here Anymore	WB	S;FI;CNF	WHV;SVR
Taxi Driver	C	S	RCA/COL; SVR
The Last Waltz	MGM/UA	MGM/UA	CBS/FOX
New York, New York	MGM/UA	MGM/UA	CBS/FOX
Raging Bull	MGM/UA	MGM/UA	CBS/FOX
The King of Comedy	20th	FI	RCA/COL

SHORT FILMS

What's A Nice Girl Like You Doing	NA	McG/H;	GPS
In A Place Like This?		GPS	
The Big Shave	NA	KPF;GPS	GPS
Italian American	NA	FI	NA

American Boy--A Portrait of Steven Prince and It's Not Just You, Murray are unavailable in any format

MICHAEL CIMINO

Thunderbolt and Lightfoot	MGM/UA	MGM/UA	20th CFV;
			MGM/UA VR
The Deer Hunter	U	S	MCA;SVR
Heaven's Gate	MGM/UA	MGM/UA	MGM/UA V

FILMS WITH SCRIPTS BY CIMINO

Silent Running	U	S	MCA;SVR
Magnum Force	WB	S;CWF;T	WHV;SVR

RECOMMENDED FILMS FROM CHAPTER 12

Stardust Memories	MGM/UA	MGM/UA	20thCFV
Cruising	L	S	MGM/CBS

KEY TO ABBREVIATIONS

C	Columbia Pictures, 71 5th Avenue, New York, NY 10022
CBS/Fox	CBS/Fox Home Video
CWF	Clem Williams Films, 2240 Noblestown Rd., Pittsburgh, PA 15205. Phone: 800-245-1146; (Central States only; call toll-free information--1-800-555-1212--for CW's toll-free number in your area)
D	Direct Cinema, Ltd., P.O. Box 69589, Los Angeles, CA 90069. Phone: (213)656-4700
FI	Films Incorporated (main office), 733 Green Bay Rd., Wilmette IL 60091. Phone: (312) 256-6600; (800)323-1406 (Central States only; call toll-free information--1-800-555-1212-- for FI's toll-free number in your area)
GPS	Glenn Photo Supply, 6924 Canby Avenue, #103, Reseda, CA 91335. Phone: (213) 981-5506
KP	Kit Parker Films, 1245 Tenth Street, Monterey, CA 93940. Phone: (408)649-5573; (800)538-5838
L	Lorimar Pictures, 3970 Overland Avenue, Culver City, CA 90230
MCA	MCA Videocassettes
McG/H	McGraw/Hill, 110 15th Street, Del Mar, CA 92014. Phone: (714)453-5000
MGM/CBS	MGM/CBS Video

MGM/UA	MGM/United Artists, 1350 Avenue of the Americas, New York, NY 10019; 10202 West Washington Blvd. , Culver City, CA 90203. Phone: (800)223-0933
MGM/UA V	MGM/UA Video
MGM/UA VR	MGM/UA Video Rentals (same information as MGM/UA)
RCA/COL	RCA/Columbia Pictures Home Video
S	Swank Motion Pictures (main office), 201 S. Jefferson Ave. , St. Louis, MO 63103. Phone: (call collect) (314)534-6300; (800) 325-3344 (Central States only; call 1-800-555-1212 for Swank's toll-free number in your area)
SVR	Swank Video Rentals (same information as above)
20th	20th Century-Fox Film Corporation, 9440 Santa Monica Blvd. , Beverly Hills, CA 90210; 1345 Avenue of the Americas, New York, NY 10019
20th/CFV	20th Century-Fox Video (same information as above)
T	Twyman Motion Pictures, Box 605, 4700 Wadsworth Rd. , Dayton, OH 45404. Phone: (513)276-5941; (800)543-9594
U	Universal Pictures, 445 Park Avenue, New York, NY 10022
V	Vestron Videocassettes
WB	Warner Brothers Pictures, 4000 Warner Blvd. , Burbank, CA 91522
WHV	Warner Home Video

SELECTIVE, ANNOTATED BIBLIOGRAPHY

The reader will note the non-standard, highly selective nature of this bibliography. My view is that while there are a great many articles on Martin Scorsese and Michael Cimino, most of them are of little use to the viewer interested more in these directors' films than in their personal lives. Apposite references regarding the films have been provided in the body of this book. In this bibliography, I am endeavoring to sketch a critical context against which Scorsese and Cimino's films may profitably be "read" and appreciated.

BOOKS

Fiedler, Leslie. Love and Death in the American Novel. New York: Dell Publishing, 1969.
An excellent literary study whose insights into the symbolic underpinnings of American literature (especially regarding its homophilic aspects) also have relevance to the thematic concerns of many contemporary American filmmakers.

Fielding, Raymond, ed. A Technological History of Motion Pictures and Television. Berkeley: University of California Press, 1967.
A collection of technical/historical papers culled from the Journal of the SMPE (Society of Motion Picture Engineers) and SMPTE (Society of Motion Picture and Television Engineers). Provides an historical appreciation of the development of the film and television media as well as interesting glimpses of the men involved in the growth of these media.

Freud, Sigmund. Leonardo Da Vinci--A Study in Psychosexuality, translated by A. A. Brill. New York: Vintage Books, 1955.

_____. Moses and Monotheism, translated by Katherine Jones. New York: Vintage Books, n. d.

Initially, I hesitated to include these works for two reasons: their apparent anachronistic nature in the context of
a book on film and the possibility that their presence here
might seem somewhat pretentious. However, in terms of
their instructive, and exhaustive, consideration of "facts" relating to the particular issue with which each book deals,
Freud's books--aside from their questionable psychological
premises--recommend themselves as enviable models of analysis. The books' status in this respect overrides any potential objections to their usefulness for the student of either
film or literature. Readers sympathetic to the view of film
as a series of unified texts that demand comprehensive approaches to appreciation should familiarize themselves with
Freud's highly enviable method.

Limbacher, James. Four Aspects of the Film. New York:
Arno Press, 1978.
   A detailed, exhaustive source of information on color,
3-D, various widescreen processes, and sound. Limbacher's
book provides an important background in these areas, one
that is essential for anyone interested in approaching film
critically. A most useful bibliography is included.

Monaco, James. American Film Now. New York: New
American Library, 1979.
   Although sketchy on Scorsese and Cimino (the latter is
only mentioned in passing as the scriptwriter/director of
Thunderbolt and Lightfoot), Monaco's book nonetheless pro-
vides important insights into the economics of contemporary
American filmmaking.

_____. How to Read a Film. New York: Oxford Univer-
sity Press, 1977.
   Rather over-involved and tedious study of filmic variables,
although valuable as a source not only for cross-references
on technical aspects of film but as a basic resource on subjects like aspect ratio, color processes, lenses, etc.

Sylbert, Paul. Final Cut. New Jersey: Seabury Press, 1974.
Weinberg, Herman G. The Complete Greed. New York:
Arno Press, 1972.
   Two instructive books on the making and breaking of Amer-
ican films. Comparisons with the Heaven's Gate debacle are
noteworthy and instructive.

PERIODICALS

American Cinematographer.
A professional journal for members of the American Society of Cinematographers and, also, for interested readers.
The magazine's November, 1980 issue is especially significant since it contains four articles on the shooting of Heav-
en's Gate. Foremost among the articles is "Behind the Cameras on 'Heaven's Gate,'" by the film's Director of Photography, Vilmos Zsigmond, which details camera set-up techniques and methods employed on the production.

American Film.
Cf. Sight and Sound for comments.

Box Office.
Invaluable journal which provides information on films and,
most importantly, on exhibitors' viewpoints concerning various
productions' marketability.

Journal of the Society of Motion Picture and Television Engineers.
The foremost technical periodical for individuals interested
in the latest film and television technical developments. An
essential complement to the Limbacher and Fielding books
listed above.

Monthly Film Bulletin. Published by the British Film Institute.
Critically predictable, albeit always well-informed, the
MFB is an indispensable source for motion picture credits,
easily besting Variety's shoddy reporting in this respect.

Sight and Sound. Published by the British Film Institute.
The BFI's film publication makes its American counterpart, American Film, look like what it really is: an etio-
lated collection of puffs and promos. Sight and Sound is critically incisive and witty, possibly the best high-visibility
film publication in the world.

Variety.
The show business bible and still the definitive source for
information on the entertainment field. Regrettably, the current issues of Variety stocked by many libraries are not yet
available on microfilm; the result is that one must sift through
increasingly tattered volumes (many of them often unbound and
simply tied together with string) to find the issue one seeks.

Further, no comprehensive index of Variety's contents exists. Research involving the use of Variety is invariably an extremely taxing experience.

FILM INDICES

Betty, Linda, ed. Retrospective Index to Film Periodicals. New York: R. R. Bowker, 1975.

Film Literature Index. Published by the State University of New York at Albany, Box 22477, 1400 Washington Avenue, Albany, NY 12222.

MacCann, Richard Dyer and Edward S. Perry, eds., The New Film Index. New York: E. P. Dutton, 1975.

These are three important bibliographic sources for film criticism literature; the Film Literature Index, which appears as separate volumes for each year, is by far the most comprehensive and useful.